2ND EDITION

A MODERN APPROACH TO

CLASSICAL GUITAR

By CHARLES DUNCAN

Composite

I0802490

ISBN 979-8-3501-6741-2

HAL•LEONARD®
A Muse Group Company

Visit Hal Leonard Online at
www.halleonard.com

World headquarters, contact:
Hal Leonard
7777 West Bluemound Road
Milwaukee, WI 53213
Email: info@halleonard.com

In Europe, contact:
Hal Leonard Europe Limited
Dettingen Way
Bury St Edmunds, Suffolk, IP33 3YB
Email: info@halleonardeurope.com

In Australia, contact:
Hal Leonard Australia Pty. Ltd.
4 Lentara Court
Cheltenham, Victoria, 3192 Australia
Email: info@halleonard.com.au

Table of Contents

BOOK 1

BOOK 2

BOOK 3

About the Author

For over 40 years Charles Duncan has sought to discover the beauty of the classical guitar and to share it with others through playing and teaching. A 1970 scholarship recipient to the Musica en Compostela "Andres Segovia" Master Class in Spain, he has also studied with teachers such as Jose Tomas in Spain, John Duarte in England, and Aaron Shearer and John Marlowe in the United States. His knowledge of guitar technique has been further enriched by more informal teaching from concert artists such as Frederic Hand, Carlos Barbosa-Lima, Evangelos Assimikopoulos, Alirio Diaz, Oscar Ghiglia, and Michael Lorimer.

During the course of his development as a performer and teacher, Charles Duncan's quest has also included broad research into the technique of other musical instruments, music performance practices, the physiological aspects of instrumental technique, and the history of music. It is through applying this body of knowledge to his own personal development as well as that of his students that he has gained most of his unique insight into the art and craft of classical guitar playing.

Based in Atlanta, Georgia, Charles Duncan's playing career includes numerous concerts and commercial performances throughout the eastern United States, as well as radio and public television appearances. His teaching career includes extensive studio teaching as well as university-level guitar instruction. Besides serving as an adjunct guitar instructor for several colleges, he directed the guitar studies program at Emory University for more than 25 years. He has also given master classes at various colleges and universities in the United States, Canada, and France.

However, it is through his books that Charles Duncan is most widely known, especially through the popular and highly-acclaimed series published by Hal Leonard Corporation, *A Modern Approach to Classical Guitar*, used nationwide by hundreds of studio and college teachers. Other noteworthy pedagogical works include *The Art of Classical Guitar Playing* and *Classical Guitar 2000* (Alfred Music) and *Guitar at Sight* (Guitar Solo Publications), which are standard texts in college and university guitar programs. For more information about Charles Duncan, including performance videos, go to *www.duncanguitar.com.*

BOOK 1: Before You Begin...

You're beginning the study of an instrument that has a rich and varied history and a wealth of music written by hundreds of composers, including some of the world's greatest. Learning to play the classical guitar can give you a lifetime of musical enjoyment.

Your playing skill and knowledge of music will show impressive growth if you'll follow a few simple practice suggestions:

- ✓ Practice at least a half hour a day on a regular schedule
- ✓ Avoid distractions—stay mentally focused while you're playing
- ✓ Use good playing posture (see page 8)
- ✓ Follow all fingering and playing suggestions closely
- ✓ Learn new material thoroughly before moving on to the next section

An important feature of this book is the use of *interactive units* (look for the pencil icon). These begin on page 18 with the "Music Review" and continue with shorter interactive units throughout the book. Be sure to fill in the blanks *before* playing the exercise or piece. This will reinforce your mental command of music and technique.

The Classical Guitar

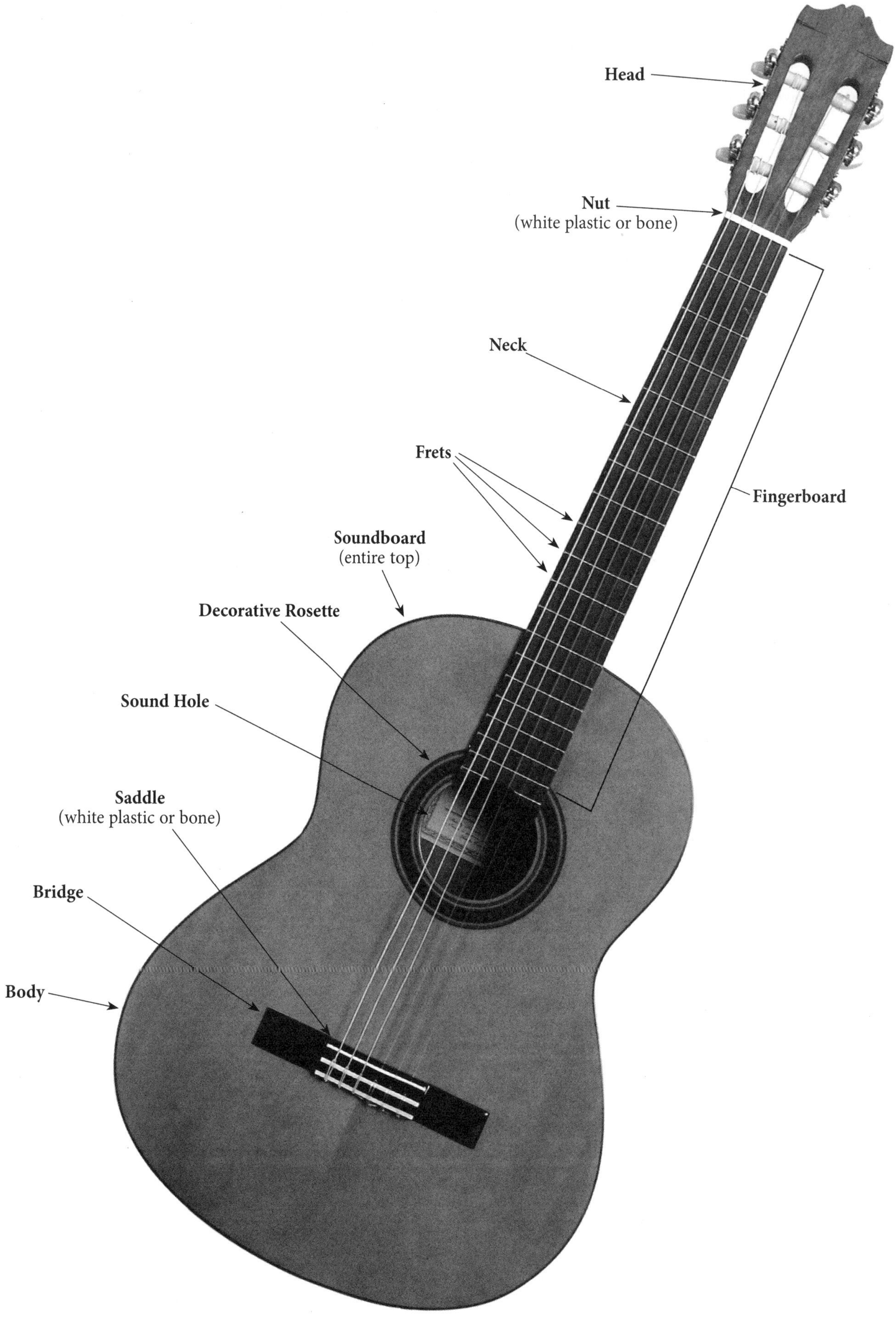

Tuning

The musical pitch to which each string is tuned is shown below. Memorize the names of the notes. Also, learn to associate each string with its proper number, shown in circles.

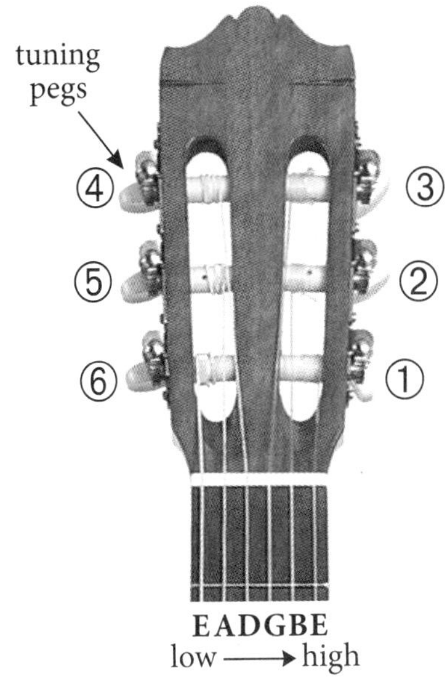

	E	A	D	G	B	E
strings:	⑥	⑤	④	③	②	①

low ⟶ high

The **tuning pegs** are used to adjust the pitch of each string so that the instrument is correctly tuned. You'll also need a pitch reference, such as a keyboard or pitch pipe.

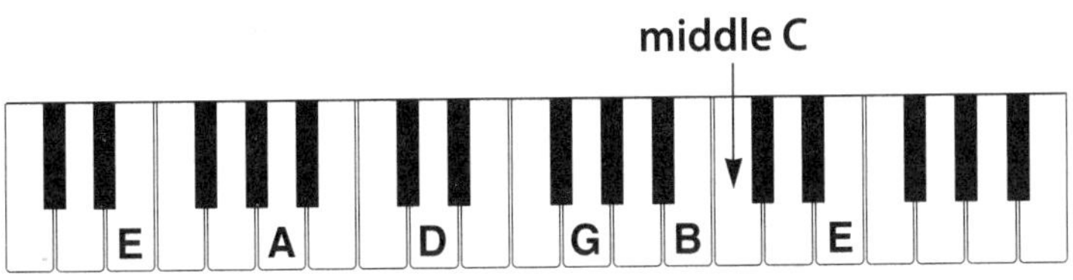

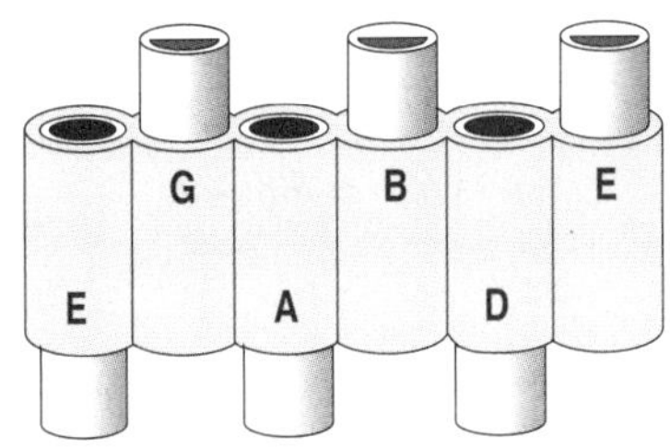

Then, use the tuning pegs to match the sound of each string to the pitch-reference, starting with the sixth string. Turn the appropriate key to raise or lower the pitch as needed.

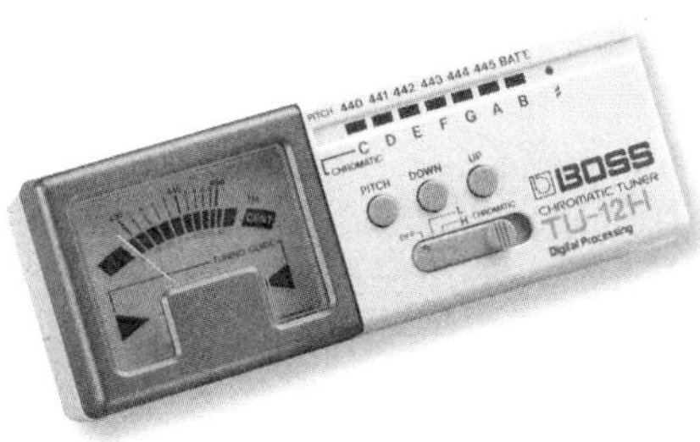

Many guitarists prefer to use an electronic guitar tuner (available in guitar shops and music stores for under $40). Electronic tuners are very popular, because they have a dial or LED display that show when you're perfectly in tune.

RELATIVE TUNING

To check or to correct your tuning when no pitch source is available, follow these steps:

- ✓ Assume the sixth string is tuned correctly to E.
- ✓ Press the sixth string at the 5th fret. This is the note A. Match the open fifth string to it.
- ✓ Repeat this procedure for the other strings, as shown. Notice that each open string is tuned to the string below at the 5th fret—except for the second string, B, which is tuned to the 4th fret of the G string.

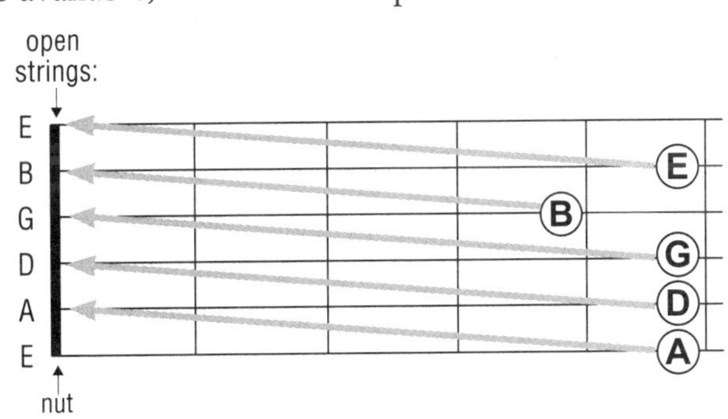

Playing Position

First, you'll need the following:

- An armless chair such as a desk or dining room chair
- A music stand (not shown), available at guitar shops and music stores for under $30
- A guitar footstool (shown below), available at guitar shops (and some music stores) for under $20

Then, seat yourself and position the guitar as you see below. Keep the following points in mind:

The Right Hand

Correct right-hand position is essential to good playing. Use the following procedure to get started:

1. Place your hand on the strings in the form of a loose fist, as shown. (Make sure the forearm, not the upper arm, is resting on the guitar.)

2. Push up with the fingers so that they uncurl, placing the tip of your thumb on the sixth string and the tips of your fingers on the treble (clear nylon) strings. Your hand should look very much like this, with your wrist 2–3 inches from the top of the guitar.

This is the basic position used for most playing. Practice it until your right hand goes into the correct position easily and naturally.

ABOUT FINGERNAILS

Classical guitar is played with the fingernails of the right hand, for good tone and accuracy of touch. Correct filing and use of the nails is a subject which we'll explore in *Book 2*; for now, you can play with your fingertips. However, you should begin using a multi-grit soft nail file (available in the cosmetic section of department stores and drugstores) to take good care of your nails. Shape them to the contour of the fingertip so that as they grow out, they extend slightly beyond the tip as shown.

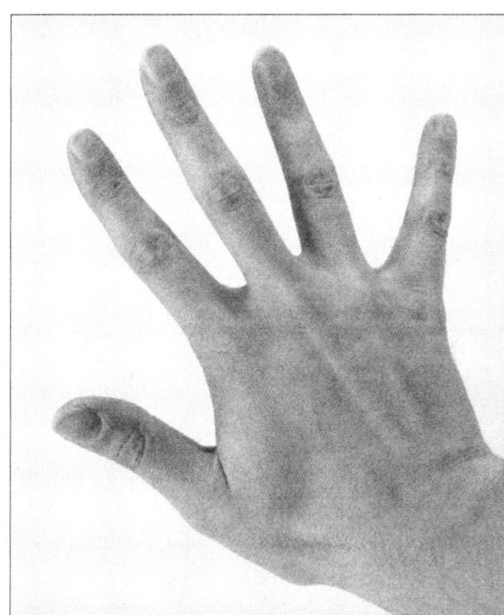

The Rest Stroke

The basic right-hand technique you'll be using in this book is the **rest stroke**. It's called "rest stroke" (*apoyando* in Spanish) because the finger comes to rest on the adjacent string. The rest stroke produces a clear, strong tone and is especially useful in the early phase of your study.

WITH THE INDEX AND MIDDLE FINGERS

Notes on the treble strings (the highest three strings) are played by the index and middle fingers in **alternation**.

As shown in the photos, rest your thumb on the sixth (or fifth) string for support, and then:

- Place the tip of your index finger (*i*) on the first string.
- Play by pulling your fingertip across the string, coming to rest against the second string. Notice that the middle finger (*m*) is now slightly extended and ready to play.

- Now play the first string with *m*, exactly as you did with *i*. Notice how the fingers exchange places; *i* is once again ready to play.
- Practice alternating *i–m* on each treble string *separately*, as shown below. Try to produce an even, steady rhythm (like walking: left–right, left–right, etc.).

string 1 i m i m i m i m i m i m
or 2
or 3

In classical guitar music, the fingers of the right hand are designated by the letters *p*, *i*, *m*, and *a*, which are abbreviations of their Spanish names:

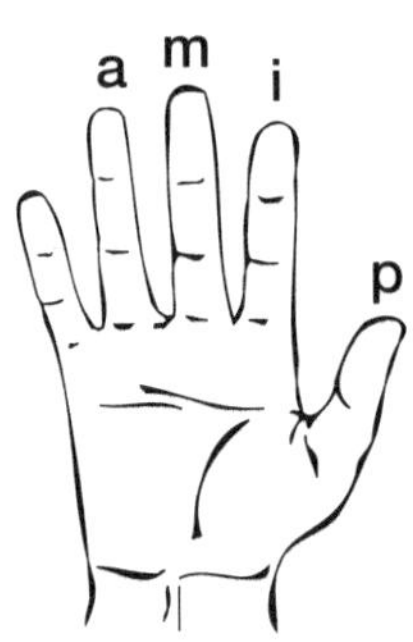

p (*pulgar*) = thumb

i (*indice*) = index

m (*medio*) = middle

a (*anular*) = ring

In this book, we'll be using only *p*, *i*, and *m*. (You'll begin using *a* in *Book 2.*)

Now, try "walking" from string to string; repeat this pattern until it feels comfortable.

string 1	i	m	i	m								
string 2					i	m	i	m				
string 3									i	m	i	m

It may seem a bit strange to play this way, since most people think "plucking" is the natural way to play. Plucking—which is called **free stroke** *(tirando* in Spanish)—will be introduced in *Book 2*. For now, just practice the alternating rest stroke with *i–m* until it feels comfortable and natural.

WITH THE THUMB

The thumb is generally used to play the bass strings (the lowest three strings). To play a rest stroke with the thumb, first place *i* and *m* on the treble strings for support, and then:

- ✓ Place the tip of the thumb (*p*) on the sixth string.
- ✓ Push down gently with the thumb until the tip comes to rest against the fifth string.
- ✓ Make sure that the tip stays relaxed; that is, turned back slightly (not hooked).

Do the same for the fifth string, then the fourth. When you get the feel of the movement, try the "walking" pattern below. Repeat it until you're comfortable with it.

string 4					p	p		
string 5			p	p			p	p
string 6	p	p						

Reading Music

PITCH NOTATION

Music for guitar is written using a **staff** with five lines and four spaces. At the beginning of the staff is a **treble clef** sign. Notes higher in pitch appear higher on the staff; notes lower in pitch appear lower on the staff.

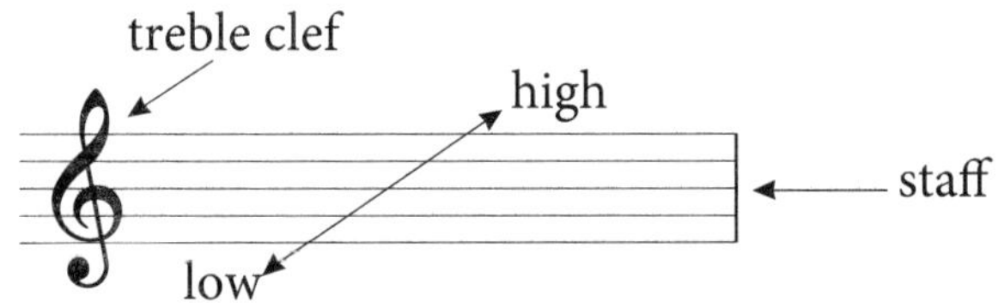

Each line and space on the staff has a letter name. The lines, from bottom to top, are **E–G–B–D–F.** The spaces are **F–A–C–E** (easily remembered as "face").

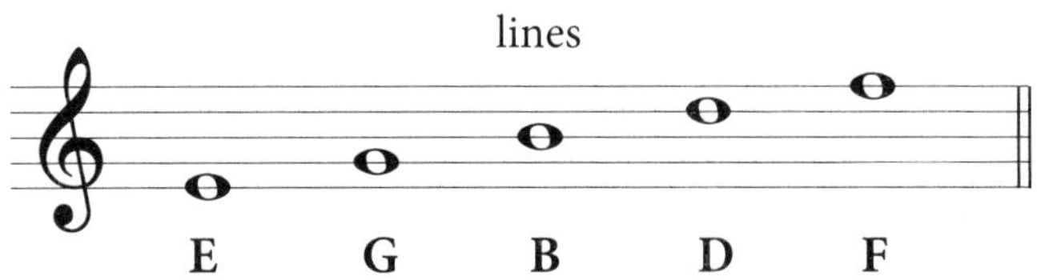

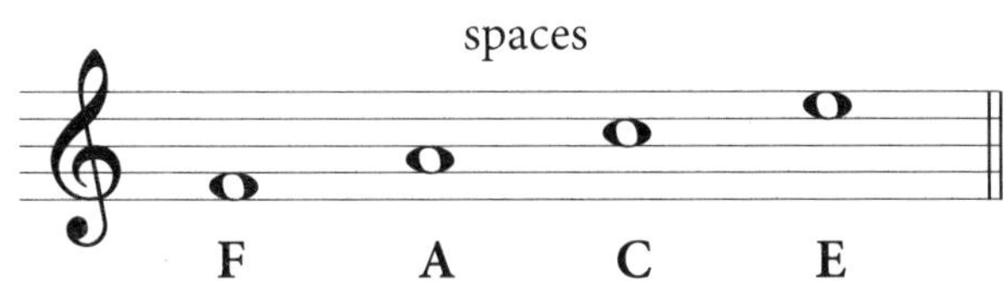

Notice that E and F appear at different places on the staff. That's because the musical alphabet has just seven letters, A to G, and repeats itself every eight notes. The space between higher and lower notes of the same name is called an **octave**.

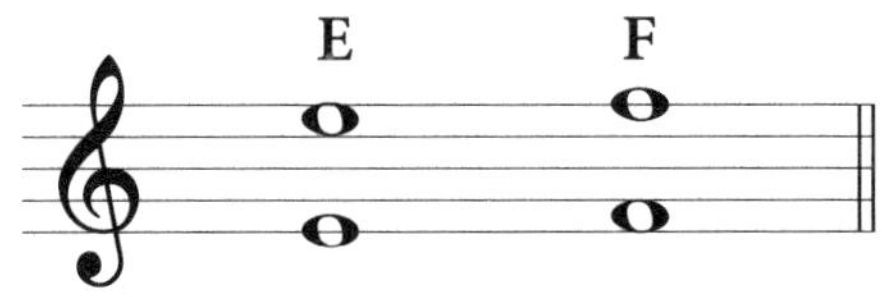

Octave 1 **Octave 2** **Octave 3**

A B C D E F G →A B C D E F G→ a b c d e f g →(etc.)

To accommodate the full range of pitch, **ledger lines** are used to extend the staff both higher and lower. The notes above and below the staff that you'll be learning in this book are shown below.

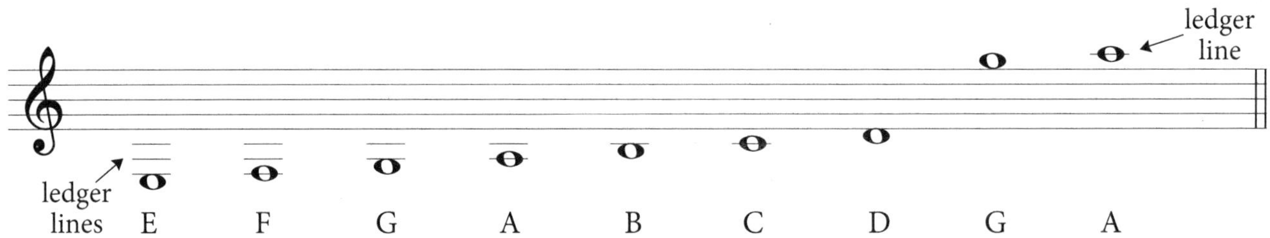

RHYTHMIC NOTATION

Musical rhythm is based on beat (also called pulse). Beats are counted by using **measures** (or **bars**), separated by **bar lines**. A **double bar line** indicates the end of a section and a **terminal bar line** indicates the end of a piece.

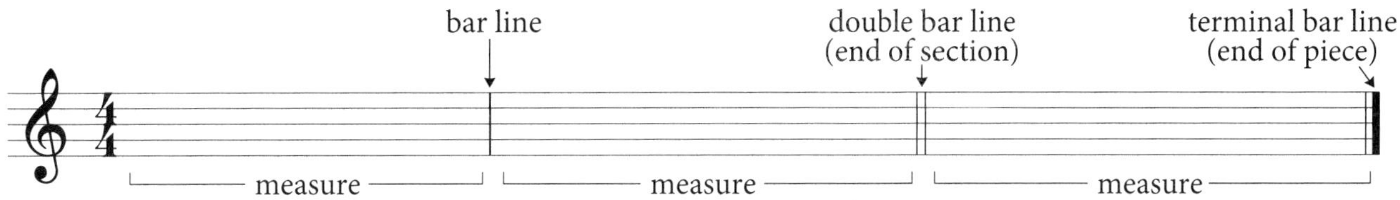

A **time signature** always appears at the beginning of a piece. The upper number indicates how many beats are in a measure. The lower number indicates the duration (or note value) of each beat. For example:

time signature → 4/4 = four beats to a measure
= **quarter note** gets one beat (1/4 measure)

4/4 is the most common time signature; **3/4** is the next most common. Count them as shown below, with a slight emphasis on the first beat (called the **downbeat**).

quarter note

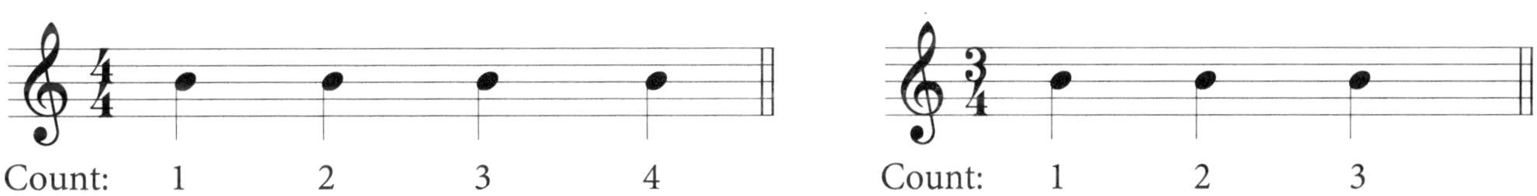

Notes can be of any duration. These are the most basic note values:

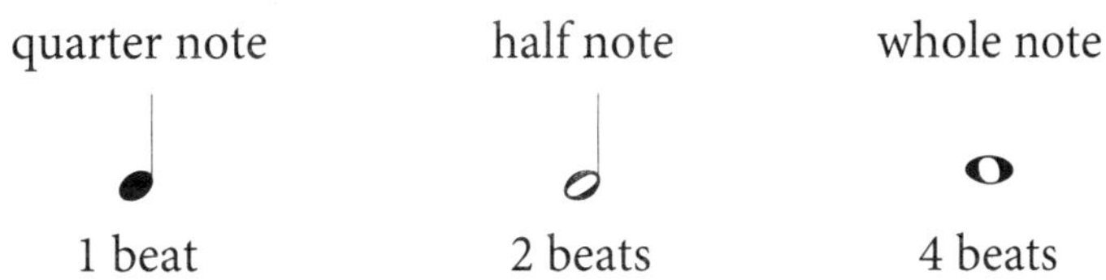

For a note that gets three beats, the **dotted half note** is used. A dot (·) after any note extends the note value by one half.

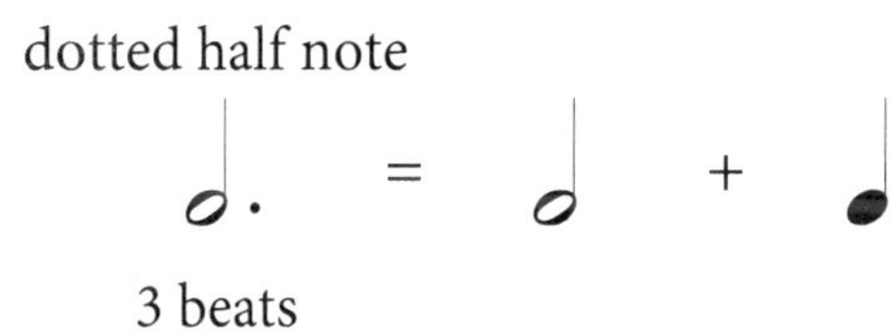

TIP: You'll master rhythmic notation and improve your "feel" for rhythm by *counting aloud* as you practice, beginning with the exercises on the next page.

Open Strings 1, 2, and 3

The following exercises are played on the open treble strings. (Strings are referred to as "open" when they are played without being fretted by the left hand.)

Use the alternating *i–m* rest stroke, and count aloud as you play.

First String E

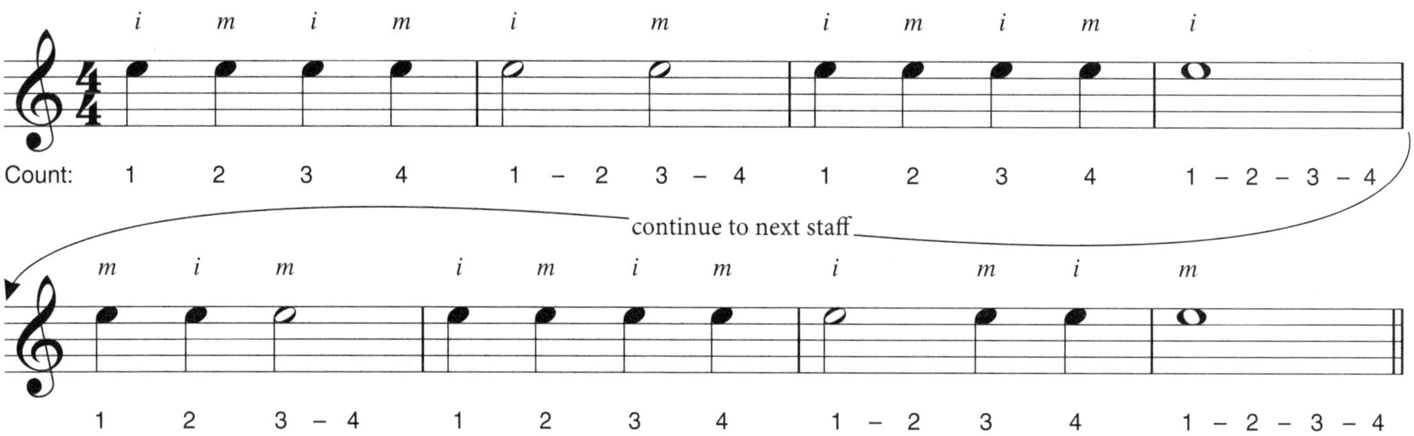

Second String B

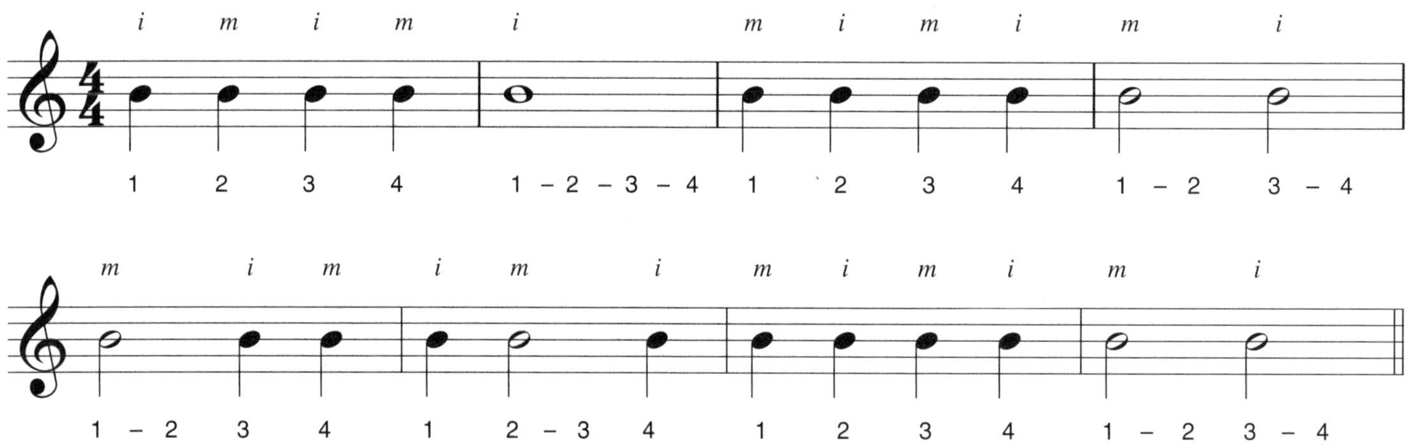

Notice the 3/4 time signature below. (Remember, the dotted half note equals three beats.)

Third String G

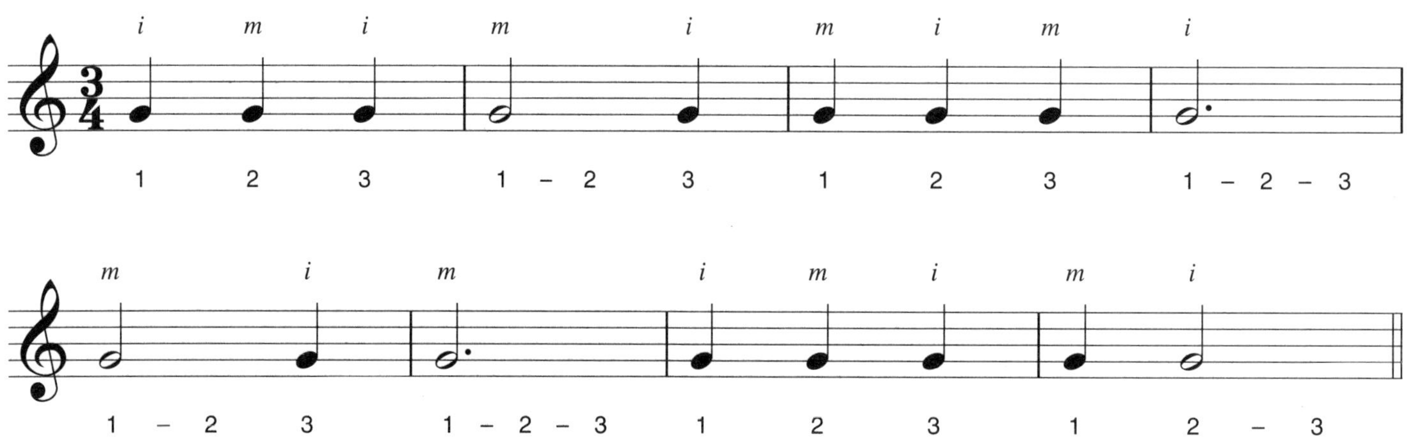

COMBINING STRINGS

Now try "walking" across the strings. You'll be playing only quarter notes here, so instead of counting aloud, say the letter names of the notes as you play.

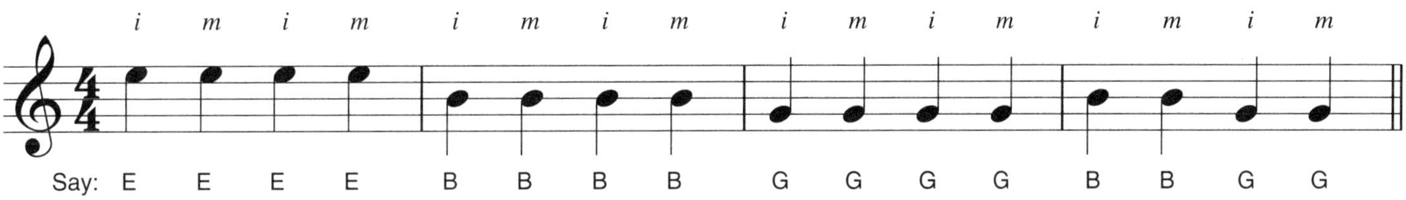

Be sure to keep alternating *i* and *m* as you cross from string to string.

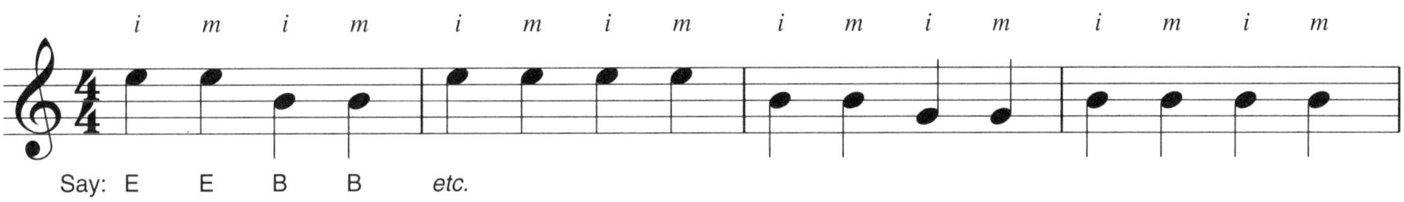

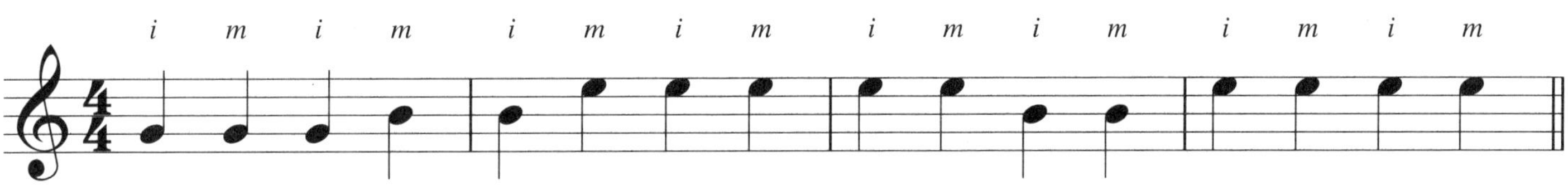

Combine walking across the strings with the different kinds of note values.

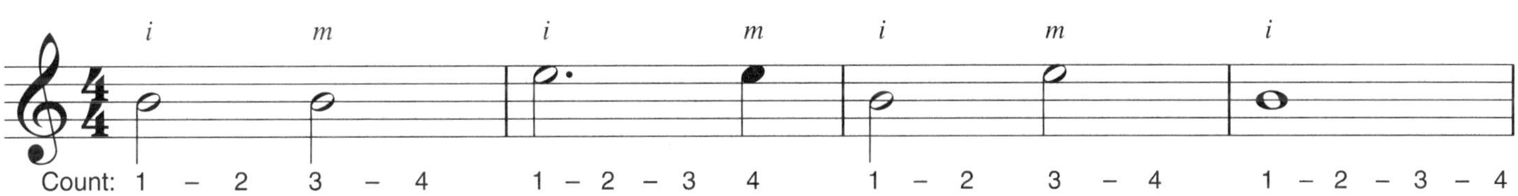

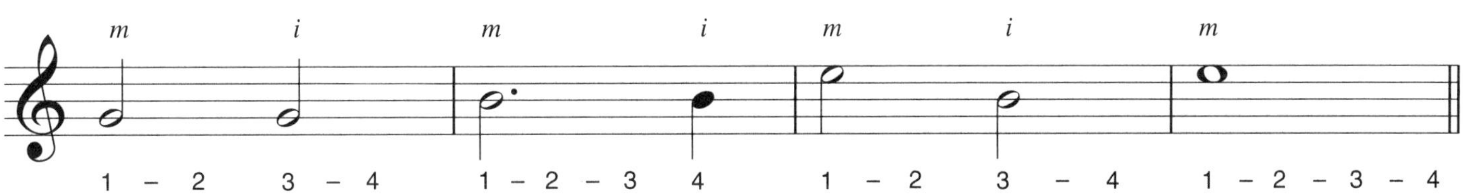

Notice that the next exercise begins with the middle finger.

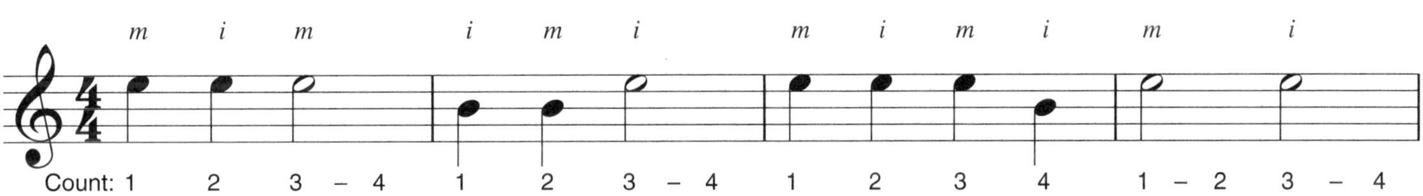

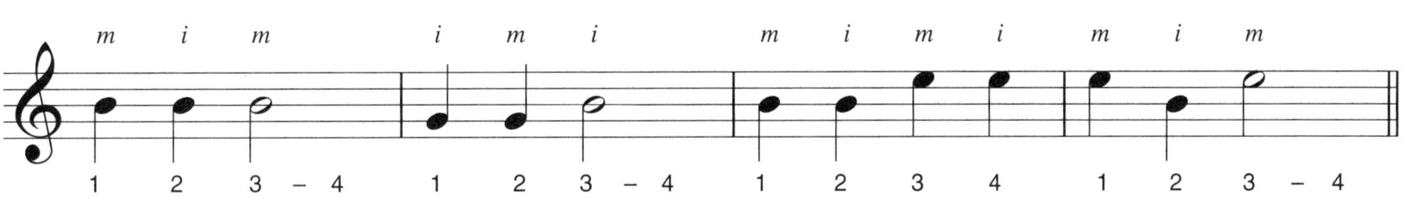

The Open Bass Strings

Practice the following exercises with your thumb (*p*) rest stroke, as shown on page 11.

Sixth String E

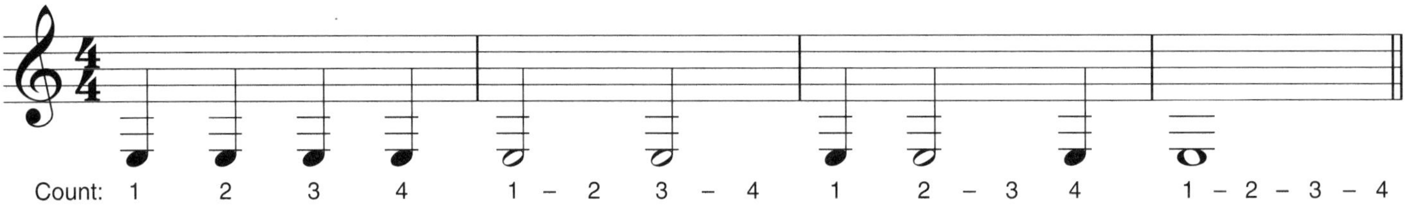

Fifth String A

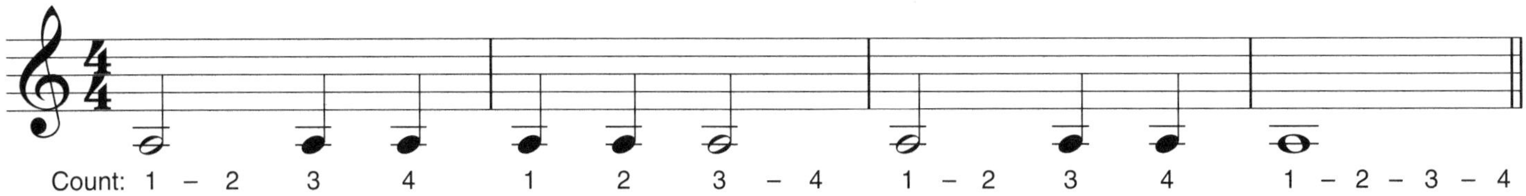

Fourth String D

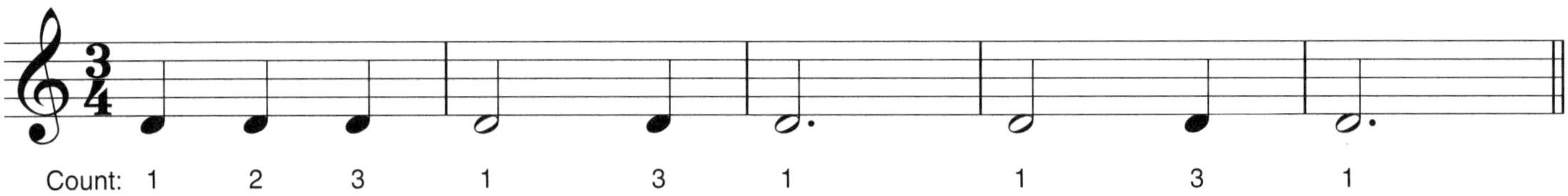

E, A, and D

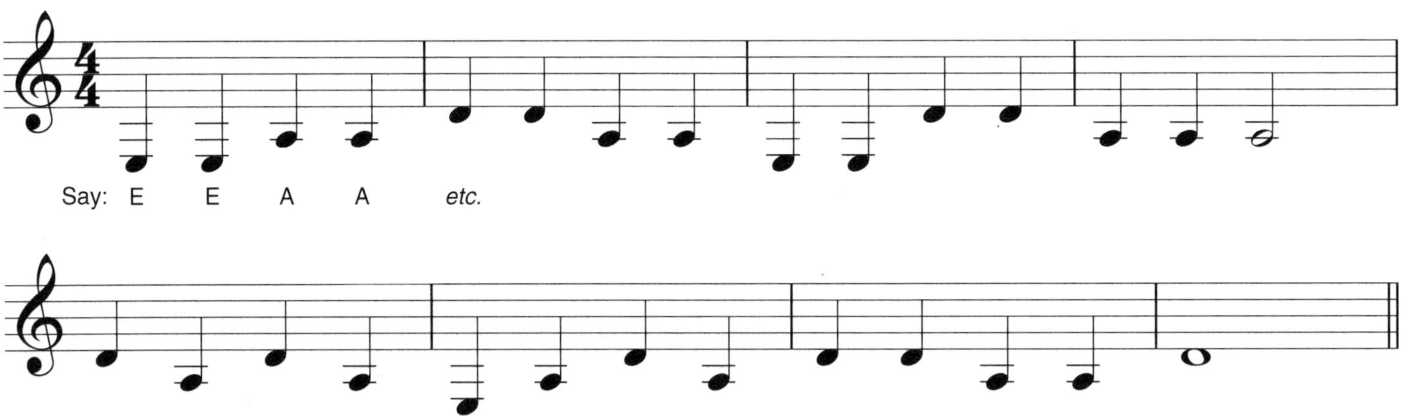

Combining Thumb and Fingers

To play with both the thumb and the fingers, you'll need to learn the free stroke with *p*. (It's possible to use the rest stroke, but most players prefer a free stroke *p* when playing in combination with a rest stroke *i* and *m*.)

FREE STROKE THUMB

The free stroke with *p* uses the same kind of thumb movement as the rest stroke, except that the tip doesn't come to rest against the next string. Instead, it moves toward the tip of the index finger and completes the stroke with an economical return to playing position.

In the following two exercises, you'll be learning how to play a treble string melody with bass accompaniment (the first piece is on page 23). Be sure to maintain strict alternation of *i* and *m*.

1

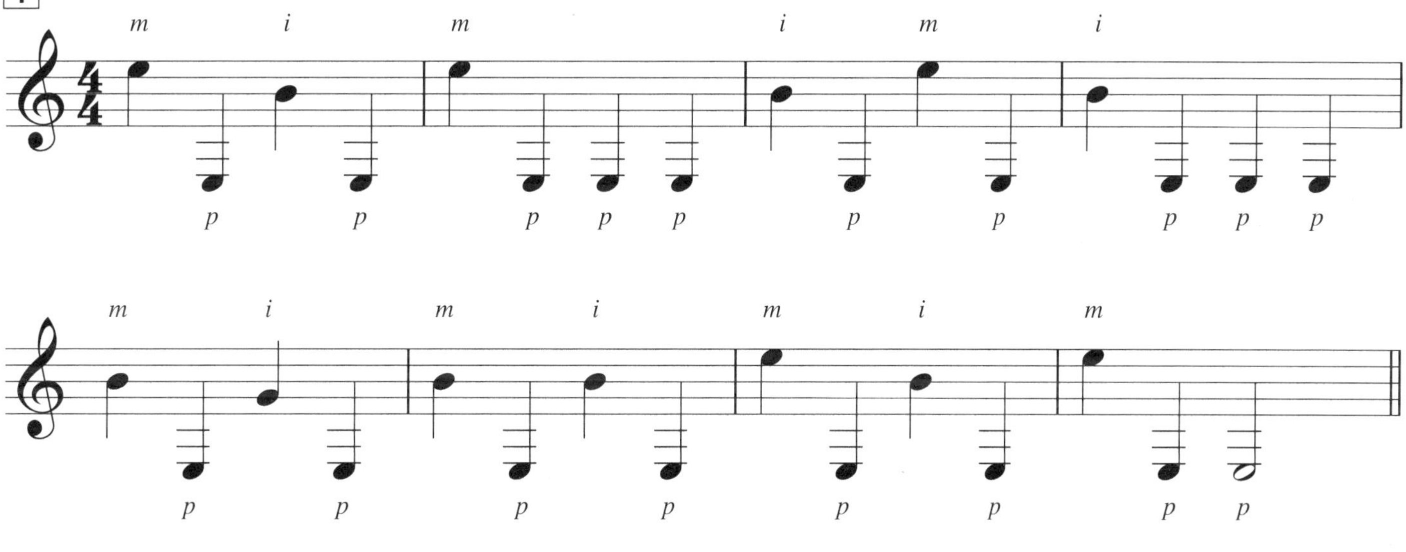

2

Music Review

Write in the correct time signatures.

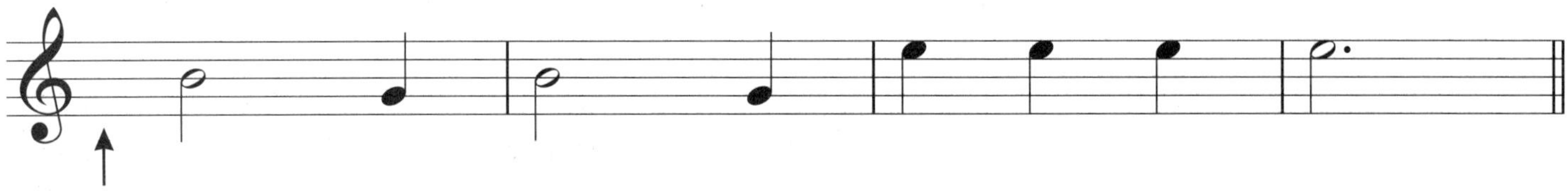

Write the letter name under each note.

B ___ ___ ___ ___ ___ ___ ___ ___ ___

Write the string number under each note.

6 ___ ___ ___ ___ ___ ___ ___ ___ ___

Name the staff lines and spaces.

E ___ ___ ___ ___ ___ ___ ___ ___ ___

How many beats does each note get?

___ ___ ___ ___ ___ ___

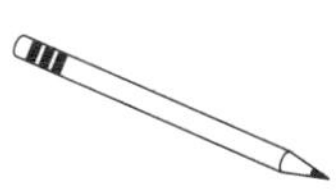

Throughout the book, you'll frequently see short interactive units similar to the above. Look for the pencil icon, and fill in the blank spaces.

The Left Hand

Now it's time to begin using the left hand.

In the correct left-hand position (a) your fingers are curved, and (b) the thumb is partly on its side, with the tip turned back. You'll see that in this position, the fingers and thumb oppose each other like a pair of pliers, as in the first photograph below.

✔ Proper Thumb Position

⃠ Bad Thumb Position

FINGER POSITION

To learn what good finger position looks like, try putting all your fingers on the third string, with a finger on each fret. Try to curve and separate them as shown. If you find this difficult at first, don't be concerned—most students do. Strength and separation will come with good practice.

ARM POSITION

Your arm position should be relaxed and natural, with the elbow pointed generally downwards, or toward the floor.

Notes on the First String

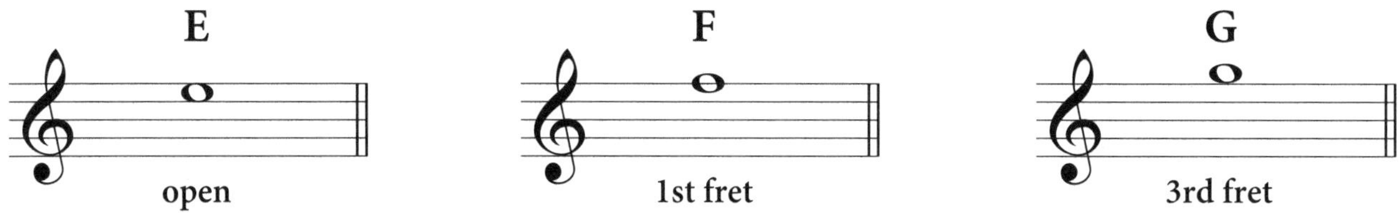

Practice the following exercises to learn the new notes, using the *i–m* rest stroke (begin with either *i* or *m*). Keep your left-hand fingers curved and well spaced, and play close to the metal frets—not in the middle of the space between frets. Use your first finger on the first fret (F) and your third finger on the 3rd fret (G).

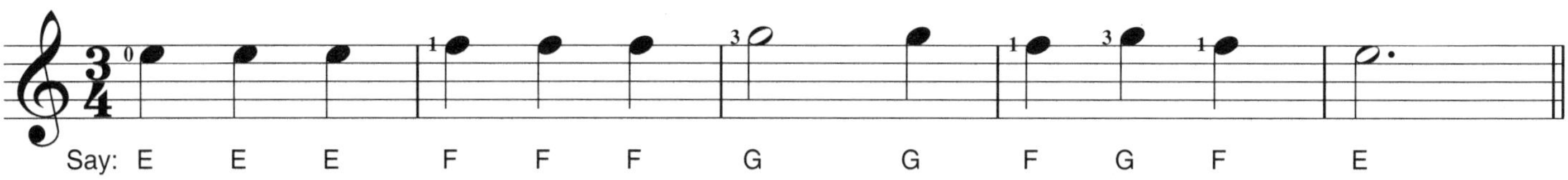

Write in the names of the notes, then play.

Write in the fret/finger numbers, then play.

Notes on the Second String

B

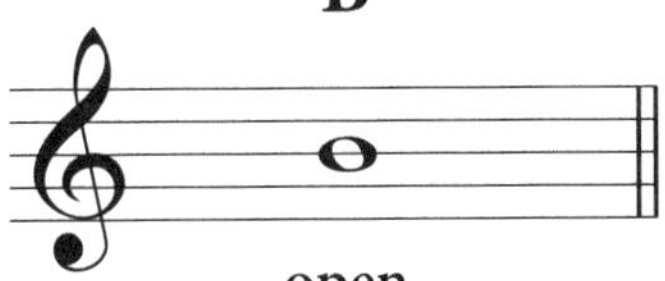

open

C

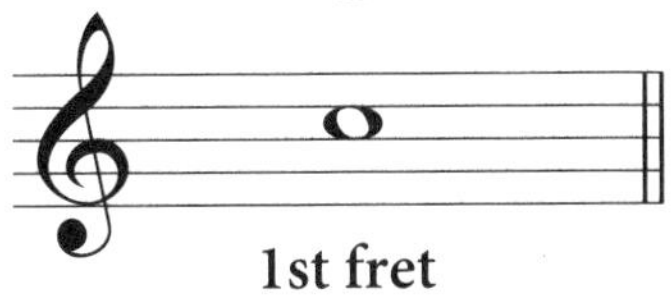

1st fret

D

3rd fret

This time, keep your first finger on the 1st fret (C) while your third finger plays the third fret (D). This will prevent unnecessary finger action and help you maintain a good hand position.

Say: B B B B C C C C D D C C B B B

TIP: It's usually a good idea to leave a finger in place until necessary to move it. Moving a finger requires effort; don't move fingers unnecessarily. (For further practice, repeat the exercises on the previous page, using this technique.)

Write in the names of the notes, then play.

B ___ C ___ ___ ___ ___ ___ ___ ___ ___ ___ ___ ___

Write in the fret/finger numbers, then play.

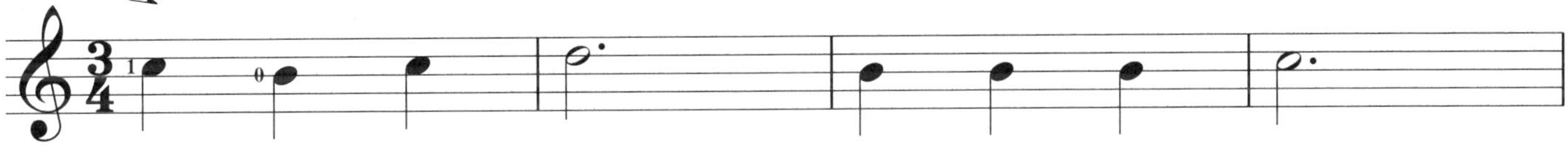

1 0 ___ ___ ___ ___ ___ ___

___ ___ ___ ___ ___ ___ ___ ___ ___ ___

Combining Strings 1 and 2

MELODIC MOVEMENT

When notes move from space to line or line to space, we call it movement by **step**, or **scalewise** movement. (The musical term "scale" comes from Italian *scala*, a set of steps or a ladder.) The following exercise combines the new notes you've learned into ascending and descending scale patterns. Begin on *m* and continue alternating.

When notes move by more than one line or space, we call it movement by **skip**. (Most melodies, like the ones on the next page, move by a combination of steps and skips.) This exercise is more difficult—take it slowly, and begin with *i*.

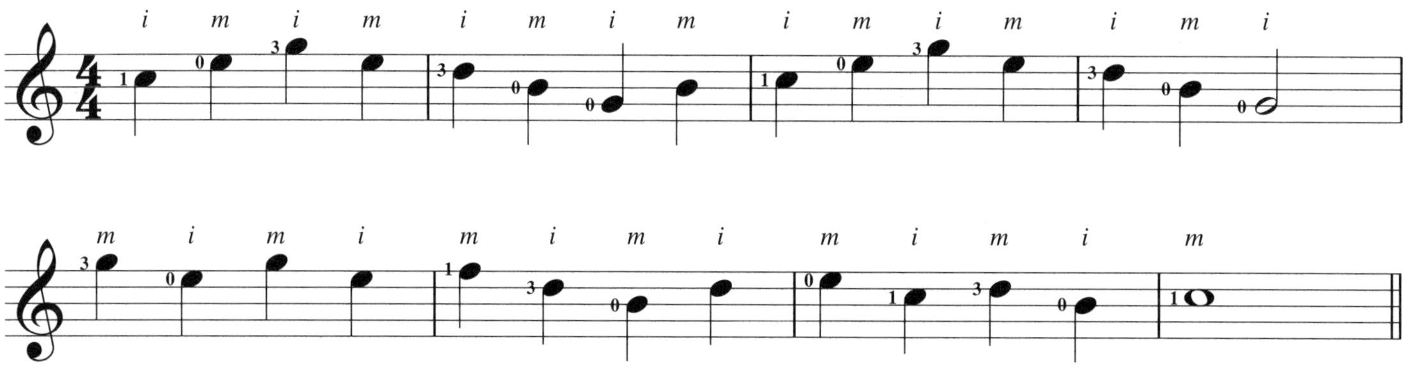

ABOUT CROSS FINGERING

Cross fingering occurs when *i* crosses over *m* to reach a higher string, or when *m* crosses under *i* to reach a lower string. It's very common in scale playing—in fact, you've already used it in measures 3 and 4 of the first exercise above. But frequent cross-fingerings are awkward, so it's usually a good idea to begin with the finger that produces the fewest of them. (The second exercise actually contains no cross-fingerings if you begin with *i*, whereas if you begin with *m* and alternate correctly, you'll find that the string changes feel very unnatural.)

For the same reason, occasionally it makes sense to repeat a finger (after a long note or a phrase ending). You'll begin using this exception to the rule of alternation in "Merrily We Roll Along" on the next page—look for the (*) in measure 5.

First Songs

These familiar melodies will develop your knowledge of the new notes. Notice also the way they combine steps and skips (or, **conjunct** motion and **disjunct** motion).

Lightly Row

Go Tell Aunt Rhody

Sur le Pont d'Avignon

Merrily We Roll Along

Notes on the Third String

G

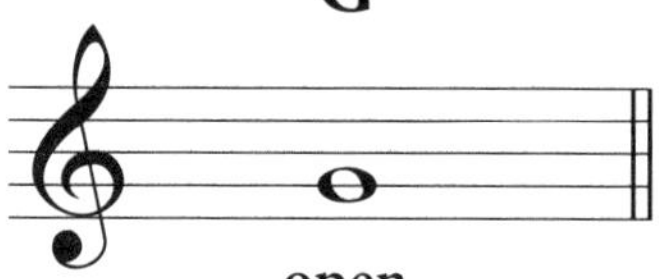

open

A

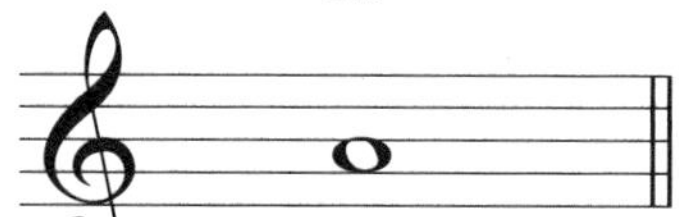

2nd fret

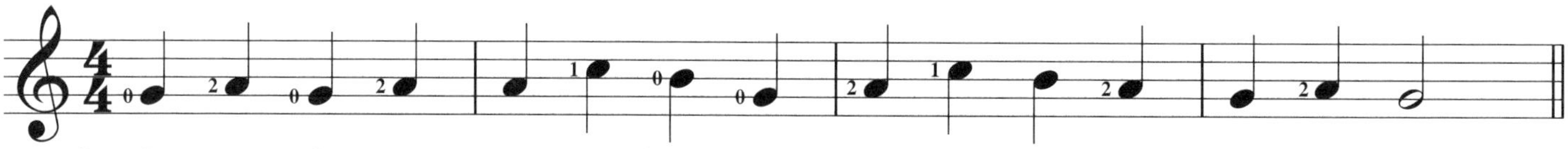

Twinkle

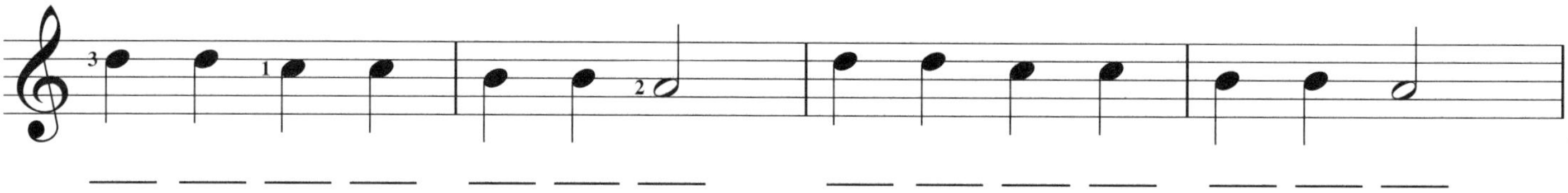

Yankee Doodle

Besides solo playing you'll enjoy **ensemble playing** with one or more players (duo, trio, quartet, etc.). Ensemble playing will also improve your sight reading and musicianship. From here on, this book will include duets for you to play with your teacher or a more advanced student.

Au Clair de la Lune
(DUET)

Melody with Bass Accompaniment

In the following two solos, you'll begin to play music in the classical style by combining a treble-string melody with a bass-string accompaniment. The first piece is an **etude** (French for "study")—that is, a piece intended to develop technique and/or musicianship. Etudes are usually based on a repeated musical idea, as this one is.

Use the right-hand technique you've practiced on the open strings (p. 17)—*i–m* rest stroke on the treble strings, free stroke *p* on the bass strings. (As a reminder, bass string numbers are included.)

Etude

"Slavonic Dance" is a bit more complex and makes an interesting performance piece, especially if you play it with a repeat. Some left-hand fingering is given; write in a more complete fingering if you think you'll need it.

Tip: Even advanced players write in their fingerings. It's always a good idea to do this whenever you think it will help you learn a piece.

Slavonic Dance

A **repeat sign** appearing at the end of the piece means to "play again" from the beginning. Many of the short pieces in this book can also be played to good effect with a repeat, even though the repeat may not be indicated.

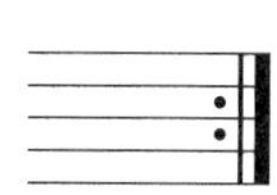

Rests

A **rest** is the symbol for a musical silence. The length of a rest is the same as the corresponding note—quarter, half, and whole.

Quarter rest

1 beat

Half rest

2 beats

Whole rest

4 beats

The whole rest indicates a complete measure of silence in both 4/4 and 3/4. Quarter rests and half rests are used to fill incomplete measures, or to indicate an exact cut-off of sound (called **note-stopping**). For now, just learn to recognize rests when you see them. Practice the following two lines of music, counting aloud; they should sound the same.

1

2

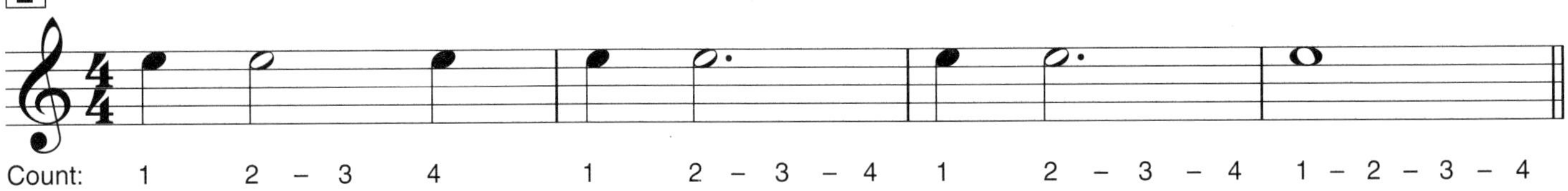

Pickup Notes

Frequently, you'll see an **incomplete measure** at the beginning of a piece. When you do, count aloud from the *beginning* of the measure and start playing on the correct beat. Notes in an incomplete measure are called **upbeats**, or **pickup notes**.

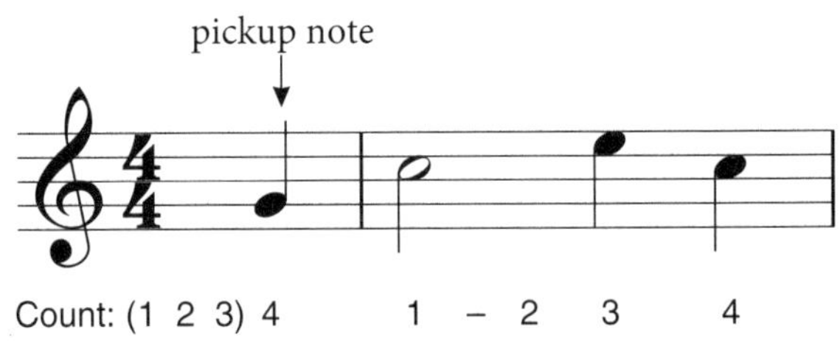

For He's a Jolly Good Fellow

Ties

Notes can be connected over the bar line by a curved line called a **tie**. When you see a tie, don't play the second note; ties are used to extend a note into the next measure. Play the first note, and hold it for the duration of both notes combined. (Be sure to count aloud as you play.)

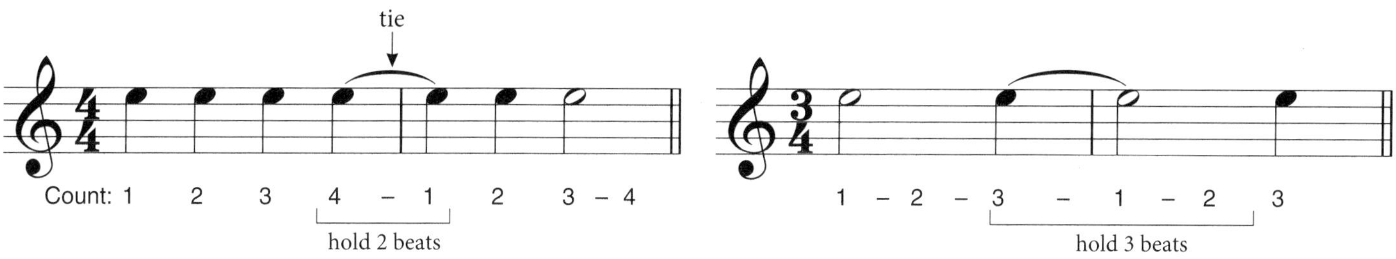

Down in the Valley

Write in the counts below, then play.

When the Saints Go Marching In

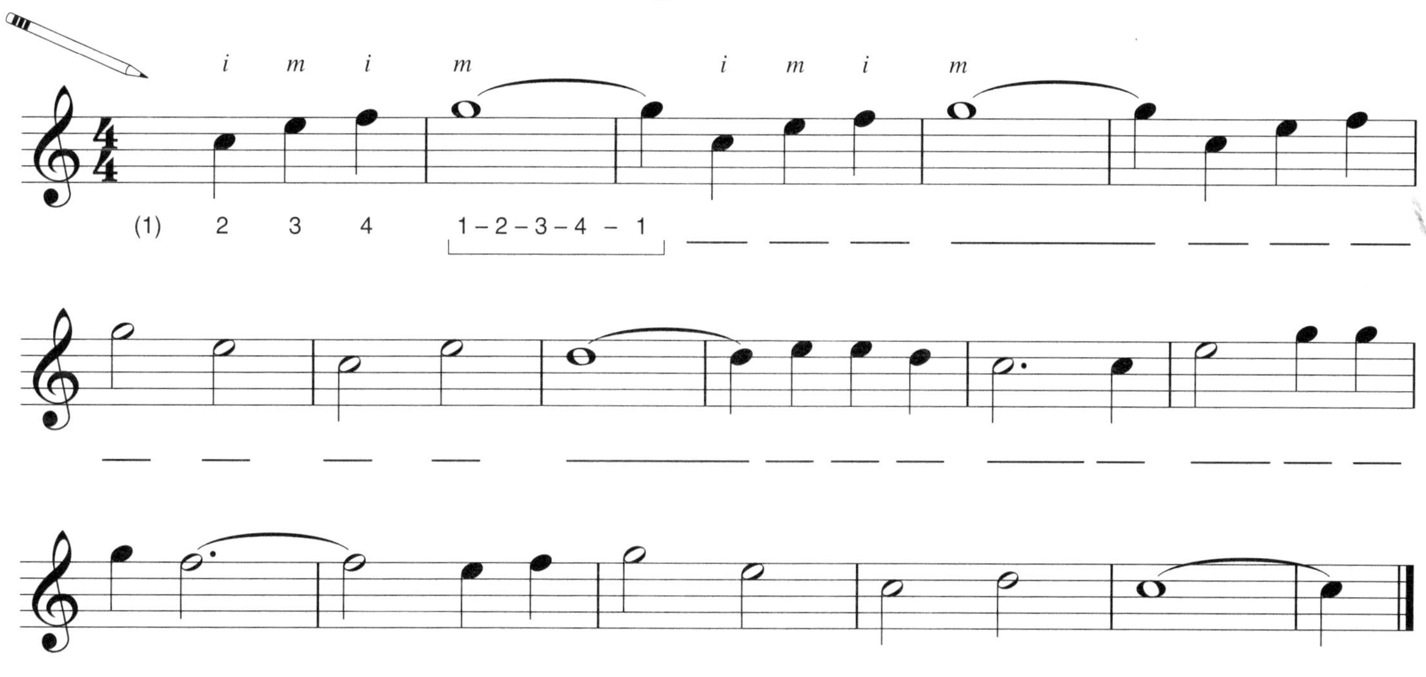

Eighth Notes

So far, we've used whole notes, half notes, and quarter notes. The quarter note can also be subdivided into **eighth notes**. Single eighth notes have a flag on the note stem; groups of eighth notes are connected by a beam. The corresponding rest is an **eighth rest**:

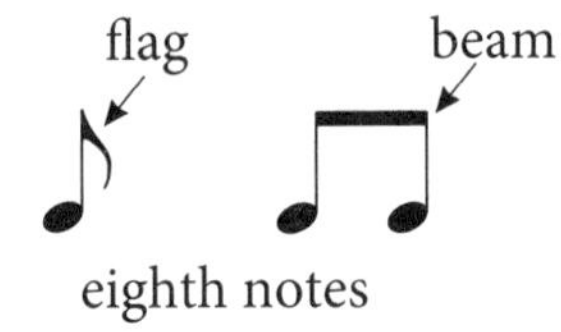

Count eighth notes in 4/4 and 3/4 as shown:

Count the following exercises carefully while you play; be sure to keep a steady beat.

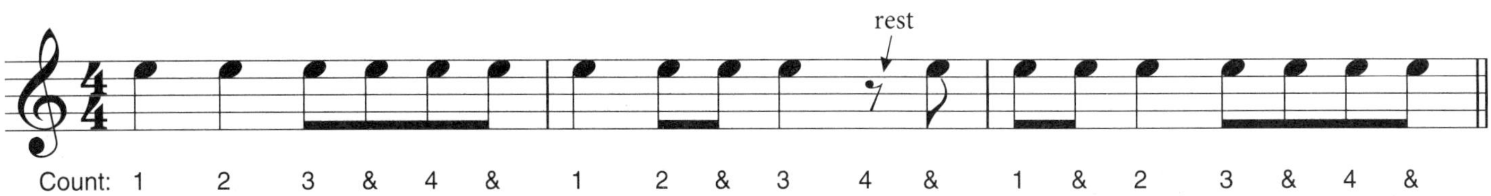

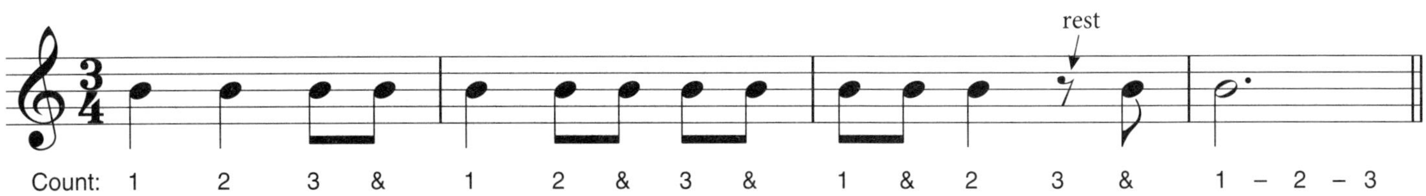

2/4 TIME

The 2/4 time signature is based on the quarter note, with *two* beats to the measure. Like 4/4, 2/4 is a form of **duple meter** (i.e., the measure is divisible by two). It's often used instead of 4/4 for music with a lively tempo, like the following two pieces. Count as shown, and complete the count by filling in the blanks before playing.

Bingo

Good King Wenceslas (DUET)

Music in Two Parts

You've learned how to combine melody with bass in solo playing, using a simplified style of notation. Now it's time to learn how such music is customarily written. First, play this line of music:

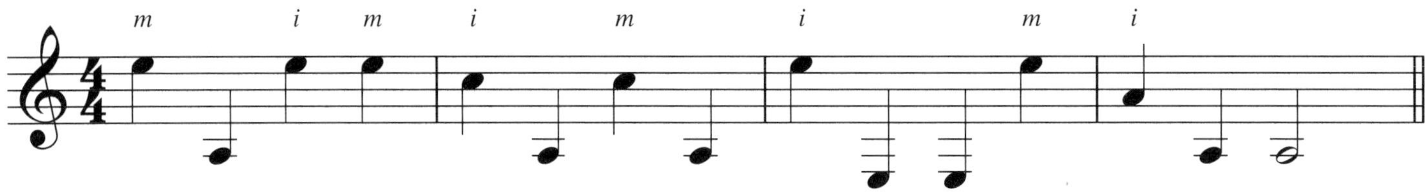

Now play this line—it should sound identical to the first. The only difference is the style of notation; here, the melody and bass are written as two separate **voices**, or parts. Note stems point *up* for a melody; stems point *down* for the bass.

This style of notation may seem more difficult at first, but you'll soon appreciate the way it clarifies the musical texture and represents the true note values.

TIP: Students are sometimes confused by the overlapping time values of the two voices. Notice that each part is counted *separately* to reflect the number of beats in the measure.

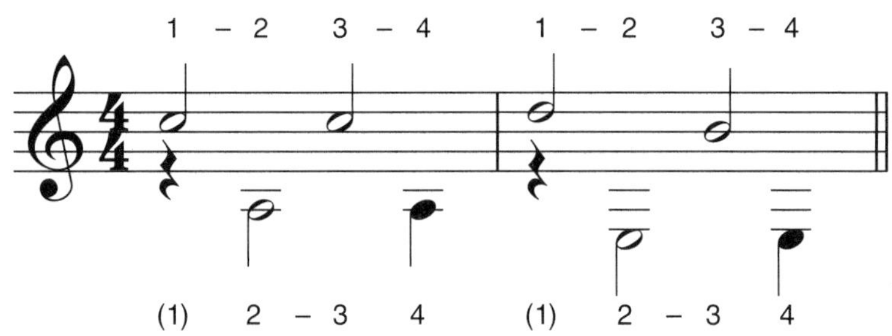

BASS-STOPPING

Bass-string notes will usually continue to ring unless you make an effort to stop them; therefore, the preceding example will probably sound more like this when you play:

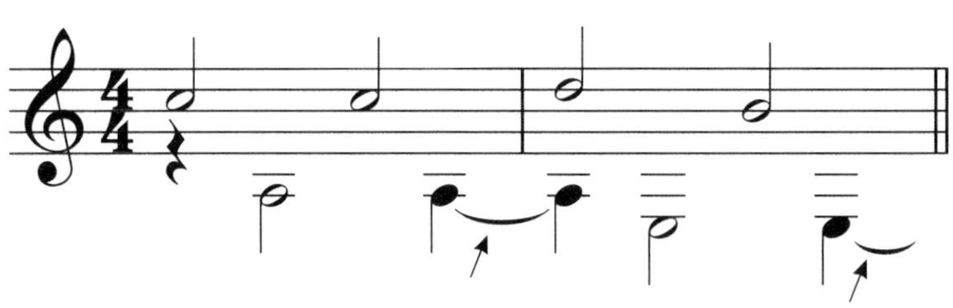

Bass-stopping is a more advanced technique that you'll be learning at a later stage. For now, unless your teacher wants to introduce you to the technique early in your study, you can just let them ring. The slight overlapping of sound is natural to the classical guitar.

A **motive** is a short musical idea. The repeated **rhythmic motive** (𝅗𝅥 ♩ ♩) of this short etude will help you get used to the new style of notation.

Etude

Now, try a somewhat more complex piece. "Chanson Russe" is another French musical term that means "Russian Song"—it's used in classical music for pieces based on the style of Russian folk music.

Chanson Russe

Dotted Quarter Notes

Dotted quarter notes are often used together with eighth notes to create rhythmic variety. Remember, a dot after a note increases its value by half. Thus, a dotted quarter note equals one and a half beats (quarter note + eighth note):

dotted quarter note 1 1/2 beats

Look carefully at this line of music, then practice it several times *counting aloud.* Note that the third measure (dotted quarter + eighth) should sound the same as the second measure, which uses tied notes.

You'll get a "feel" for this kind of rhythm by practicing the following well-known tunes. Count aloud as indicated, and write in the count for "Auld Lang Syne" before playing.

Deck the Halls

Alouette

Auld Lang Syne

The "Ode to Joy" from Beethoven's Ninth Symphony uses the dotted quarter/eighth note for rhythmic emphasis at the end of each four-bar **phrase** (except the third). The tied quarter note on the third phrase-ending creates even more emphasis through **syncopation** (i.e., a melodic accent on an upbeat, which is tied to the next downbeat). This can be tricky, so be sure to count aloud.

Ode to Joy (DUET)

"The Streets of Laredo," a fine old song of the American West, provides excellent practice in playing dotted quarter notes. Notice also the use of regular quarter notes—the alternating style of note values gives the piece its distinctive "swing."

The Streets of Laredo (DUET)

"Shenandoah," another great song of the American West, uses frequent tied notes to create a lyrical and somewhat syncopated melody. This one will test your skill at reading and playing tied notes; be sure to count aloud.

Shenandoah (DUET)

More Advanced Solo Playing

The pieces on this page and the next will further develop your skill as a soloist. The first, "Berceuse," uses a variety of note values and phrase-shapes, and has a double ending. The title means "lullabye"; several great composers have been attracted by this kind of musical form, which captures the gently rocking rhythm of a cradle song.

Berceuse

1ST AND 2ND ENDINGS

In the piece above, the repeat sign is combined with a 1st and 2nd ending. Play the first ending and return to the beginning; on the repeat, skip the first ending and play the second ending.

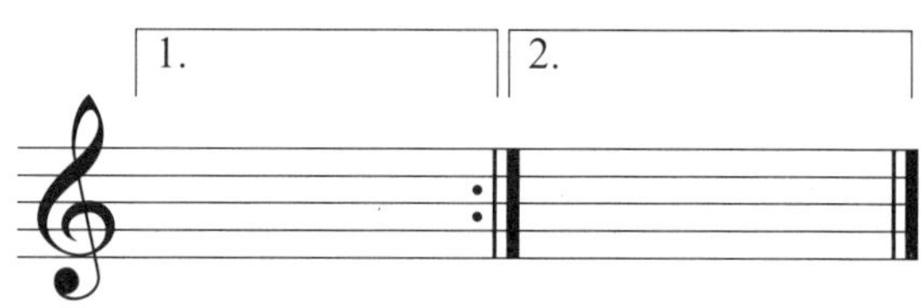

"Song of the Silk Road" is somewhat more difficult, but not as difficult as it may look. This piece uses a **drone bass** and repetitive scale patterns to suggest the exotic musical sounds of the famous caravan route. Keep a steady beat, and remember that in the case of ties, you play only the first note. (This piece does not require you to play *p* together with *i* or *m*.)

Song of the Silk Road

Notes on the Fourth String

D

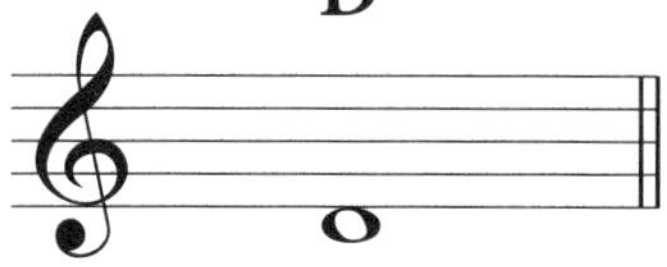

open

E

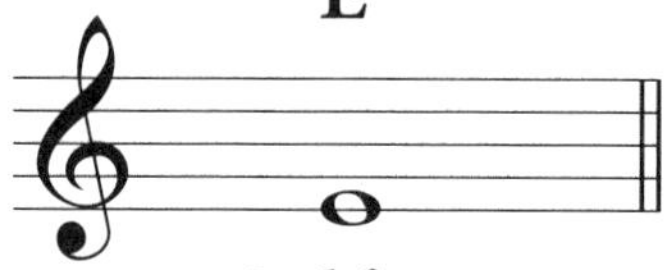

2nd fret

F

3rd fret

Fill in the blanks for each exercise, then play with *p* (rest stroke or free stroke).

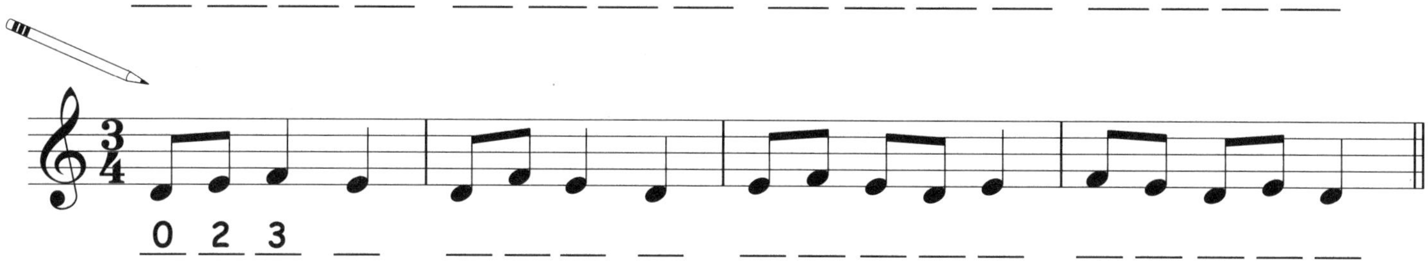

Besides practice for the new notes, this short **estudio** (Spanish for "etude") will give your thumb a workout. Play it entirely with *p*, keeping your fingers "planted" on the treble strings for support.

Fourth-String Estudio

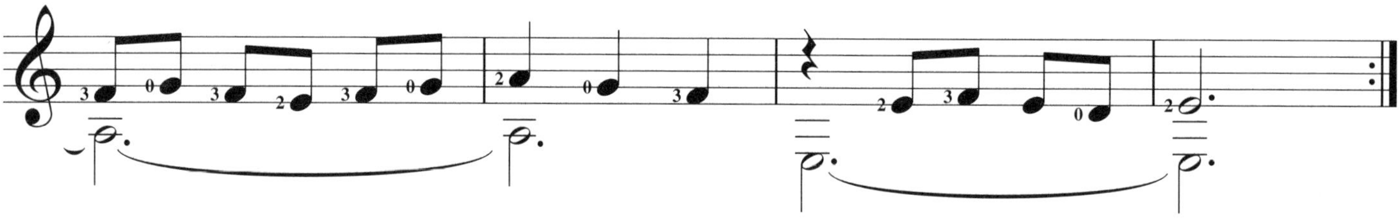

Use *i–m* rest stroke to play the melody of this classic Appalachian folk song.

The Riddle Song (DUET)

Notes on the Fifth String

A

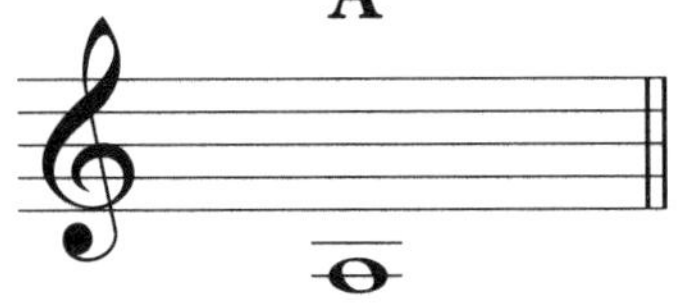

open

B

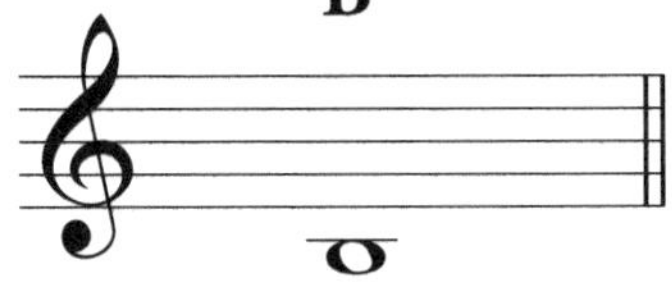

2nd fret

C

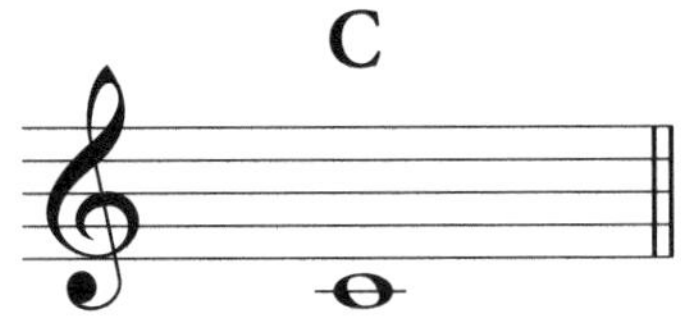

3rd fret

Fill in the blanks for each exercise, then play with *p*.

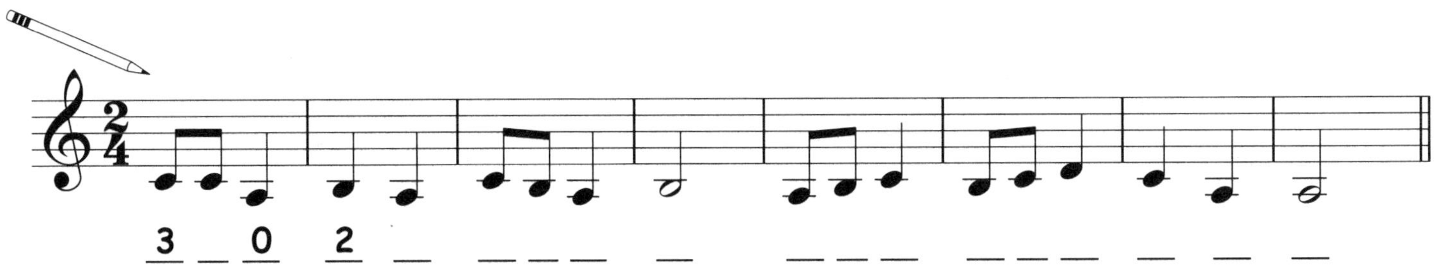

The following exercise is adapted from the first eight bars of a beautiful estudio by Fernando Sor. Sor was one of the greatest Spanish composers for the classical guitar, and is often referred to as "the Beethoven of the guitar." (Play entirely with *p*.)

Soriana

Write in the note names, then play.

Hymn

The following study is adapted from one of the most famous pieces in the classical guitar repertoire—"Asturias" by Isaac Albeniz (also known as "Leyenda"). It's also a workout for *p*, but not as challenging as it may look—there's a lot of repetition. Notice also the use of the *first finger* to play the fifth-string B in the second and third lines. (This prevents awkward, unnecessary movement of the second finger.)

"Asturias" Theme

Use *i–m* to play "Jingle Bells" and the beautiful Thanksgiving song "We Gather Together" by Lowell Mason on the next page. (Lowell Mason, a 19th century New England composer and music educator, is often called "the father of American music education.")

Jingle Bells (DUET)

We Gather Together (DUET)

Sharps and Flats

The notes you've learned so far are the **natural** notes of the musical alphabet. The complete musical alphabet also uses **accidentals**, which are indicated by a sharp (♯) or a flat (♭) after the letter name of the note (A♯, B♭, etc.).

- The sharp sign (♯) raises the pitch of a note by one fret.
- The flat sign (♭) lowers the pitch of a note by one fret.

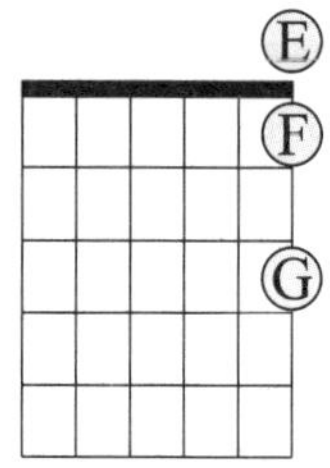

For example, consider the first-string notes you've learned: E (open), F (1st fret), and G (3rd fret). Between F and G there's a second-fret note that's called either F♯ or G♭:

- Moving up one fret from F, the note is called F-sharp (F♯),
- Moving down one fret from G, it is called G-flat (G♭).

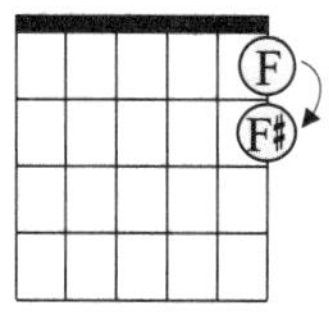

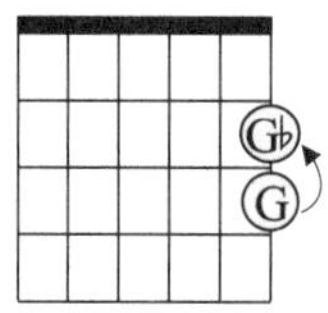

Sharped and flatted notes that identify the same musical pitch, like the F♯ and G♭, are called **enharmonic tones**. Both sharps and flats are used in classical guitar music, but sharps occur more frequently.

We'll start by learning the accidentals on strings 1 and 2:

FIRST STRING

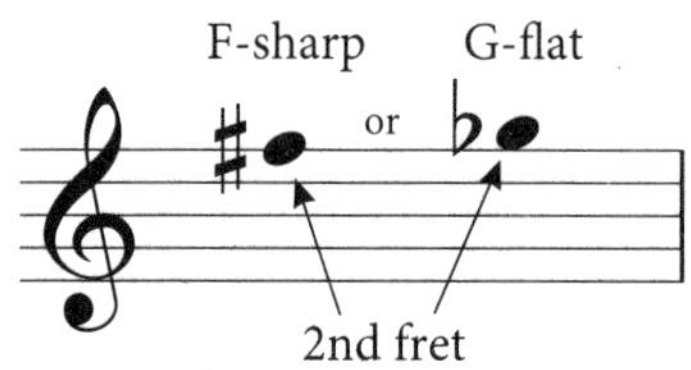

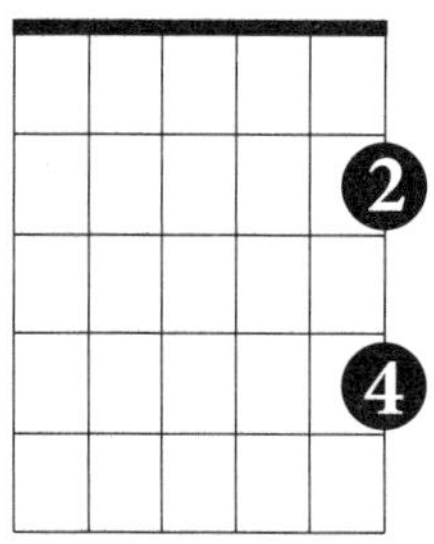

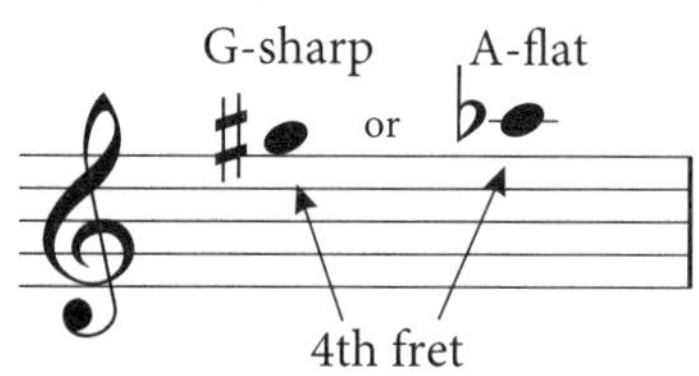

Notice the use of a ledger line above the staff for the fourth-fret A flat. (You'll be learning to use the fifth-fret A natural a bit further on.)

SECOND STRING

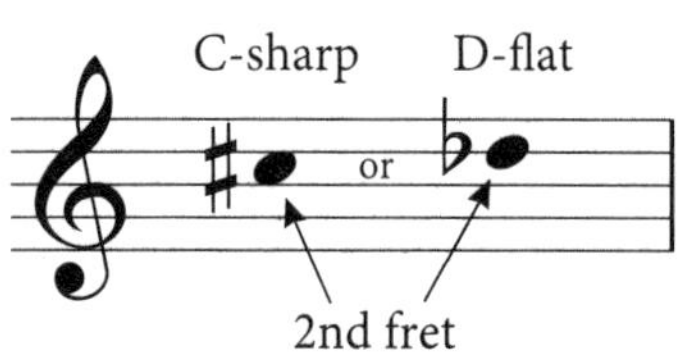

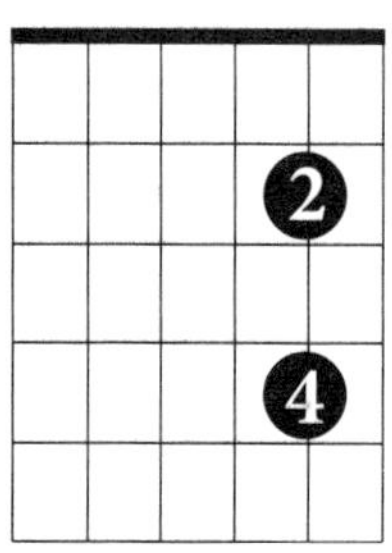

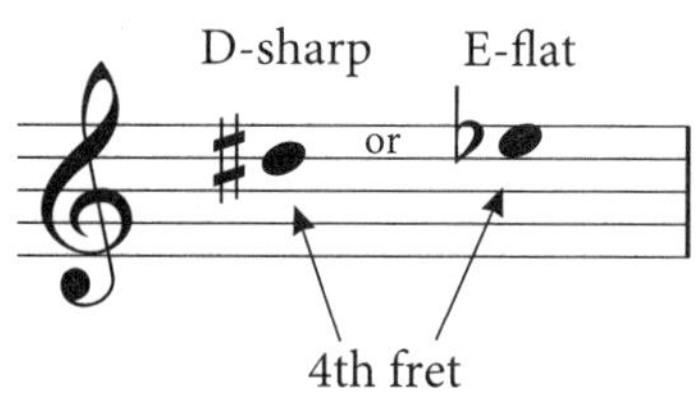

Learn to use the sharped notes on the first two strings by practicing the following scale-pattern exercise. Remember, you'll be using only your *second* and *fourth* fingers.

Chromatic scales are scales that move up or down one fret at a time, using both the natural notes and the accidentals. The following chromatic scale contains all the notes you've learned on the first two strings, with sharps ascending and flats descending. Write in the finger numbers, then practice for additional left-hand development.

The following piece illustrates an important rule: when a note is sharped or flatted in a measure of music, it remains sharp or flat for the whole measure. Since the sign isn't repeated, you'll need to look carefully at measures where a note has been **chromatically altered** by a sharp or flat.

Aura Lee

The Natural Sign

The natural sign (♮) is used to *cancel* a previous sharp or flat within the measure. Also, to avoid possible confusion, the natural sign is often used when a note that was sharped or flatted in the *preceding* measure is used without chromatic alteration. You'll see both uses of the natural sign in the following exercise.

Beethoven's "Für Elise" provides good ensemble practice; when coordinated properly, the two parts create the sound of the original piano solo.

This piece also introduces you to sectional form. Repeat the first section (called the A section); the second ending takes you to the B section, which is also repeated. (The second ending of the B section is also the end of the piece.)

Für Elise (DUET)

1.
2.
p m
p m i m i m i
1.
2.

Besides increasing your knowledge of the fingerboard, the new notes you've learned also open a door to more varied solo playing. The next piece is in the style of a Renaissance dance called "Alman" in England and "Allemande" in France—a stately, 4/4 dance of German origin. (The Renaissance period in music is approximately 1500–1650.)

This piece also requires a little more left-hand control. Look closely at the measures where you see a fifth-string B in the bass. Here, you'll need to hold down the B with your first finger so that you can finger the treble notes comfortably. Even more important, this will allow the bass note to **sustain** (i.e., keep ringing) while you play the treble notes.

Alman

ACCIDENTALS ON STRING 3

The chromatically-altered notes on the third string are shown below:

Third String

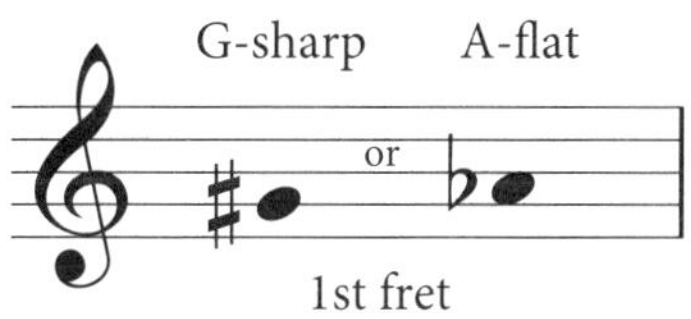

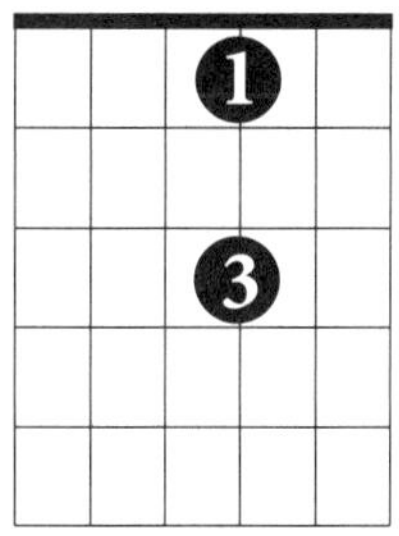

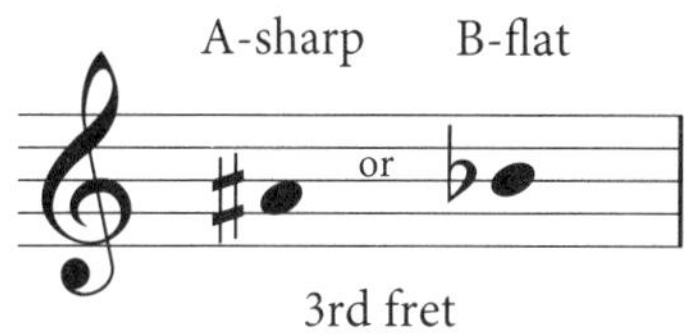

Practice the following exercise to become familiar with G♯ and A♯. (Be sure to play with repeats, as indicated.)

This familiar carol uses the third-string B♭ and also the second-string E♭. Write in the fingering, then play.

We Three Kings

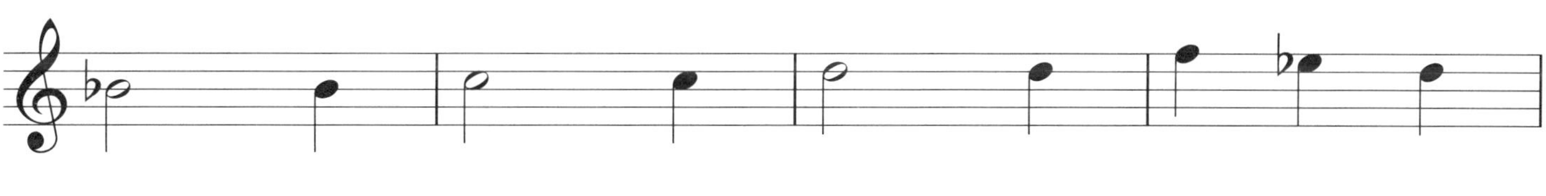

Write in the fingering for the following scale-pattern exercises, then practice for technical development.

KEY SIGNATURES

When the same notes are sharped or flatted throughout a whole piece, as in the exercises above, a key signature is normally used. For example:

This key signature  means that you sharp all of the Fs.

This key signature  means that you flat all of the Bs.

You'll begin playing music with key signatures in *Book 2*; for now, learn the following one-octave scales. The first (G major) uses one sharp, while the second (F major) uses one flat.

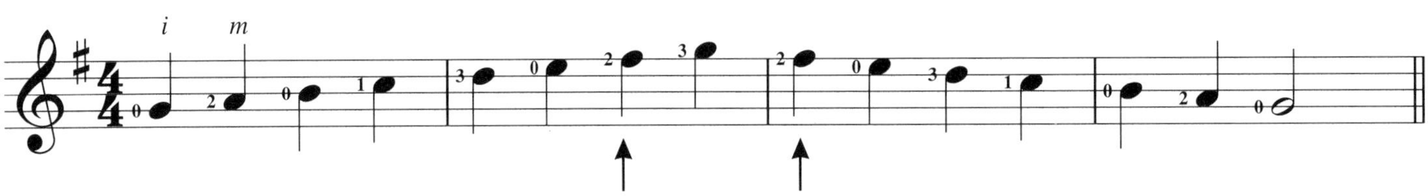

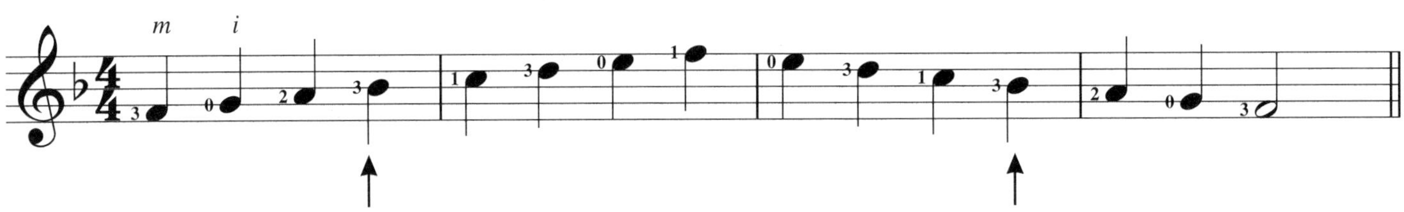

Right-Hand Development

Until now, you've played solos using the thumb and fingers separately. Playing with thumb and fingers together requires a little more skill, and opens another door to more varied playing. Practice the exercise below until you're comfortable with it; then try "The Coventry Carol."

TIP: When you're first attempting the exercise, it may help to get the fingers going first (*m–i*, *m–i*, etc.) on the C and then come in with your thumb when you feel ready.

The Coventry Carol

Accidentals on Strings 4 and 5

The first and fourth fingers play the chromatically-altered notes on the 4th and 5th strings.

FOURTH STRING

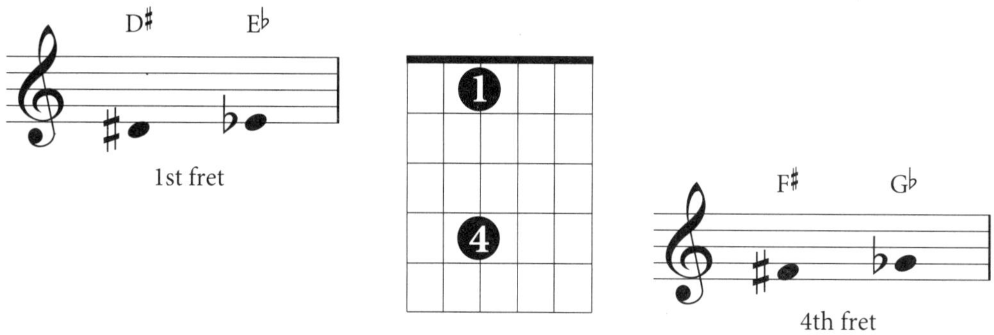

FIFTH STRING

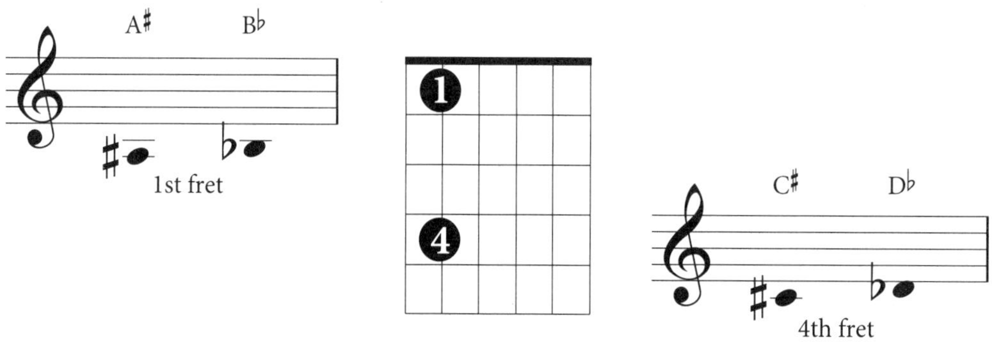

Since classical guitar music uses sharps more frequently than flats, the music on this page and the next contains only sharped notes. You'll be learning music that uses flatted notes on the bass strings at a later stage of your development. For now, just learn to recognize them.

Practice using the new fourth-fret notes C♯ and F♯ by fingering and playing the theme of Jean Sibelius's beautiful tone poem "Finlandia."

Finlandia

"All Through the Night," a beautiful Welsh song, uses several of the sharped notes you've learned. It's also a good example of **AABA song form**. The first four measures, called the A section, are repeated (**AA**). Then, there's a contrasting B section, and the song concludes with a repeat of the A section.

Before you begin practicing the piece, use it for a review of note names by filling in the blanks.

All Through the Night (DUET)

PLAYING BEYOND FIRST POSITION

The notes you've learned so far are all in **first position**, because your first finger plays the first fret. Each time your first finger moves up to the next fret, you're in the next fingerboard position—for example, second position = frets 2-3-4-5; third position = frets 3-4-5-6; all the way up the fingerboard.

We'll begin the study of **position playing** in *Book 2*. For now, learn to use the first-string A in a basic **second position** fingering by practicing the theme from "Joy to the World."

A

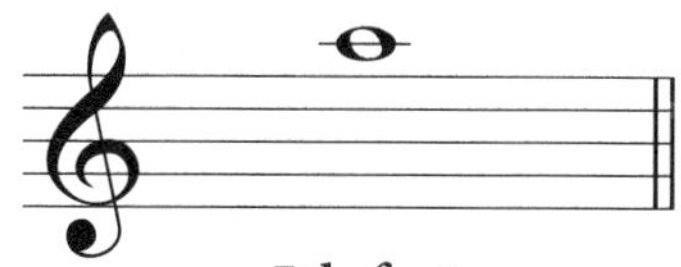

5th fret

Joy to the World

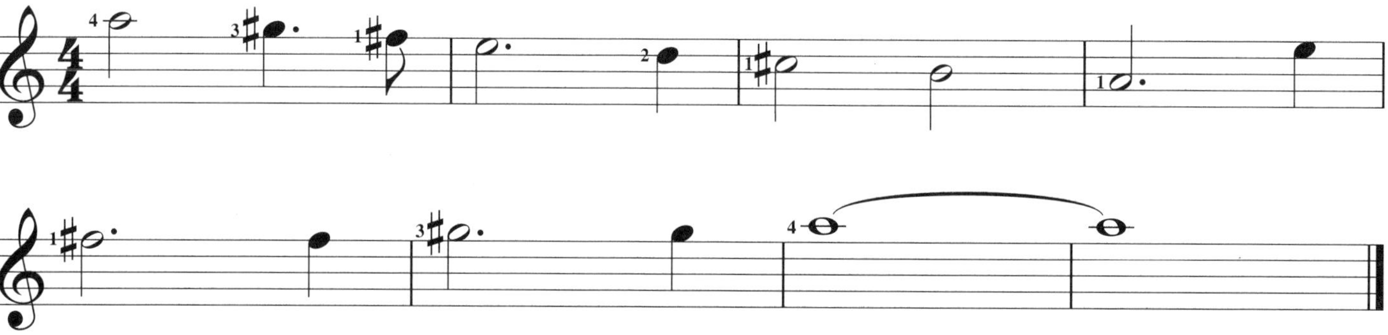

TWO-OCTAVE CHROMATIC SCALE

The A chromatic scale contains all the notes you've learned and makes an excellent exercise for the left hand. To play the high A, use (depending on the size of your hand) either a fourth finger extension, or a temporary shift from first to second position.

✔ **TIP**: To develop strength and separation, keep the fingers well-curved and well-spaced. Also, leave each finger pressing down on its respective fret as you ascend, then lift all four fingers together to play the next string.

One of the most famous pieces for classical guitar is "Romanza" (or "Romance de Amor," as it's usually called in the Spanish-speaking countries). If you continue to make good progress, you'll soon be able to play the standard, intermediate-level **arrangement**. For now, enjoy this simplified version.

TIP: Watch for the second-position fingering in the next-to-last line of music.

Romanza

Notes on the Sixth String

The notes on the sixth string have the same letter names and are played at the same frets as the first string.

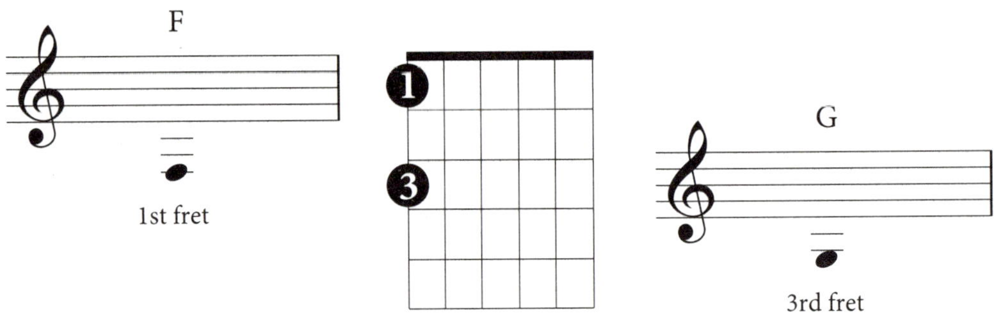

Fill in the blanks, then play with a *p* rest stroke.

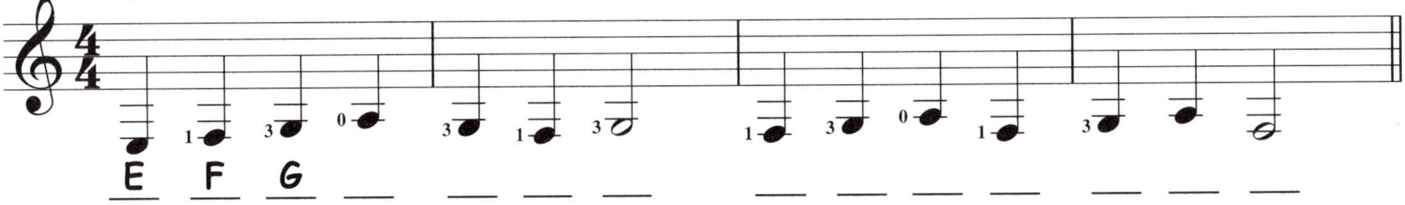

When you're practicing the Brahms "Lullabye," watch out for the fifth string B♭. Also, look closely at measures 3 and 4—here, you'll be using the *fourth* finger to play F and C. (This will prevent awkward repetition of the third finger.)

Lullabye

"Noche en España" ("Night in Spain") is based on a flamenco dance known as *Fandangos de Malaga*—i.e., the fandango as played in the city of Malaga. For variety, and to test your musical ear, try playing it an octave higher as well—use the range of notes shown below. Learning to play by ear will increase your enjoyment of the guitar and improve your overall development as a musician.

Noche en España (DUET)

Accidentals on String 6

The chromatically-altered notes on the sixth string also have the same letter names and are played on the same frets as the first string.

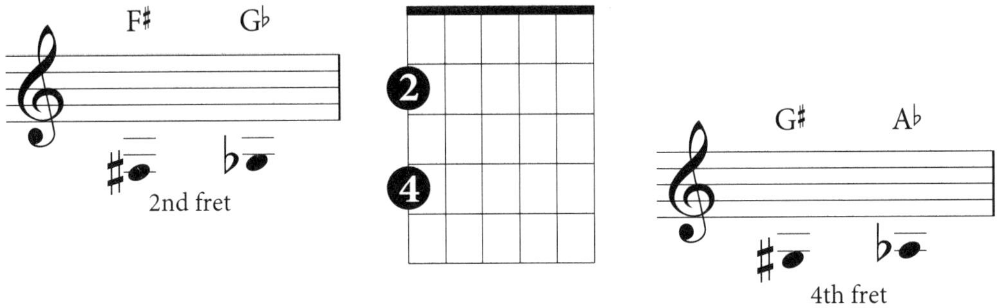

Complete the exercise, then practice “Malagueña Theme” and “Celtic Ballad” on the next page. “Malagueña” is probably the most famous Spanish popular melody of all time; “Celtic Ballad” is an arrangement of “Slane,” a relatively unknown but beautiful ballad named for a famous castle in Ireland.

Malagueña Theme

Celtic Ballad

New Finger Combinations

Certain finger combinations come up again and again in classical guitar playing because the harmonies that they produce are pleasing to the ear. The following exercise is a good example and should be memorized. Watch out especially for the paired second and fourth fingers (in measures 1 and 3, for example). The fourth finger is used here on the third fret for better finger position and better transition to the next pair of notes.

CONTINUING YOUR STUDY

The following arrangement of "Greensleeves" will make a strong finale to your beginning study of the classical guitar. It's an effective performance piece, and it's challenging—in fact, the first pieces in *Book 2* are easier to play.

In *Book 2*, you'll begin by learning a new right-hand technique (free stroke with *i*, *m*, and *a*) in order to play chords, arpeggios, and more complex musical textures. But before going on to *Book 2*, look at the section on "Playing Chords" on the last two pages. Many beginning students of the classical guitar already have a basic knowledge of common guitar chords. For those who do not, the chords on pages 64–65 should be mastered before going on to the next level.

Greensleeves

Playing Chords

For students who do not already have a basic knowledge of **chords**, the following section will provide a practical and helpful introduction to chord playing. Chords such as these are the harmonic basis of a great deal of the classical guitar repertoire, especially from the beginner to the intermediate level.

Three or more notes played at the same time are called a chord. Some chords are very common and are used again and again in classical guitar music. Here are your first two:

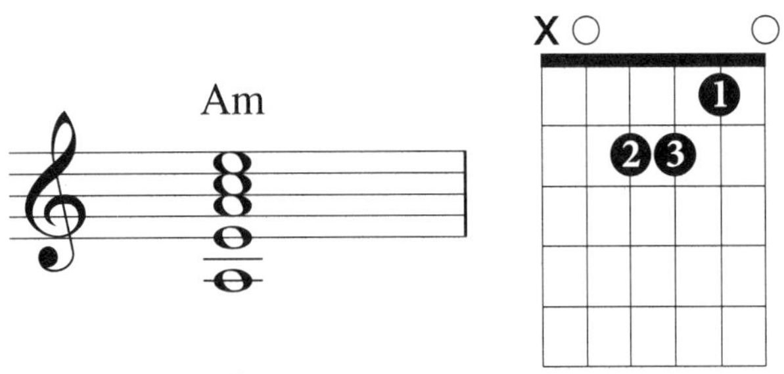

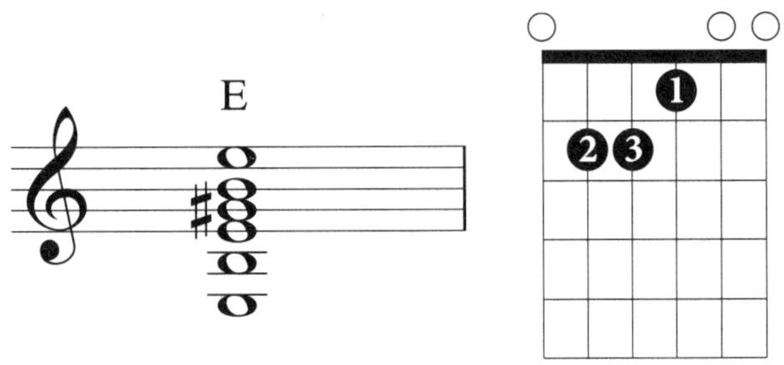

Since **Am** (A minor) and **E** (E major) have identical chord shapes, changing from one to the other is simple. Just raise your fingertips off the strings, *keeping your fingers together*, and reposition them on the next chord. Make sure that your thumb stays in place on the back of the neck; only the fingers move. Practice changing back and forth as shown in the diagram.

You can strum these for now using a simple **brush stroke** with *p*—just brush your thumb lightly over the correct number of strings. Try to get each note to sound clearly.

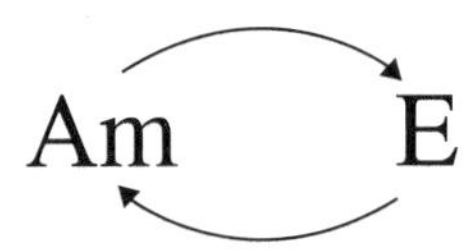

Now try another chord, **D minor**.

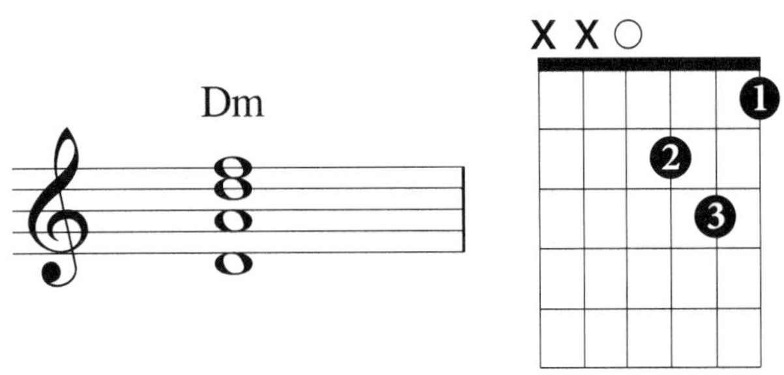

Practice changing back and forth from Am to Dm, which will be a little more difficult.

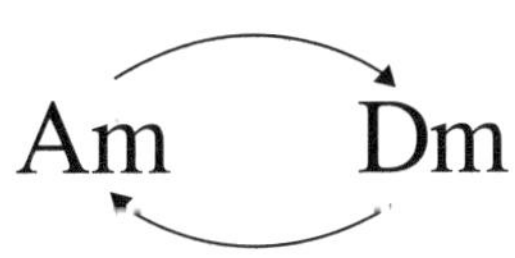

Notice that fingers 1 and 2 stay in the same relationship; concentrate on the placement of the third finger.

TIP: Always try to move your fingers simultaneously from one chord to another—not one finger at a time.

Now try a slightly more difficult pair of chords, C (C major) and G7 (G seventh).

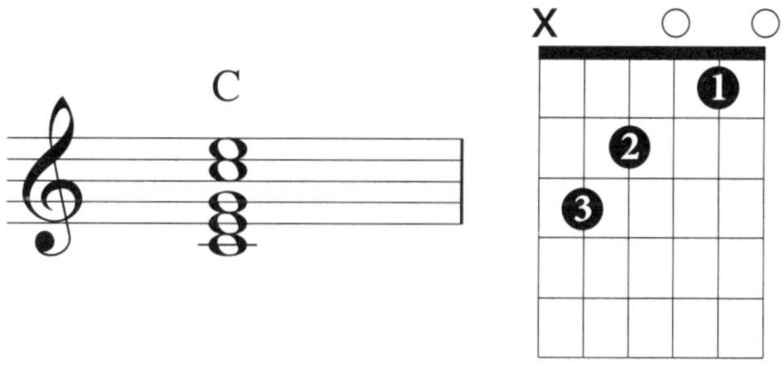

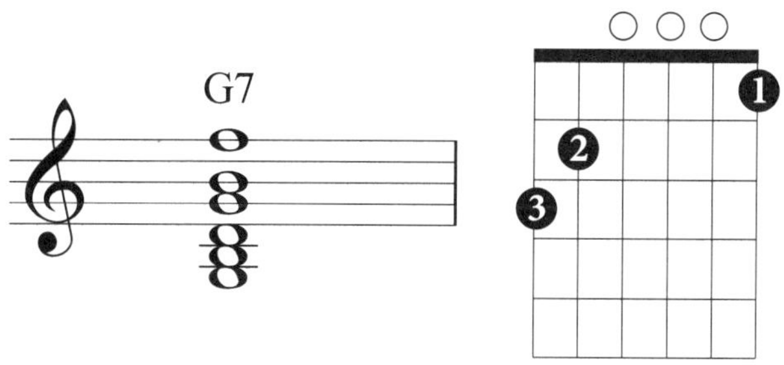

Again, notice the similarity of the chord shapes—the G7 looks like an expanded C chord. However, learning to move the fingers simultaneously will take a little longer for these chords.

TIP: Until you can move the fingers simultaneously, lead with your third finger, not your first. (Leading with the first finger results in one-at-a-time finger placement.)

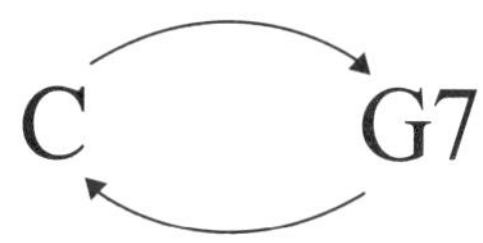

Now practice the following chord progressions until you can make the changes easily.

BOOK 2: Before You Begin...

If you've mastered the skills developed in *Book 1* of this series, you're ready to move up to a more advanced level of classical guitar playing. In this book, you'll be learning a lot of new skills—see the book contents on pp. 2–3 for an overview of what they are. You'll also begin exploring the classical guitar repertoire, with over two dozen pieces chosen for their superior musical quality as well as some of the author's own compositions. Since the use of right-hand fingernails is usually recommended for students at this level, a thorough discussion of nail usage is included as an appendix (pp. 126–128).

You'll use this book to best advantage along with its companion volumes *A Modern Approach to Classical Guitar Repertoire, Part 1* (second edition, 2009) and *Easy Classical Guitar Duets.* Besides the enjoyable and progressively more difficult pieces, the accompanying audio with these companion books will give you a good idea of how much beauty can be found in the easy-to-intermediate repertoire.

Students at this level should also recognize and begin using the interpretive terms and symbols that are usually incorporated into classical guitar music. You'll see them throughout this book; the following two sections provide a handy reference guide to their meaning.

✔ **TIP:** It's also a good idea to have a basic music dictionary in your personal book collection. The *Hal Leonard Pocket Music Dictionary* is a handy and inexpensive option.

TEMPO MARKINGS

Composers and music editors use a variety of tempo terms to indicate the speed at which a piece should be played. Since Italian is the international language of classical music, they're usually in Italian. From slowest to fastest, the most common ones are the following:

Grave	Slow and solemn
Largo	Slow and stately
Lento	Slow but with a lighter emotional tone
Adagio	Slow but with a stronger rhythmic flow
Larghetto	Somewhat faster and lighter in mood
Andante	At an easy, walking pace
Andantino	Somewhat faster than Andante
Moderato	At a moderately brisk pace
Allegretto	Fairly fast; light and charming
Allegro	Fast and joyful
Presto	Very fast
Prestissimo	As fast as possible

A more objective measure of tempo is the **metronome setting** that sometimes appears along with the tempo marking; you'll see it used throughout this book for all the pieces. Look for the abbreviation **M.M.** followed by the number of beats per minute. (The abbreviation M.M. stands for "Maelzel's Metronome" in honor of Johann Maelzel, the 19th century inventor of the metronome.) For example, a metronome setting of M.M. ♩=80 tells you to set the metronome to click (or pulse) at 80 BPM, and then play along with the beats to get the feel of the correct tempo. Electronic metronomes from $25–$50 are available at most music stores.

INTERPRETIVE MARKINGS

You'll also be seeing a number of interpretive markings, most often in the form of abbreviations or symbols. These are used to guide the player's control of rhythm and dynamics in order to interpret the music with feeling and good musicianship. The most common are the following:

Abbreviation	Italian Term	Meaning
p*; *pp	*piano; pianissimo*	soft; very soft
mp	*mezzo piano*	rather soft
mf	*mezzo forte*	moderately loud
f*; *ff	*forte; fortissimo*	loud; very loud
sfz	*sforzando*	suddenly louder
acc. or >	*accento*	play with an accent
dim. or >	*diminuendo*	getting softer
cresc. or <	*crescendo*	getting louder
accel.	*accelerando*	speeding up
rit.	*ritardando*	slowing down
rall.	*rallentando*	gradually fading away
espr.	*espressivo*	expressively; with feeling
𝄐	*fermata*	hold for longer than the literal note value

In addition, terms such as the following are used without abbreviations or symbols:

animato	lively; with animation
con moto	with a strong sense of rhythmic drive
maestoso	with majestic feeling
affetuoso	with tender feeling
poco; molto	a little; very much
a tempo (after a ***rit.*** or ***accel.***)	play at the original tempo

Of course, when you're learning to play a piece, you must always practice much slower than the indicated metronome setting, and you needn't be concerned with the fine points of interpretation. However, once you've mastered the technical requirements of a piece, practicing it for control of rhythm and dynamics will provide even more enjoyment. If you're interested in playing for people, this kind of practice will also help develop the kind of professionalism and emotional warmth that listeners expect.

Playing with Free Stroke

Except for scales and accented notes, most classical guitar playing past the beginner level is based on the **free stroke**, which enables you to play chords, arpeggios, and counterpoint. To play with free stroke, you'll need to keep your wrist and forearm a little higher than for rest stroke. For most players, the best position is around three inches from the top of the guitar.

Notice that the wrist is only slightly arched, and that the knuckles are fairly high, positioned almost directly over the fingertips. This allows space for your fingers to escape the strings toward the palm of the hand while you maintain a strong, natural right-hand position.

You should avoid flattening the knuckles and curling the fingers, because this creates tension in the hand and tends to produce poor string tone. When positioned correctly, the fingers should escape the strings at a fairly shallow angle, as shown in the first illustration.

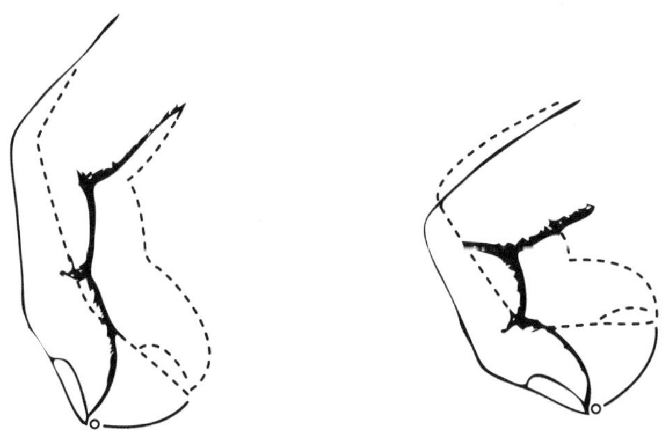

TIP: You can think of a good free stroke as a modified rest stroke. As the illustrations indicate, the correct finger motion is actually more like a down-and-in push than a strictly upward pluck.

Open-String Free-Stroke Exercises

Practice the following open-string chordal exercises slowly and carefully to get the feel of free-stroke playing. In the first one, place your thumb on the fifth string for support. If you're playing with nails, pay close attention to how the nails engage the strings.

TIP: It's like notching, drawing, and releasing an arrow—the "arrow" being the resulting tone.

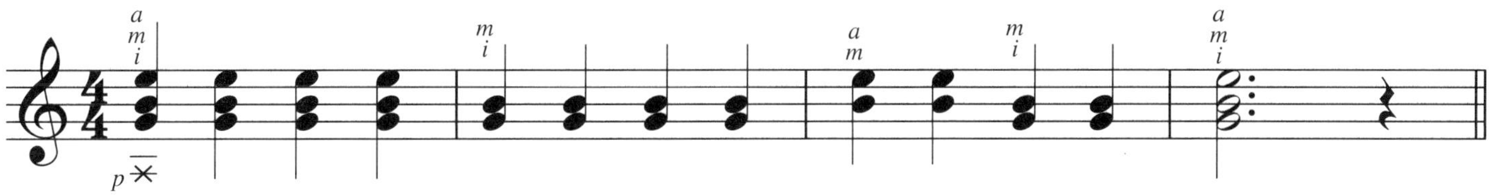

Now try adding the thumb. If the opposed movement of the thumb and fingers seems a bit awkward at first, just experiment with your touch until you can produce clean-sounding chords.

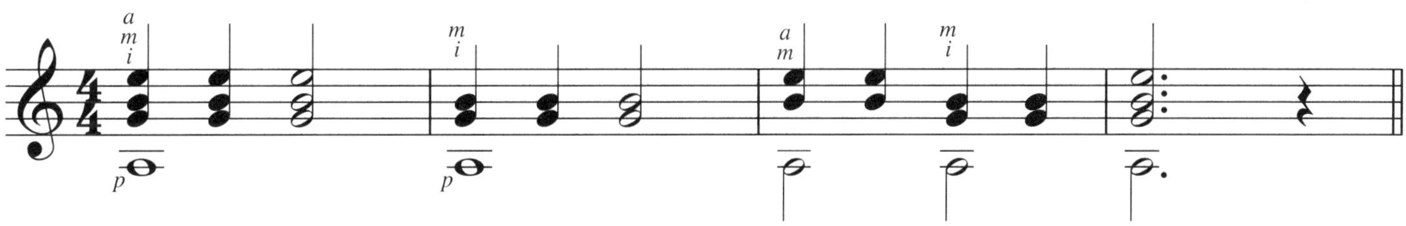

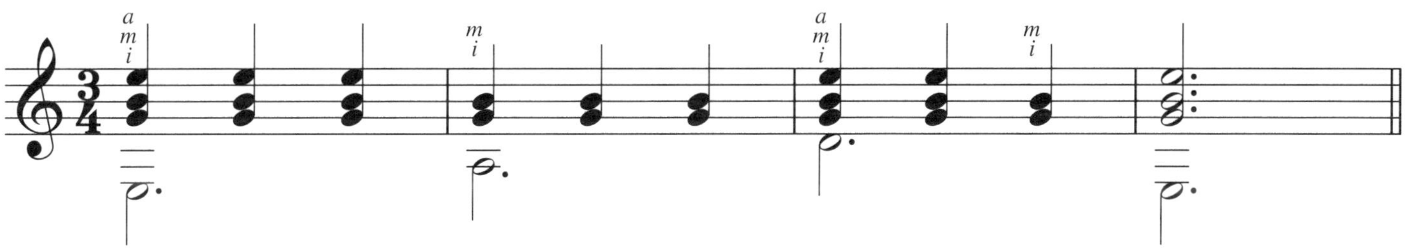

Now try a couple of basic **arpeggio** exercises.

TIP: "Plant" your fingernails (or fingertips) on the strings at the beginning of each measure, just as if you were going to play a four-note chord. The technique of **planting** helps develop secure touch and can be used whenever notes of an arpeggio are in an ascending direction. Also, the doubling of the bass notes does not mean that they are played twice! This is merely a device used in arpeggiated music to indicate the actual duration of the bass note which supports the arpeggio.

Giuliani's Arpeggio Exercises

Mauro Giuliani (1781–1839), one of the great guitar composers, wrote numerous excellent short pieces for students. You'll be playing some of them very soon, but a few of his *120 Studies for the Right Hand*, which are comparable to the famous Hanon and Czerny exercises for piano, will complete your basic introduction to free-stroke playing. Besides being fun to practice, these exercises will develop your technical skill while you're studying the more theoretical material on the next four pages. Thereafter, they can serve as useful daily warm-up exercises.

Each exercise is based on a simple alternation between the C and G7 chords shown below, along with the corresponding chord diagrams. (Memorize and practice until you can make the chord changes easily before attempting the exercises.)

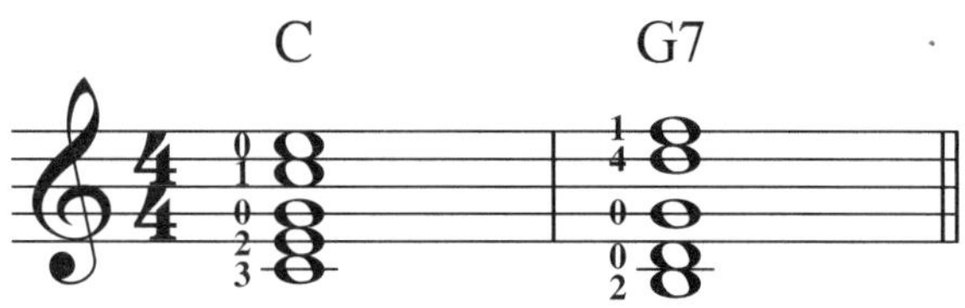

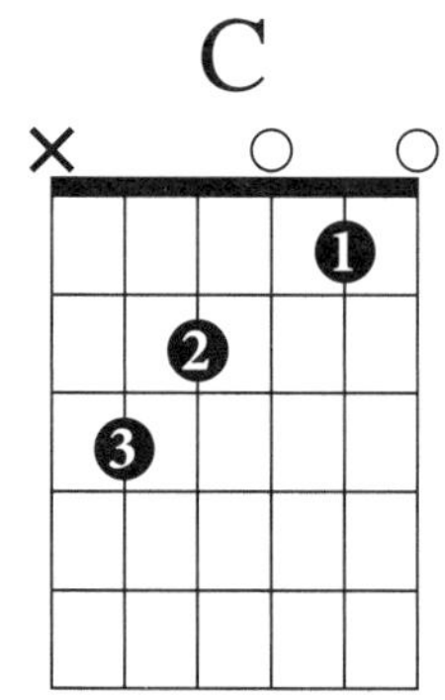

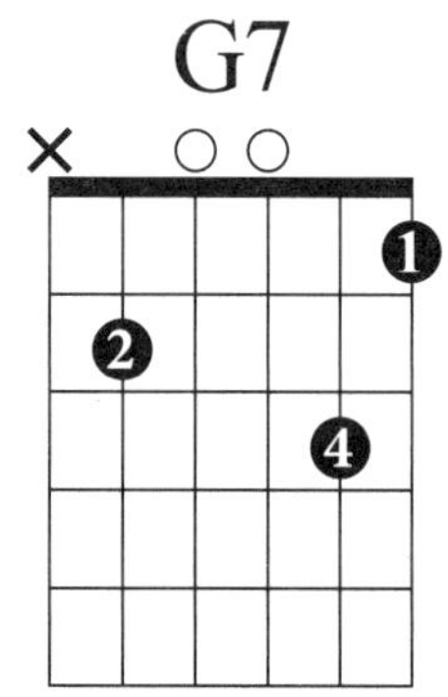

Notice also that these exercises are written in **eighth-note triplets**. The eighth-note triplet is used to subdivide a beat into thirds in 2/4, 3/4, and 4/4 and is very easy to count. You can count triplets by saying either "one-trip-let, two-trip-let," etc., or "one-and-a, two-and-a," etc., as shown below:

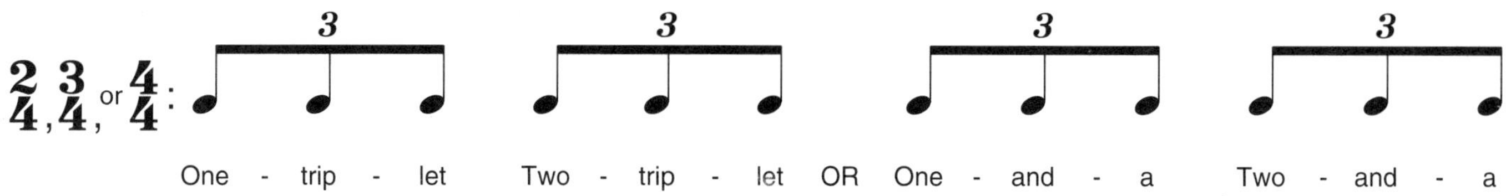

Practice these exercises slowly and carefully. Play each exercise at least twice, concluding with the final C chord.

TIP: Look for opportunities to practice planting the ascending notes of an arpeggio whenever you see the fingerings *p–i–m*, *p–i–a*, or *p–i–m–a*.

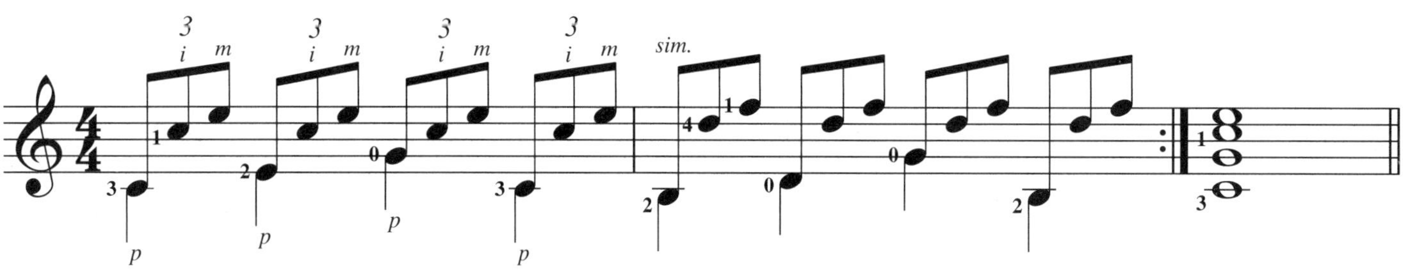

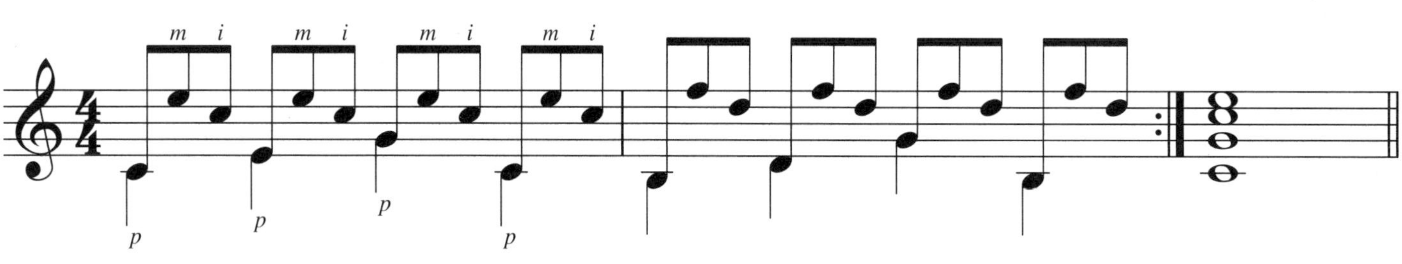

i a i m i a i m
p p p p

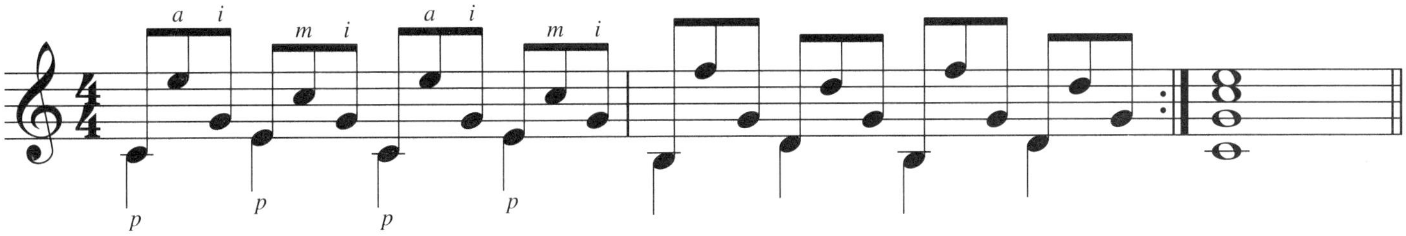
a i m i a i m i
p p p p

i m a m i i m i m
p p p

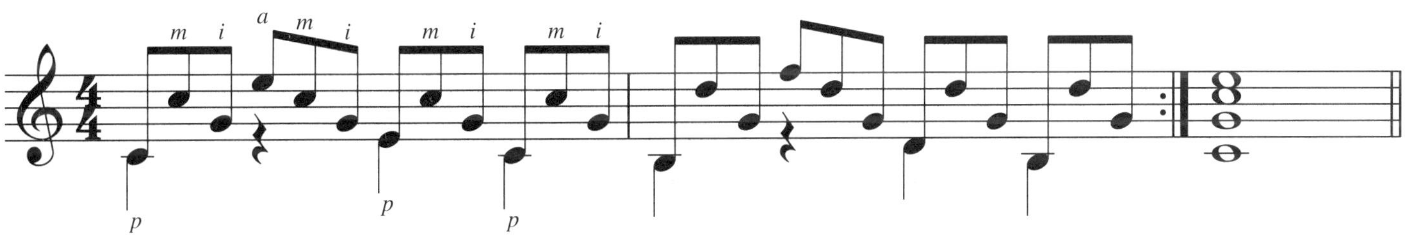
m i a m i m i m i
p p p

i m a i m a
p p

a m i a m i
p p

Scale Construction

You'll need to practice the preceding exercises for a while before you move on. In the meantime, let's pause for a look at some basic music theory, beginning with how scales are constructed. In this section, you'll also learn an important new left-hand technique: the **half-barre** (or half-bar).

The most common scales in classical music are the **major** and **minor diatonic scales**, composed of seven scale tones (or scale degrees) with a specific pattern of **half steps** and **whole steps**. On the guitar, a half step is the musical distance between notes on neighboring frets; a whole step is the musical distance between notes separated by a fret.

For all major scales, the pattern of half and whole steps is the same as for the C major scale shown below (**W**=whole step, **H**=half step):

Major

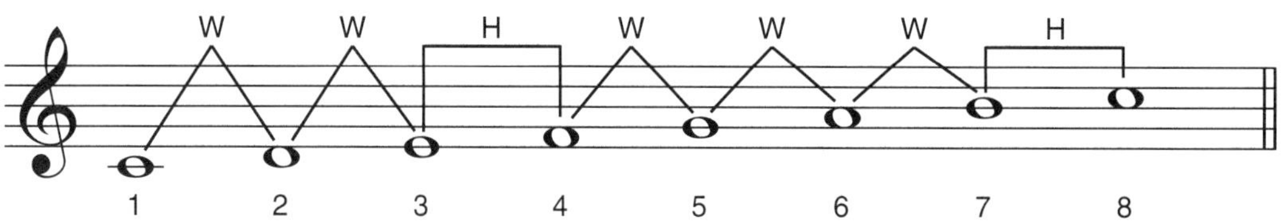

For all minor scales, the pattern is the same as for the A minor scales below. However, minor scales are a bit more complicated. Notice that there are three of them: the natural minor, the harmonic minor, and the melodic minor. The natural minor is the foundation, while the harmonic minor raises the 7th degree by a half step.

Natural minor

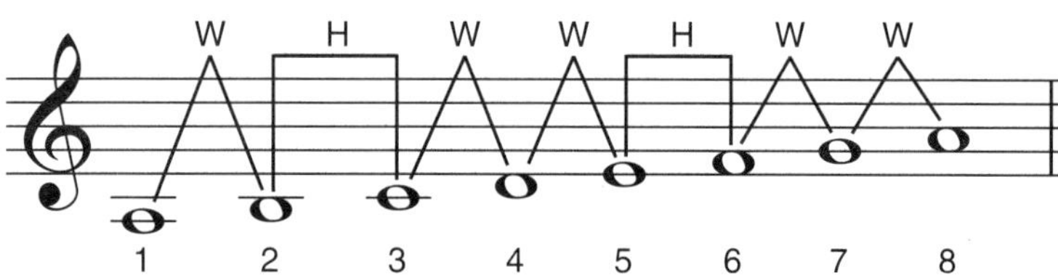

Harmonic minor

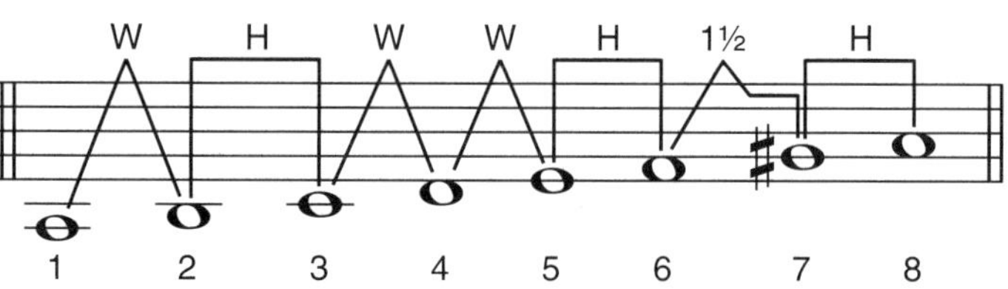

The chords in minor keys are based on the harmonic minor scale. However, since the raised 7th creates an awkward 1½ step melodic interval between scale degrees 6 and 7, for melodies in minor keys the melodic minor is preferred. The melodic minor uses both a raised 6th and 7th degree ascending; when descending, it uses the natural 6th and 7th degrees.

Melodic minor

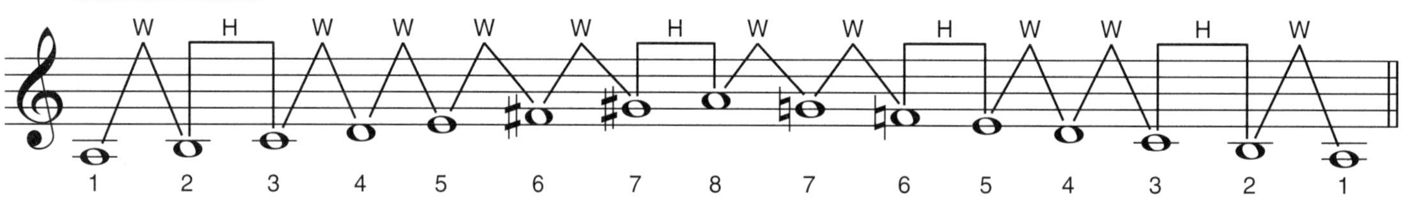

Key Signatures

In order to keep the correct pattern of half and whole steps, all major and minor scales (except C and Am) require a **chromatic alteration**. The number of sharps or flats needed to produce the correct pattern of intervals also designates the **musical key** that the scale defines. The key is indicated by a **key signature** at the beginning of each line of music, consisting of one to six sharps or flats—for example:

Most music for the classical guitar is written in keys with no more than four sharps or two flats. Because of the abundance of good pieces in C and Am and G and Em (one sharp), in this book you'll only need to recognize the first key signature above. (*Book 3* will provide a progressive introduction to music in the other principal keys.)

To learn all the first-position notes in the new keys of G and Em, memorize and practice the following two-octave scales, using the *m–i* rest stroke. To continue improving the strength and coordination of the *a* finger, practice with *a–i* and *a–m* rest stroke as well.

TIP: Remember that *all* the Fs are sharped—look for the reminder sharps over the lower-octave Fs.

G Major

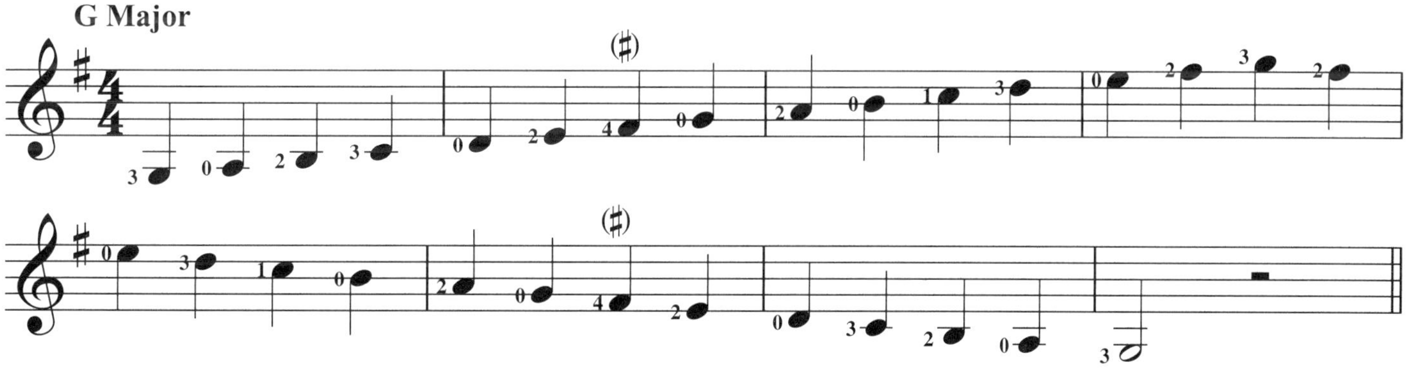

E Melodic minor

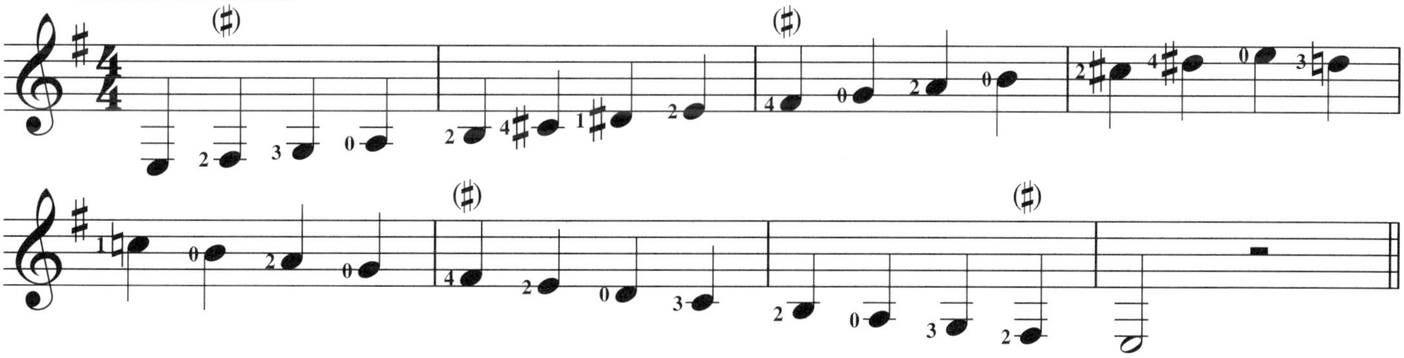

Chord Construction

All chords are composed of the intervals defined by major and minor diatonic scales, as shown below for the C scale. The interval from scale tone one (the **root**) to scale tone two is a **second**, from the root to scale tone three a **third**, and so on up the scale.

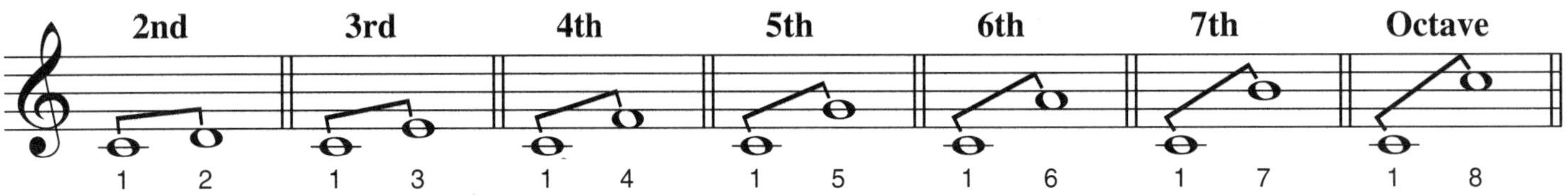

Any of these intervals may appear in major, minor, or seventh chords, depending on how the chords are **voiced**. However, **stacked thirds** are the basis of chord construction. Two stacked thirds produce a **triad**, containing both the third and fifth tones above the root. The common guitar chord is derived by doubling and rearranging the triad tones, as shown below for the C and D minor chords:

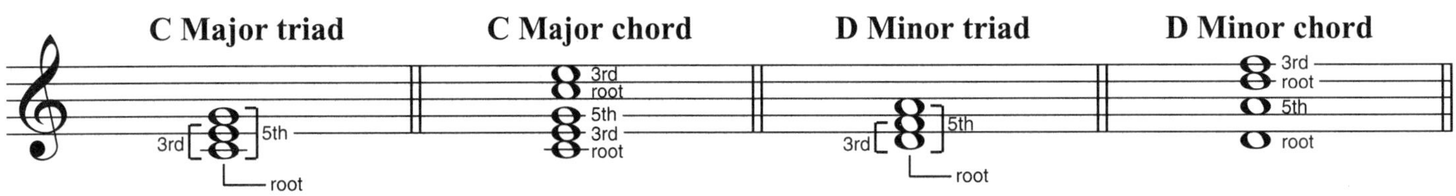

When three thirds are stacked, the resulting chord is called a **seventh** chord, because the interval between the root and the highest note is a seventh. However, you'll very seldom see seventh chords in this form in guitar music. Because of the way the instrument is tuned, you'll usually see them in a more **open voicing**, as shown below for G7 and E7 chords:

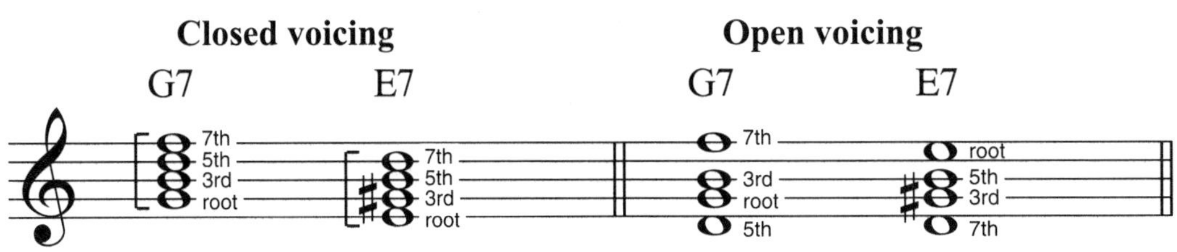

The chords build on the first, fourth, and fifth notes of the scale are known as **primary chords**, because they provide the basic harmonic skeleton of most classical and popular music. Respectively, they're called the **tonic**, **subdominant**, and **dominant** chords, and the dominant is often a seventh chord. They can also be designated by Roman numerals as **I**, **IV**, and **V(7)**. Although you'll usually play them in more formal voicings, you should memorize the common primary chords for the keys of A minor, G, and E minor.

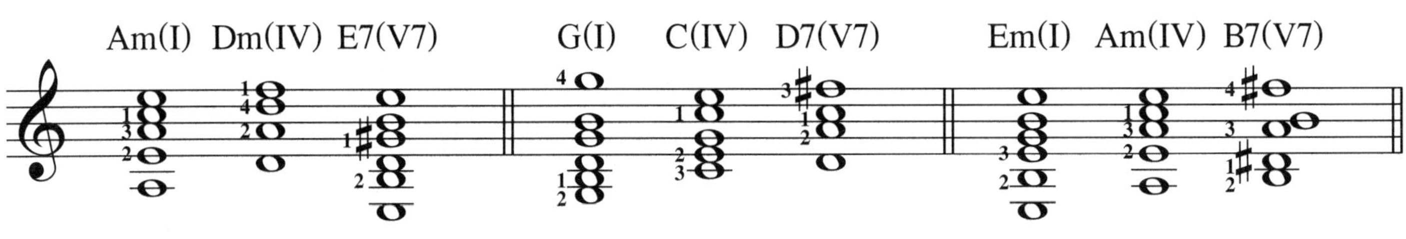

Barred Chords: The Half-Barre

The primary chords for the key of C major are C, F, and G7. Look closely at the fingering shown for the F chord. To play the F chord, you'll need to learn an important new left-hand technique—the **half-barre**, indicated here by the bracket in the music and the curved line in the corresponding chord.

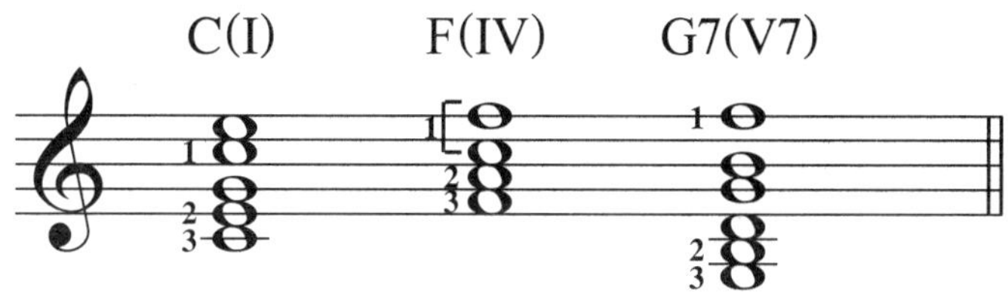

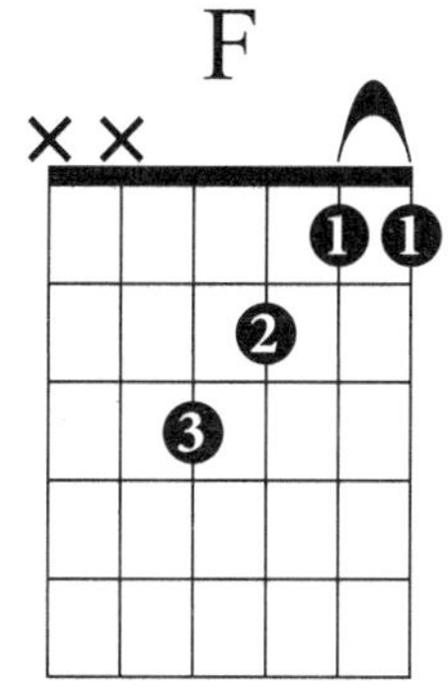

In this book, you'll be using the half-barre from time to time, so start practicing it now; it takes time to develop the necessary strength and coordination. Also, you'll be developing the kind of skill needed for the **full barre**, which is introduced in *Book 3.*

To make the half-barre, flatten the finger from the middle joint to the tip as shown below in the first photograph.

TIP: The knuckle should be sharply bent so that it can exert the necessary leverage from above. Leverage from below is provided by the thumb, which opposes the first finger as shown in the second photo.

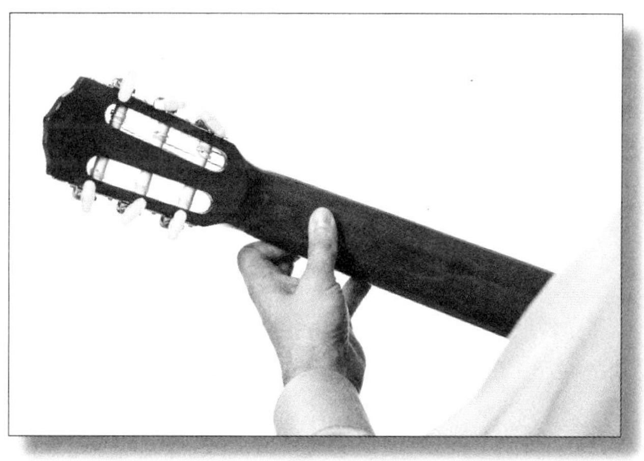

Now memorize and practice the following two **cadences** in the key of C major. Cadences are I–IV–V7–I progressions that use the kind of voicing common to classical music. Each note of the chord can be considered a separate voice, as in four-part vocal harmony. Notice also the ¢ over the F chord. In most guitar music, the symbol for the half-barre is ¢ or ½ C (for *ceja*, the Spanish word for "bar"), followed by the fret number in either Arabic or Roman numerals.

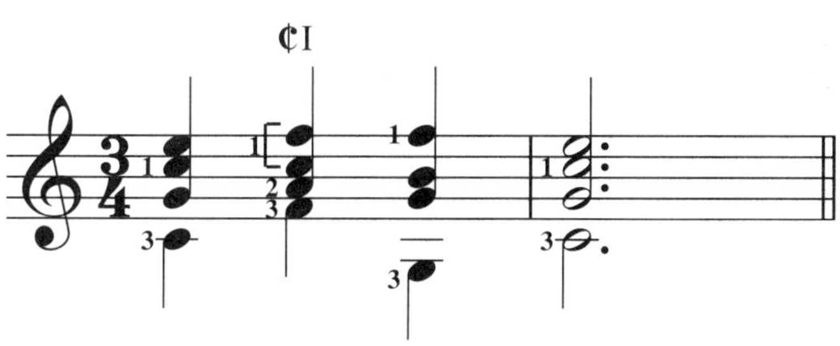

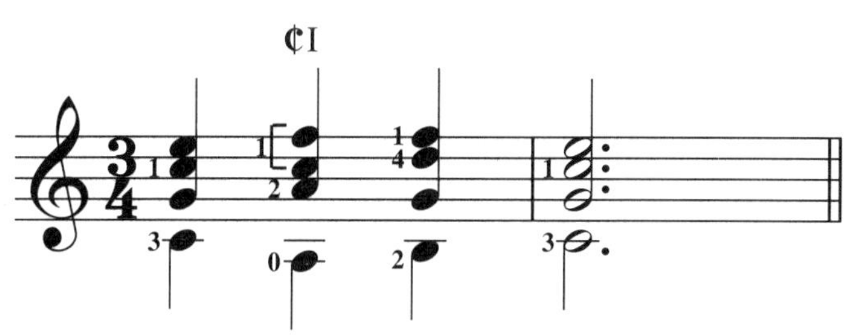

Common Musical Styles and Textures

Several musical styles and textures are so common in classical guitar music that you'll benefit from learning them before trying to learn the solos that begin on page 80. Practicing the etudes in this section will also help train your fingers for the kinds of coordination needed to play the solos.

Notice that the etudes are based harmonically on the use of **consonant intervals**, which are the foundation of traditional harmony. Consonant intervals are those that sound naturally pleasing to the ear—especially **thirds**, **sixths**, and **tenths**. The tenth has the same harmonic quality as the third, but with an additional octave between the higher and lower notes.

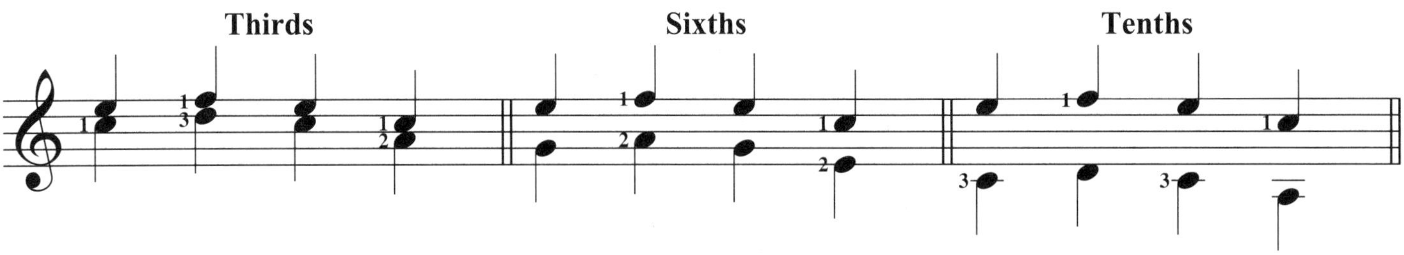

ETUDE 1—Simple two-part harmony, using primarily thirds and sixths. Play with *i–m*.

ETUDE 2—Simple two-part harmony, using only parallel sixths. **Parallel harmony** is the parallel movement of two or more voices. Play the melody using alternate *m–i* free strokes.

ETUDE 3—Simple three-part harmony based primarily on parallel tenths with an **internal pedal point**. The term "pedal point" refers to the way organists can sustain a bass note indefinitely with a foot pedal. This style of arpeggiated harmony was popularized by the composer Domenico Alberti (1710–1740) and is also known as **Alberti bass**. Guitar composers of the period 1770–1850 used this style very frequently.

ETUDE 4—Somewhat more complex three-part harmony, with movement primarily in thirds supported by an independent bass line. This too is a very typical kind of texture you'll be seeing more of. Use *p–i–m* throughout.

TIP: The thumb always plays the bass line (the downstemmed notes).

ETUDE 5—Four-part harmony, with a simple melody supported by **block chords**. Listen carefully for the melody, and be sure that the *a* finger plays with as much force as *i* and *m*.

TIP: You'll find that it helps to compress the right-hand fingers together—the more compact the hand, the more solid the stroke of the *a* finger. Note also the key signature; the etude is in E minor, and all the Fs are sharped.

ETUDE 6—Melody and bass combined in simple two-part **counterpoint**. In this kind of texture, the bass line provides a firm harmonic foundation for the independent movement of the melody. In pieces of this kind, the right-hand fingering can be tricky. Just practice slowly and carefully.

In each of the preceding etudes, the highest voice is the melody. However, the melody can also be in the bass, as seen in the two arpeggio etudes on the next page. Try to accent the bass notes and be sure to give them their full time value, as indicated by the double note values and downstems.

ETUDE 7—This etude uses the F chord, indicated by the ¢ over the measures where it is used. Also, remember that the downstem half notes are *not* to be played as separate notes. This form of notation is used only to indicate the actual duration of the bass notes.

ETUDE 8—Notice the key signature and the repeat of the first line of music. Notice also the tied notes at the end. In the last measure, you play only the fourth-string E; the other notes of the E major chord carry over from the preceding measure.

First Classical Solos

These paired compositions by Matteo Carcassi (1792–1853) and Ferdinand Carulli (1770–1841) make a good introduction to solo playing. Both are fairly easy as well as fun to play, and both illustrate the style and texture of guitar music from the **Classical period** in music (approximately 1770–1850). Music from this period tends to be very symmetrically constructed, with a melody supported by broken chords as in Etude 3.

Carcassi's simple but effective structure is based on the repetition of two complete musical thoughts. Carulli's structure is somewhat more complex, with a contrasting third section and a **da capo**, indicated by the **D.C. al Fine** at the end. "Da Capo al Fine" means "play again from the beginning to the end *without repeats*." Whenever you see this term, go back to the beginning and play up to the **Fine**, which indicates the actual ending of the piece.

Andantino

Matteo Carcassi

Country Dance

Ferdinand Carulli

Accenting a Melody with Rest Strokes

Good players often use rest strokes to provide melodic accent in pieces such as the "Waltz" below, especially for notes on the first string. For second-string notes, the **half rest stroke** is usually preferred. A half rest stroke is a free stroke with a heavier downward push into the string. With practice, you'll discover that it can sound almost identical to a rest stroke. Practice the following pattern study with *a–m* rest strokes to get the general feel of this kind of touch.

Carulli's charming little "Waltz" also illustrates another way Alberti bass can be written, using upstems instead of downstems for the internal pedal tone. Consequently, the piece looks like an arpeggio exercise, but the notes on strings 1 and 2 provide a distinct melody. See the accent marks (>) in the first line of music.

Waltz

Ferdinand Carulli

Allegretto M.M. ♩ = 104

Fernando Sor (1778–1839) was one of the very best classical guitar composers; in fact, he's been called the Beethoven of the guitar. The piece below is a good example of the many beautiful compositions he wrote for students.

More complex melodies, such as the one in this piece, offer more opportunities for variety of accent. To begin, try to use rest strokes or half rest strokes for the notes indicated by accent marks. Then experiment with your touch to see where else similar accents might sound good.

TIP: The overall effect should be a lyrical, flowing melody with lots of tonal color.

Andante

Fernando Sor

M.M. ♩ = 132

The following two pieces will introduce you to the musical styles and textures of the **Renaissance period** (approximately 1550–1650) and the **Baroque period** (approximately 1660–1750).

"What If a Day or a Month or a Year" is an anonymous instrumental version of a song by Thomas Campion, an English poet of the period. It's a good example of the kind of music composed for the **lute**, which was the most popular instrument of the Renaissance. Because the lute is so similar to the guitar, most lute music can be played without alteration on the classical guitar.

This piece is also fairly easy to play, except for the shift to the B major chord in the third line. Since the chord contains a somewhat difficult spacing of *p–i–m–a*, you'll need to practice this shift separately.

TIP: To help make the shift secure for the left hand, be sure to use the fourth finger as a **guide finger** (as indicated by the dash).

What If a Day or a Month or a Year

Anonymous
16th century English

Henry Purcell was the finest English composer of the Baroque period, and the *minuet* was one of the most popular dances of the 17th and 18th centuries. Written for harpsichord, the forerunner of the modern piano, this charming little piece is a good example of the kind of **transcriptions** that are an important part of the classical guitar repertoire. (A transcription is an adaptation of a piece written for another instrument.) Since it's based primarily on simple two-part counterpoint, it's also fairly easy to play, except for a few difficult fingerings in the third line.

TIP: Practice the third line separately as an exercise. (Practicing the more difficult passages separately is always a good idea.)

Minuet

Henry Purcell

Andantino M.M. ♩ = 112

Sixteenth Notes

When the quarter note is divided by fourths, the result is a **sixteenth note** (i.e., one-sixteenth of a whole note). Single sixteenth notes are written with a double flag; groups of sixteenth notes are written with a double beam: A sixteenth rest looks the same as an eighth rest, but with a double tail:

Groups of four sixteenth notes are counted "one-e-and-a, two-e-and-a," etc. Practice the following rhythm line with an *i–m* rest stroke, counting aloud as shown.

The following beneficial arpeggio study also provides an easy introduction to reading music written in sixteenth notes. Like Carulli, Giuliani, and Sor, Dionisio Aguado (1784–1849) was another fine guitar composer of the early 19th century who wrote many well-known short study pieces.

This piece also introduces you to the use of **position shifting** to simplify the left-hand fingering. You'll learn more about position shifting later in the book. For now, you'll enjoy using the easy shifts in the first line of music.

TIP: In the first line of music, note the use of guide fingers. Note also the circled string number ③, which indicates that you play the B in measure 3 on the third string.

Estudio in Am

Dionisio Aguado

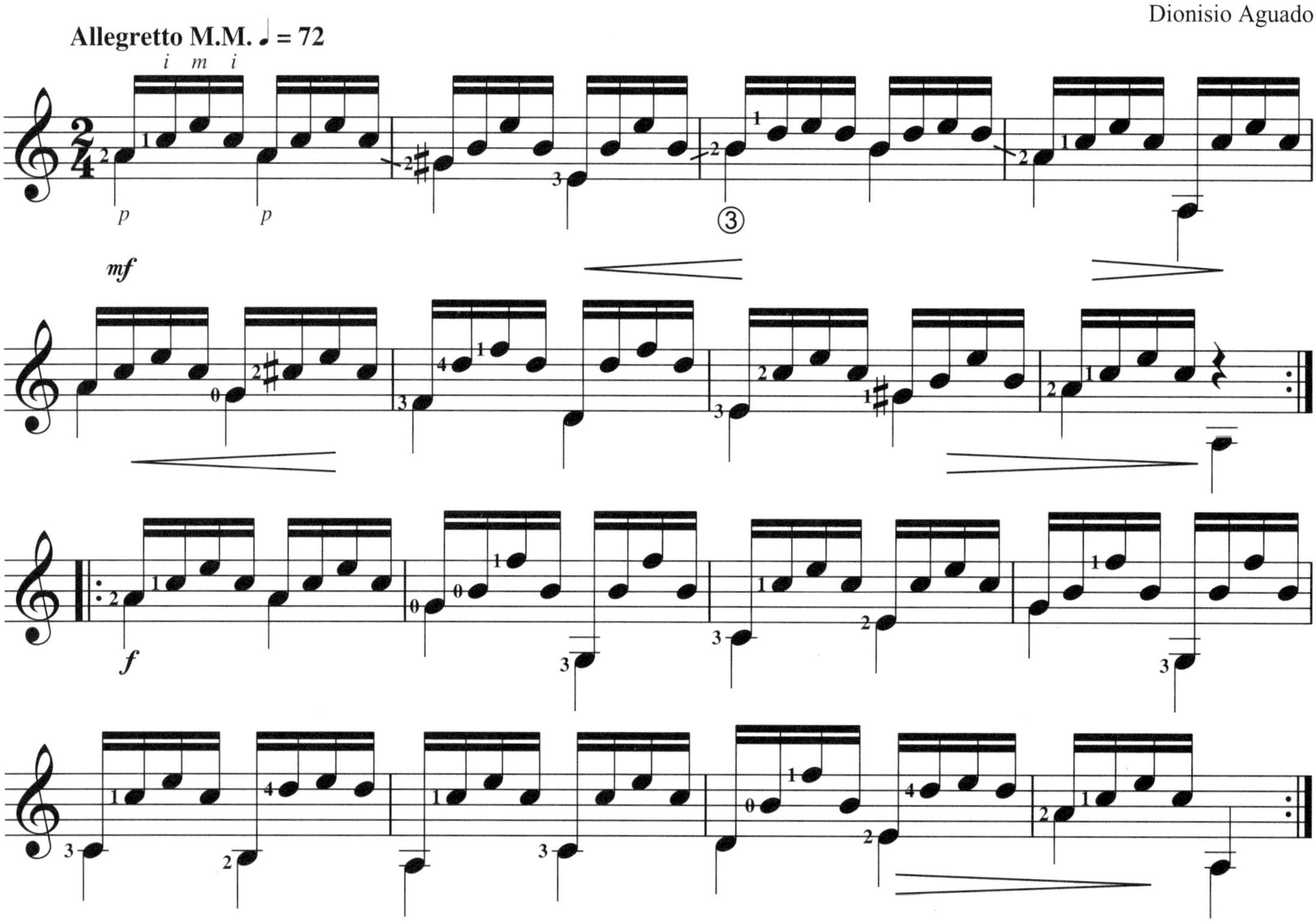

Two sixteenth notes can also be beamed together with an eighth note as shown: Count this **rhythmic figure** by saying "one—and-a, two—and-a," etc., as in the rhythm line below. Practice with *m–i* rest strokes while counting aloud.

Count: 1 & a 2 & a 1 - e - & - a 2 & 1 & a 2 & a 1 – 2

In the famous "Lone Ranger" theme from the William Tell Overture, this figure is used as a **rhythmic motive** (a motive is a short musical idea). Practice with *m–i* rest strokes while counting aloud.

Count: & a 1 & a 2 & a 1 & 2

Dotted Eighth Notes

A dot after an eighth note increases its value by half: The dotted eighth note is usually beamed with a sixteenth note to create another kind of rhythmic figure—**dotted eighths and sixteenths:** A good way to learn this figure is to practice the dotted eighth as if it were three tied sixteenths, as in the rhythm line below. Be sure to count aloud.

Count: 1 e & a 2 1 (e &) a 2 1 (e &) a 2

The "Battle Hymn of the Republic" is an excellent example of the use of dotted eighths and sixteenths. Practice with *i–m* rest strokes while counting aloud.

TIP: Although the sixteenth note is beamed with the *preceding* downbeat, it is actually an **upbeat** to the *next* downbeat. Listen for this strong rhythmic connection as you count "a-*one*, a-*two*," etc.

Count: a 1 a 2 a 3 a 4 a

Carulli's "Moderato" has a much more varied texture and complex appearance than Aguado's "Estudio." However, it's easier to count and play than it appears at first sight.

TIP: If the rhythmic coordination of the bass and treble parts in the second line seems confusing, try counting aloud as you play. You'll see that the beat is evenly subdivided between the bass and treble, and each right hand finger-stroke matches the appropriate syllable of the "one-e-and-a, two-e-and-a" count.

Moderato

Ferdinand Carulli

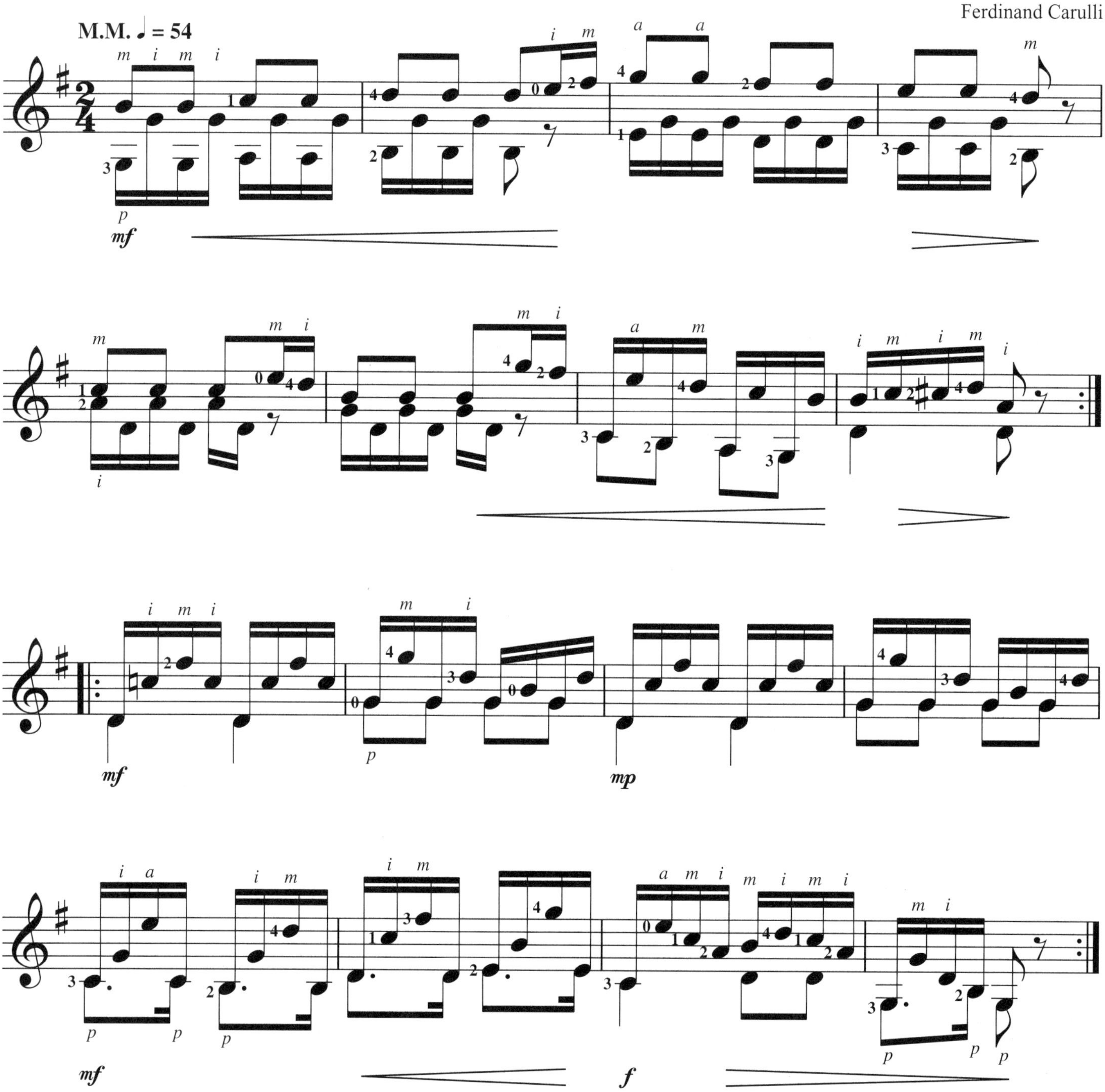

The following piece uses each division of the beat by sixteenth notes that you've learned to help create a strong melody with rhythmic variety. It's also a good example of the kind of highly original and lyrical music that Wolfgang Amadeus Mozart was writing for the piano well before the age of ten. The first measure in the second line is a bit tricky, but otherwise the piece is not difficult to play. Once you've mastered the rhythm, practice it for dynamic control to bring out the phrase shapes and song quality of the melody.

Andante

W.A. Mozart

M.M. ♩ = 52

Playing in 6/8 Time

Until now, you've played music with time signatures based on the quarter note. Time signatures based on the eighth note include **3/8, 4/8, 6/8, 9/8,** and **12/8**. The most common of these is **6/8**. In 6/8 time, there are six beats to the measure, and all note and rest values are proportionate to the eighth note: ♪ 𝄾 = 1 beat, ♩ 𝄽 = 2 beats, and ♩. 𝄽. = 3 beats. Practice the rhythm line below slowly while counting aloud:

For 6/8 music in a slow tempo, or when practicing slowly, you should simply count "1-2-3-4-5-6," as in the classic French love song, "Plaisir d'Amour."

Plaisir d'Amour

However, when 6/8 is played at a faster tempo, there is an even more obvious "feel" of two strong beats to the measure than in "Plaisir d'Amour" (beats 1 and 4). In this case, it's more convenient to count "one-and-a, two-and-a," similar to the eighth-note triplets in the Giuliani arpeggio studies. A good example is this famous Irish jig:

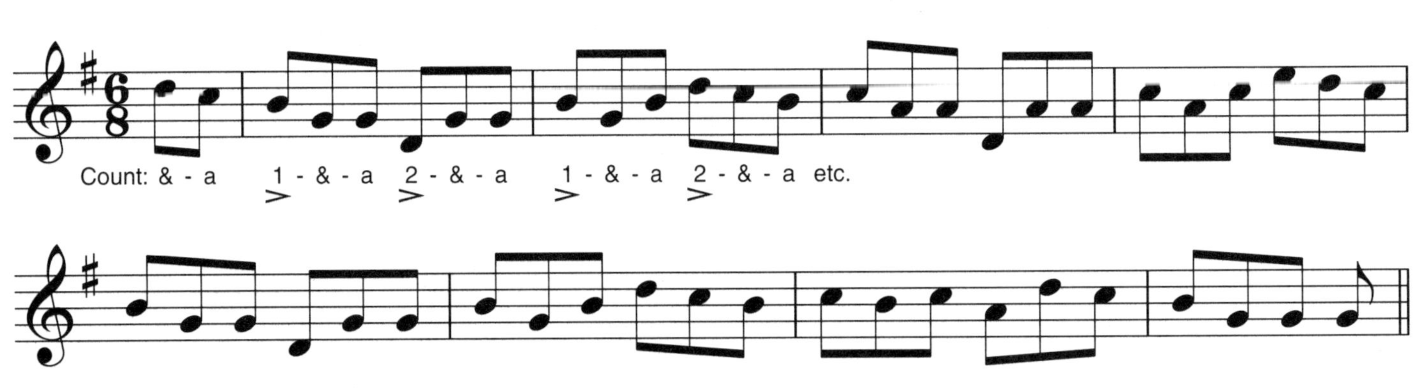

"Nocturne," on the next page, reflects the style of the 19th century Romantic composers such as Chopin, Beethoven, and Schumann who popularized the lyrical, dreamy *nocturne* form (the term means "night music"). The **Romantic period** in music is approximately 1800–1880; probably the most famous nocturne of all time is the first section of Beethoven's "Moonlight Sonata."

Nocturne

Charles Duncan

Adagio M.M. ♩. = 72

Carulli's "Barcarole" is a good example of another form used by composers to capture a lyrical, romantic mood. A *barcarole* (from Italian *barca*, meaning "boat") is a Venetian gondolier's song.

TIP: Look closely at the first line of music; the broken curved line means that you leave the first finger down as a **pivot** to anchor the hand and prevent unnecessary finger movement. Try to use this technique throughout the piece wherever the same musical figure appears.

Barcarole

Ferdinand Carulli

Larghetto M.M. ♪ = 52

Giuliani wrote many charming miniature pieces to serve as etudes; the piece below is a good example. It introduces you to a somewhat more complex musical texture in 6/8 time, and the last line is a technical challenge in itself.

TIP: Practice the chord changes used in the last line in the form of the following cadence:

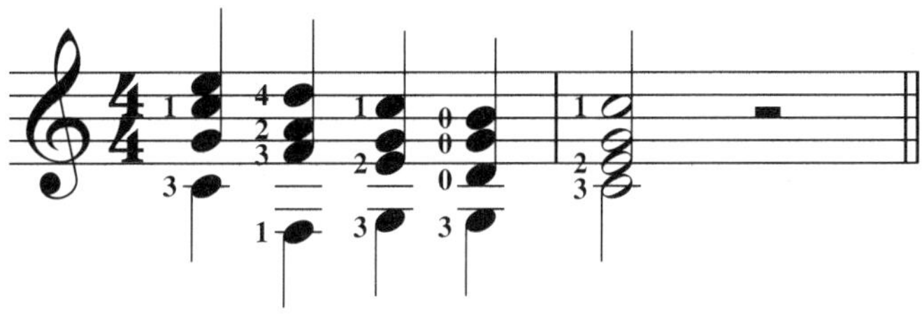

After you've mastered the technical challenges, practice for phrasing and melodic emphasis—try to make the piece "sing."

Moderato

Mauro Giuliani

M.M. ♩. = 52

Interlude: Song Accompaniments

While you're mastering the solos on the preceding pages, let's take a time-out for some enjoyable and beneficial recreational practice. If you don't already have some accompaniment skills, this section will be especially helpful.

The most widespread use of the guitar is as an accompaniment instrument, and well-rounded classical guitarists are very good at accompanying songs. The songs in this section will introduce you to the basic accompaniment styles for songs in 4/4 and 3/4, as well as provide further practice in playing arpeggios, changing chords, and using the half-barre F chord. If you're interested in developing your accompaniment skills further, several excellent Hal Leonard folk song and popular music anthologies are available.

Michael, Row the Boat Ashore

American Folk Song

Cockles and Mussels

Irish Ballad

M.M. ♩ = 104

Amazing Grace

Traditional Hymn

* The wavy vertical line is the symbol for a **broken chord**, also known as a **rolled chord**. Play it either with a brush stroke with the thumb, or a rapidly executed arpeggio with a double thumb stroke: *p p i ma.*

Scarborough Fair

Traditional English Ballad

M.M. ♩ = 104

Syncopation

The melodies of the following two pieces will also reinforce your knowledge of **syncopation**, which was introduced in *Book 1*. Syncopation occurs when normally unstressed beats or parts of a beat are rhythmically stressed. For example, in syncopated melodies, you'll often see quarter notes on an upbeat instead of the downbeat, or eighth notes tied to the next downbeat.

TIP: Whenever you see this kind of notation, remember that you'll need to play on the "ands" of the count.

Practice the two rhythm lines below, counting aloud. Then practice the melody part as well as the accompaniment part to "Hava Nagilah" and "Joshua Fought the Battle of Jericho." (Be sure to count aloud while learning the melody part.)

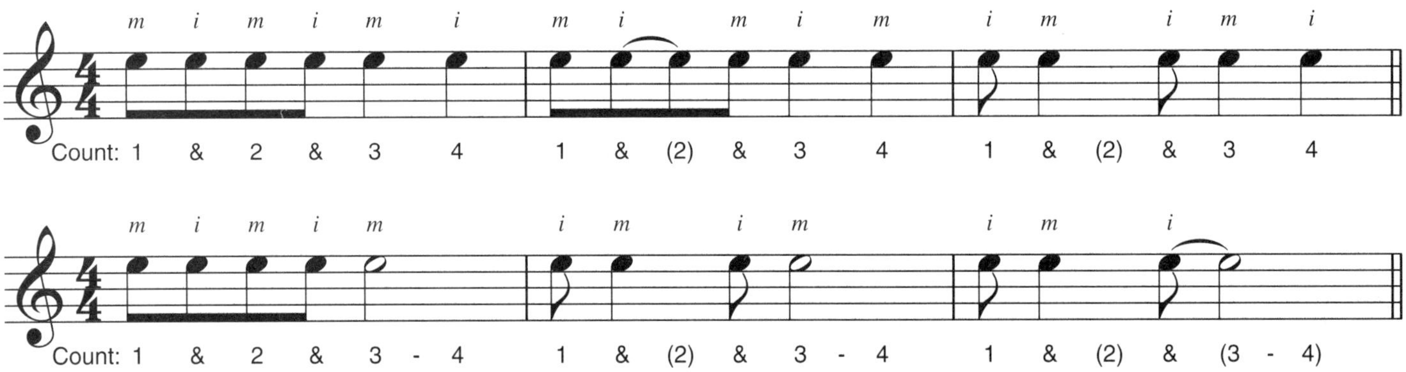

Hava Nagilah

Israeli Folk Dance

Joshua Fought the Battle of Jericho

American Spiritual

Position Playing: Second and Third Positions

Position playing is the term that guitarists use for playing beyond the first position on the fingerboard, with the fret played by the *first* finger as the reference point. For example, in **second position**, your first finger plays the *2nd* fret notes, and therefore you can play notes as high as the 5th fret without moving your hand. Similarly, in **third position**, you can play notes as high as the 6th fret without moving your hand, and so on up the fingerboard. You'll learn more about position playing in *Book 3*. For now, a good command of second- and third-position playing is enough, since most of the easy-to-intermediate classical guitar repertoire doesn't use notes past the 6th or 7th frets.

When you're playing in second or third position, open-string and 1st-fret notes are played on *the next lower string*, as shown below for the notes that you'll be playing in their next higher fingerboard positions.

TIP: This pattern of repetition up on the fingerboard is known as the **rule of five frets**—any note on strings 1, 3, 4, and 5 can also be found five frets higher up on the fingerboard on the next lower string. Second-string notes are found *four* frets higher on the third string.

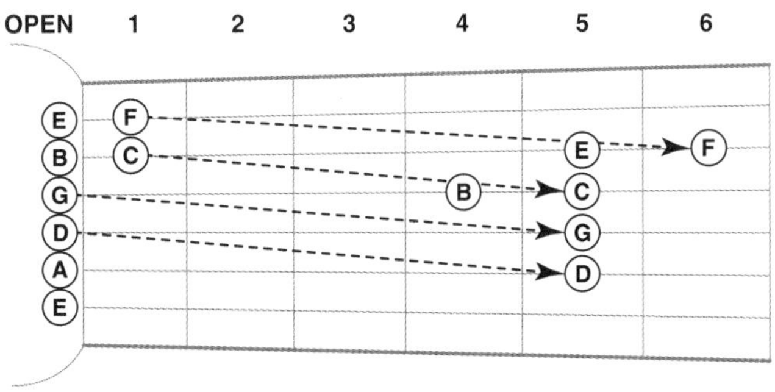

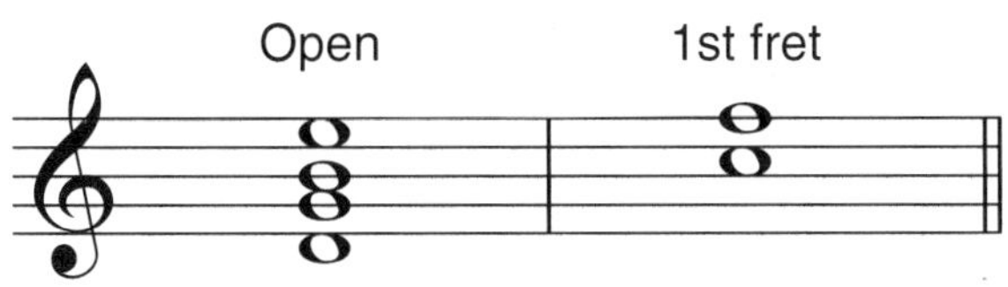

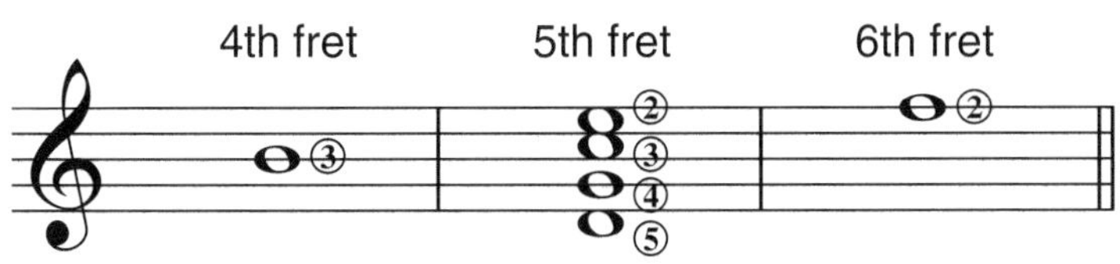

To learn the second- and third-position notes that you'll be playing, practice the following scale pattern exercises. When you're comfortable with the exercises, go on to the duets on the next five pages.

G Major, second position

C Major, third position

A Melodic minor, second and third position

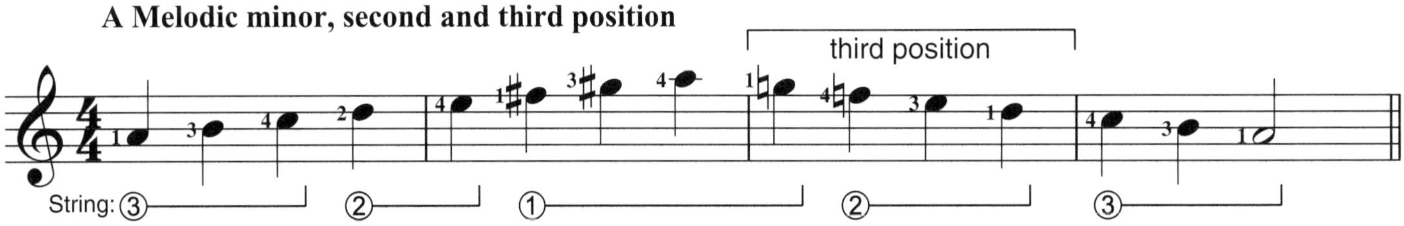

The following two etudes by the author in contrasting pop music styles will give you an easy introduction to playing in second and third position. They also illustrate the more advanced kind of accompaniment skills that you'll be capable of at a higher level of guitaristic development. Practice each melody slowly and carefully, using the position fingerings shown. For the accompaniment, you can either have an instructor play with you or play along with the recorded accompaniment.

Second-Position Etude

Third-Position Etude

The melody of this slow, majestic piece by J.S. Bach is played entirely in second position. Even though it is a rather quiet piece, use good, solid rest strokes.

TIP: Listen also for the stronger, warmer, and more uniform tone quality achieved by playing it entirely in second position. Position playing is often used for this purpose, even when it's not needed for reaching notes on the higher frets.

Chorale from *St. Matthew Passion*

J.S. Bach

The melody of this charming piano solo by Schumann is entirely in third position, except for measures 3 and 4, which are in second position. Notice also the open-string B in measure 4; it's used here for convenience in returning to the third-position fingering.

Bagatelle

Robert Schumann

In this famous Christmas carol, you'll be alternating freely between second- and third-position fingerings beginning at measure 9 (see the *).

TIP: With a bit of practice, you'll find that alternating between second- and third-position fingerings is easy and natural, because it doesn't require an actual position shift. Your thumb only needs to pivot on its tip to support the small back-and-forth hand movement.

God Rest Ye Merry, Gentlemen

19th Century English Carol

Moderato M.M. ♩ = 120

Using the Second and Third Position in Solos

A lot of the easy-to-intermediate guitar repertoire is based on first-position playing with occasional use of the higher positions. The next six pieces will introduce you to this kind of music, which requires a somewhat higher level of technique than the music you've played so far.

Gaspar Sanz (1640–1710) was the most important early composer for the Spanish guitar, and several of his pieces have become standards of the concert repertoire. The "Espanoleta" below is also well-known as one of the main themes of Joaquin Roderigo's beautiful guitar concerto "Fantasia Para un Gentilhombre."

TIP: In the 1st measure of the second line, be sure to hold down the bass note F for the whole measure.

Espanoleta

Gaspar Sanz

You've had a lot of practice in bringing out the melody in arpeggiated pieces from the 19th century. The author's composition below shows how the same technique is used to bring out the melody in modern classical guitar music of the same general kind. It also illustrates the fact that sixteenth notes don't necessarily have to be played fast; this is a fairly slow piece with a romantic feel.

TIP: In addition to the use of second position in the next to last line of music, notice where the half-barre chord is used.

Reverie

Charles Duncan

Lento M.M. ♩ = 58

The "Allemande" below is a fine example of the popular Renaissance dance form also spelled as "Alman" or "Aleman"—a stately dance of German origin in 4/4 time.

Likewise, the two transcriptions on the next page are fine examples of one of the most popular Baroque dances, the *Bourree*—a lively dance of French origin in 4/4 time. The composer of the second, Johann Krieger (1651–1735), is not nearly as well-known as J.S. Bach (1685–1750), but several of his pieces for harpsichord also make excellent transcriptions for guitar.

✔ **TIP:** Each piece uses some unusual position shifting in order to simplify the left-hand requirements. In Bach's "Bourreé," you'll also be playing the note D in the bass line on the *fifth string* where indicated.

Allemande

Anonymous
16th century

Moderato M.M. ♩ = 104

Bourreé

Allegretto M.M. ♩ = 120

J.S. Bach

Bourrée

Allegretto M.M. ♩ = 116

Johann Krieger

"Packington's Pound" is another of the excellent anonymous lute pieces of the Renaissance. Carcassi's "Caprice" on the next page is a light-hearted recreational piece designed to promote the student's technical development.

TIP: In "Caprice," notice the occasional use of the half-barre at the 2nd and 3rd frets. Notice also the 3/8 time signature, which is often used instead of 3/4 for fast pieces in triple meter. Count 3/8 the same way you would count 3/4: "1-and-2-and-3-and," etc.

Packington's Pound

Anonymous
16th century English

Allegro M.M. ♩ = 132

Caprice

Matteo Carcassi

Allegro M.M. ♪ = 138

Left-Hand Technique: Using Slurs

On the guitar, notes on the same string can be played by the left hand alone. This valuable technique is called **slurring**, and it's used for several purposes:

- ✓ To simplify right-hand fingering and give the plucking fingers a break.
- ✓ To make fast single-note passages easier to play.
- ✓ To make smoother connections between the notes of a melody.
- ✓ To create variety of melodic accent.
- ✓ To produce various kinds of ornaments, also known as **embellishments** (see p. 119).
- ✓ When practiced as exercises, to develop the strength and control of the left-hand fingers.

Slurs can be either ascending or descending. Ascending slurs are commonly called **hammer-ons**, while descending slurs are called **pull-offs**. Both are indicated by a **ligature** (i.e., the same kind of short curved line that connects tied notes).

Hammer-On

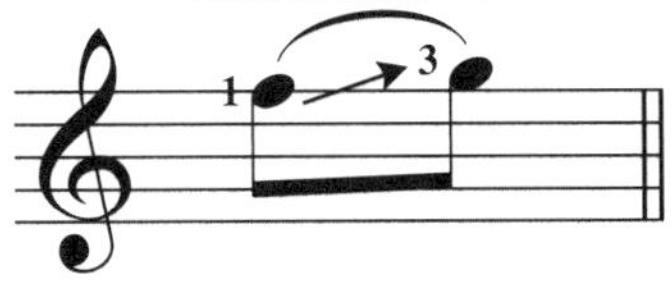

Pull-Off

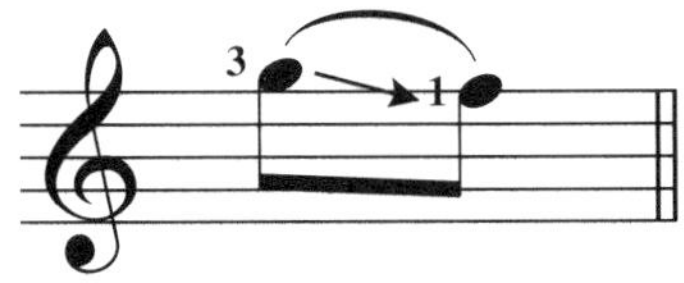

ASCENDING SLURS ("HAMMERING ON")

The common term for ascending slurs, hammer-on, tells you exactly what to do. Pluck the first note, then play the next note by sharply *hammering* your fingertip onto the string. The note is sounded by the percussive impact of the curled fingertip.

✓ **TIP:** Aim small with your fingertip and try to strike the string just behind the next metal fret—not in the middle of the fret space. This will give you a cleaner-sounding note with less effort.

Practice the following slur exercises on strings 1, 2, and 3 slowly and carefully. Try to produce clean-sounding notes with an even, steady eighth-note rhythm.

DESCENDING SLURS ("PULLING OFF")

The common name for the descending slur, pull-off, also tells you what to do, although a bit more explanation is needed. First, make sure that you're already holding down the second note when you play the first note. Then, to play the second note, pull your fingertip sharply toward the palm of the hand by flexing the tip joint. As you practice the following first-string exercise, remember that you're actually *plucking* the second note with a left-hand finger.

Pull-offs on the lower strings are somewhat trickier, because you have to play the second note without accidentally plucking the next higher string. The best solution to this problem is to pull the fingertip sharply *into* the next higher string, but not across it.

TIP: This is basically the same thing that your right-hand fingers do when playing rest strokes.

Practice the following exercises on strings 2 and 3 to develop the fingertip control that you'll need.

Now practice the following second-position exercise that combines strings one, two, and three into a scale pattern of descending slurs.

If you can play the preceding exercises, you're ready to play the melody part in the following duets adapted from well-known keyboard pieces. In Bach's "Minuet in G," slurs are used to enhance the rhythmic drive of each group of eighth notes. Slurs are often used for this purpose.

Minuet in G

J.S. Bach

Allegretto M.M. ♩ = 112

Jean Philippe Rameau (1683–1764) was a French contemporary of Bach; several of his excellent compositions have also been transcribed for classical guitar. In this one, note the use of slurs to create variety of melodic accent as well as rhythmic drive.

Rondino

J.Ph. Rameau

Andantino M.M. ♩ = 100

The following two pieces by Fabritio Caroso (1527–1605?) will introduce you to the use of slurs in solo playing. Caroso was a composer and dance instructor of the Italian Renaissance; these two pieces are from his dance manual *Il Ballarino* published in 1581.

The first piece is fairly slow and sounds almost like an improvisation. In fact, when played with feeling, it should sound as if you're improvising it yourself. Therefore, you'll need to use slurs only in the first measure of each of the last two lines of music. Here, the slurs will make the execution of the sixteenth notes much easier and more fluent.

Gratia d'Amore

Fabritio Caroso

Andante M.M. ♩ = 88

"Alba Novella" is a faster piece with a stronger beat than "Gratia d' Amore," and therefore slurs can be used to good effect at several points. However, since slurs were not commonly used in lute technique, they are indicated here by the sign for the **optional slur**—a broken ligature: ⌒ You'll see this sign frequently in modern guitar editions of early music, or whenever a modern composer feels that the choice of using the slur should be left up to the player.

TIP: Learn the piece without slurs first, then try using them as you're getting the piece up to speed. The closer it approaches the suggested metronome setting, the more natural the slurs will feel and the better they will sound.

Alba Novella

Fabritio Caroso

Allegretto M.M. ♩ = 112

The well-known first section of Beethoven's beautiful piano classic, "Für Elise," makes a very effective guitar solo. Note the optional slurs in the fourth line of music—when you get the piece up to speed, using slurs here will enhance the greater sense of rhythmic urgency conveyed by this section of the piece.

Für Elise

Larghetto M.M. ♪ = 108

Ludwig van Beethoven

Using Slurs for Ornamentation

Ornamentation (also known as **embellishment**) is the musical term for the decoration or emphasis of a melodic note with rapidly executed notes above and/or below the note. On the guitar, ornaments are usually executed with slurs. You'll learn more about ornamentation in *Book 3*; the last four pieces in this book will introduce you to the use of descending and ascending slurs for ornamentation.

THE GRACE NOTE

The most basic ornament is the **grace note** (𝆔), which you play with a *very* quick pull-off. Like most ornaments, it's written as a smaller note connected to the main note with a short ligature. Also like most ornaments, the way it looks can be confusing, especially when the melody note is combined with any lower notes. In all cases, you play the grace note *together with the lower note(s)* and pull off to the main note. The following examples show how grace notes are written and how they are actually played.

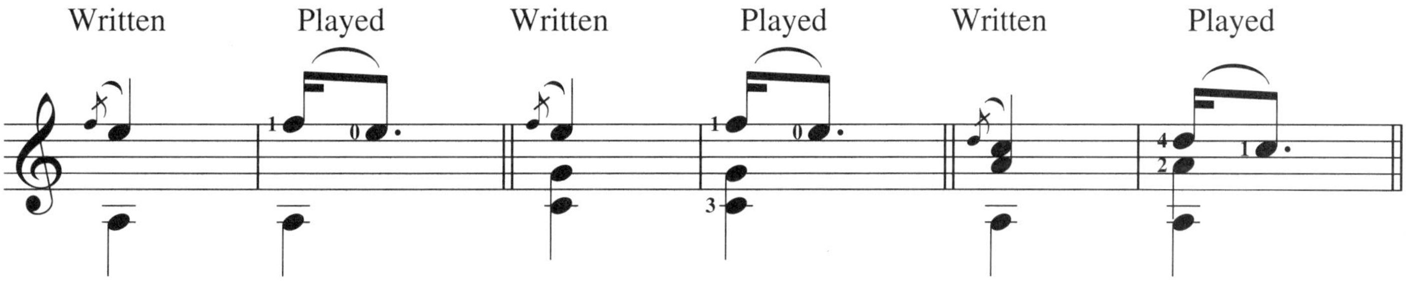

✔ **TIP:** This ornament tricks the ear. When well played, it sounds as if the main note (not the grace note) falls on the beat. This also helps explain why it's written as a small note before the beat.

THE DOUBLE GRACE NOTE

The **double grace note** takes two forms known as the **mordent** and the **inverted mordent**, shown below. The inverted mordent is more common and is the one we'll be using in the last two pieces. You play it by executing a very quick hammer-on and pull-off, as shown in the second example:

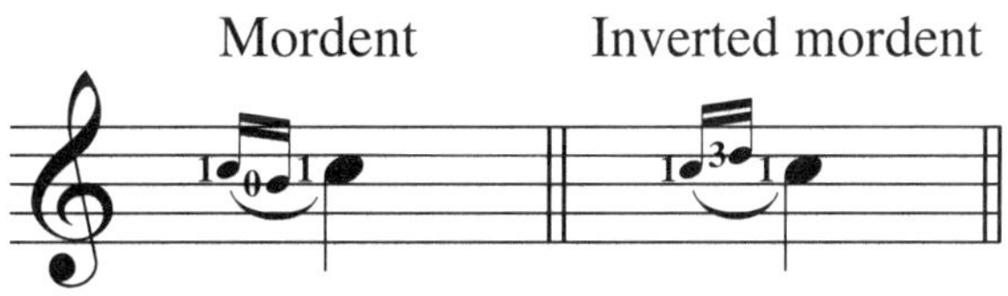

Like the grace note, the first note of this ornament is played together with any lower notes. Also like the grace note, it can sound as if the main note falls on the beat, at least when the music tempo is not very fast. However, as the tempo speeds up, the ornament will sound much more like a triplet:

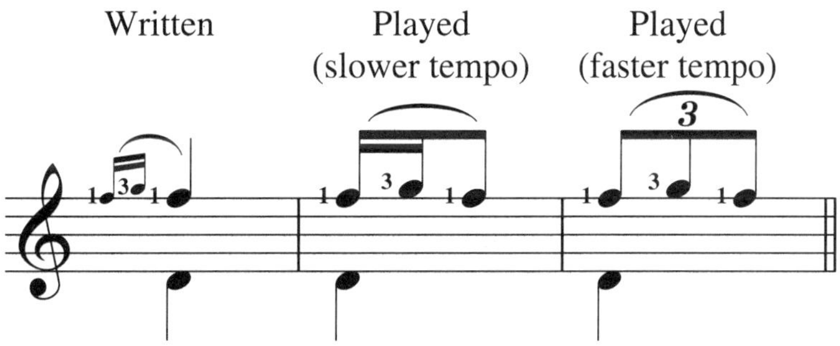

✔ **TIP:** Just try to execute the double grace note as rapidly as you can. Depending on the tempo of the music, either interpretation of the ornament is perfectly acceptable.

Besides being a very beautiful piece, Sor's "Andante" below provides an easy introduction to playing grace notes. The same grace note is used in the first, second, and fourth lines of music.

TIP: Remember to execute the pull-off as a left-hand rest stroke, which actually *plucks* the melody note (C in each case).

Andante

Fernando Sor

Coda: Spanish Music in the Phrygian Mode

A **coda** is a short concluding section at the end of a musical composition. The music symbol is the **coda sign:** 𝄌 As the "coda" to this book, let's look at what makes Spanish music sound "Spanish" and conclude with some Spanish-sounding music.

Modern Spanish music is strongly influenced by the gypsy music called **flamenco**, which is generally based on the **Phrygian mode**. The Phrygian mode is the scale pattern of intervals produced by the A natural minor scale with E (not A) as the root (shown below). When the Phrygian mode is built on any other root, chromatic alteration is needed to keep the pattern of whole steps and half steps the same. (For example, in the common key of A Phrygian, the B must be flatted.)

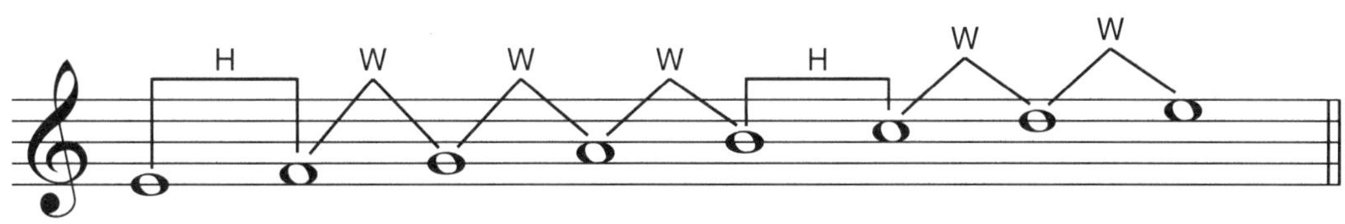

The following Spanish-sounding cadences define the keys of E Phrygian and A Phrygian. Although the other chords are built on the natural minor scale, the tonic chord in Phrygian keys is always major and therefore requires a sharp.

TIP: The G, F, and B♭ chords are in the form frequently preferred by flamenco guitarists in order to take advantage of the open strings and create an even more exotic sound.

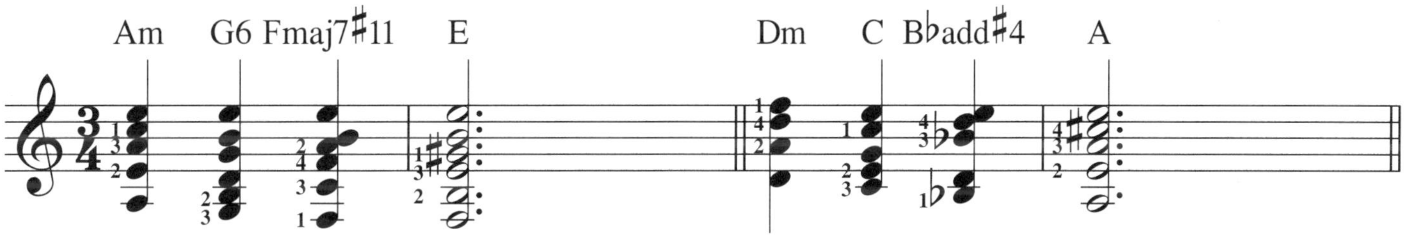

Also, Spanish guitar music often uses the flamenco technique known as **rasgueado**, in which the strings are struck with the back of the fingernails. The most basic rasgueado technique is an up-and-down strum with *i* that's similar to strumming with a guitar pick. Practice using it on the following simple but distinctive flamenco chord progression; the arrows indicate the direction of the strokes.

TIP: Notice that, on the upstrokes, you don't need to play all six strings—just four is enough. For downstrokes where the lowest note is on the fifth string, lightly plant your thumb on the sixth string to dampen it.

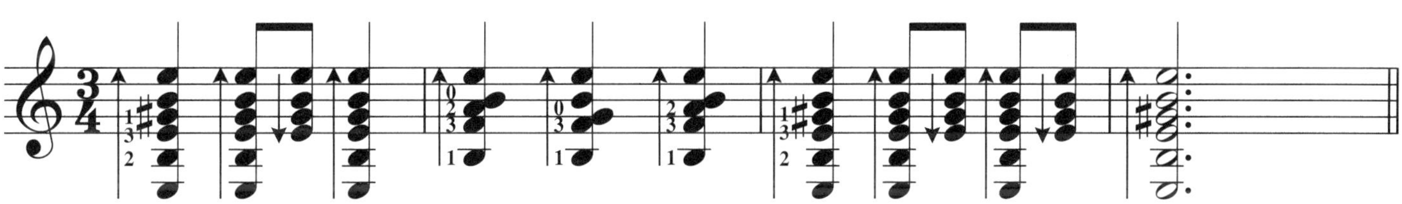

"Fiesta," on the next page, reflects the melodic and harmonic structure of lively flamenco forms in the key of A Phrygian such as the *bulerias* and *tientos*. In the repeat, both grace notes and double grace notes are used to embellish the melody, and the piece concludes with a short coda. "Malagueña," on pp. 124–125, is in the key of E Phrygian, and is based on some of the most traditional versions of this famous flamenco dance form. It also uses the same rasgueado chords shown above.

Fiesta

Charles Duncan

Allegro M.M. ♩ = 184

✔ **TIP:** Students who find the embellished repeat on the next page overly challenging can nonetheless enjoy the piece while polishing their chops. Simply take a D.C. from measure 1 at the top of the page, repeat the first page, and when you get back to the same place, go to the Coda.

Coda
rit.

Malagueña

Traditional Flamenco
(arr. Charles Duncan)

Allegro M.M. ♩ = 176-192

accel.

Appendix: Playing with Fingernails

You'll achieve the best instrumental tone and accuracy by learning to play with your fingernails. Good players vary in the ways that they use their nails, but most of them observe the following basic rules:

- ✓ For all strokes, the string should make simultaneous contact with the nail and the tip of the finger.
- ✓ The fingertip merely "cushions" the nail contact; the actual sound is produced by the nail alone.
- ✓ Even though it only takes a fraction of a second, a fingerstroke has a beginning, middle, and end. Since the quality of tone depends on how smoothly the nail engages the string from contact to release, nails must be filed carefully.
- ✓ Advanced players often vary the contact point to achieve contrasts in tone color. However, for the basic stroke, the contact point is on the left side of the nail (the side nearest the thumb); the release point is slightly past the midpoint of the nail, as shown below.

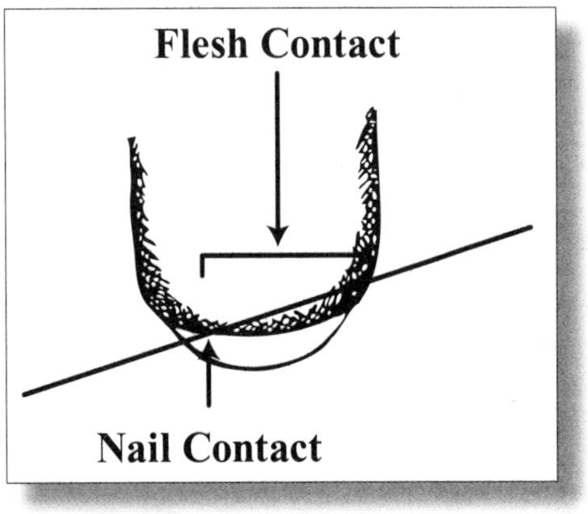

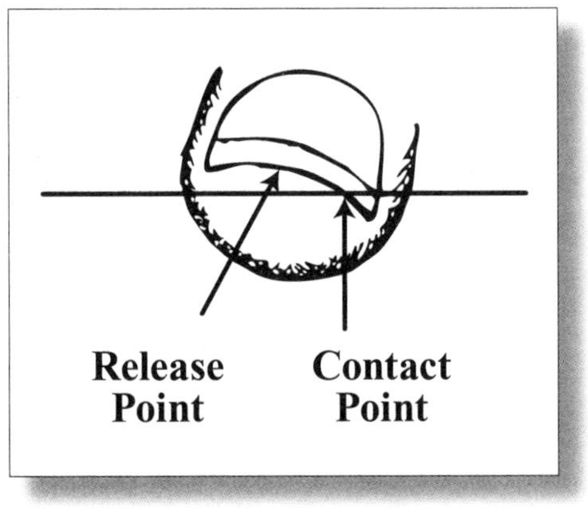

FILING THE NAILS

Various brands of useful nail files are available at nail shops, beauty supply stores, the cosmetics sections of department stores and drugstores, and even dollar stores. Avoid the common metal files; the best ones are made out of synthetic material with surfaces for shaping, smoothing, and polishing. A piece of fine sandpaper (#500 or finer) comes in handy for smoothing off edges, especially from underneath. For final polishing, Open Coat Silicon Carbide Paper is preferred by most players. (Large hardware stores and guitar shops usually carry this paper, and it's also marketed on the internet.)

Shape the nails slowly and carefully with the file at around a 45° angle with the nail. Hold the file steady while you move your fingernail across it with short, gentle back-and-forth strokes. Examine the results frequently from different angles to achieve the correct shape, as shown on the next page.

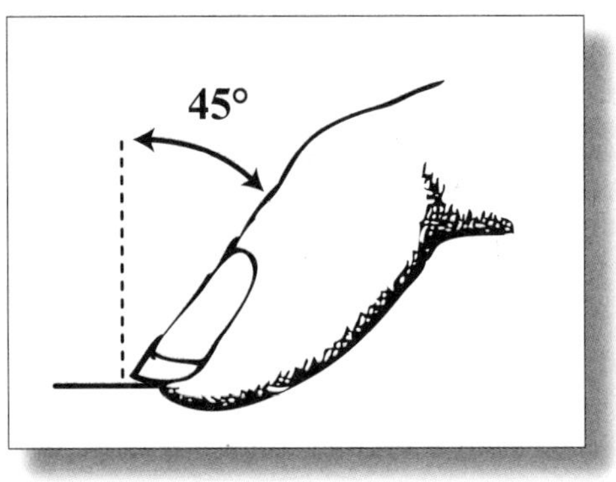

SHAPING THE NAILS

Nails need to be shaped so that they will engage the strings with gentle but firm resistance. Therefore, they should not be long and pointed, but relatively short and blunt. Seen from underneath, as in the first illustration, they should appear 1/16th–1/8th of an inch long. Seen from the side, they should closely resemble the second illustration:

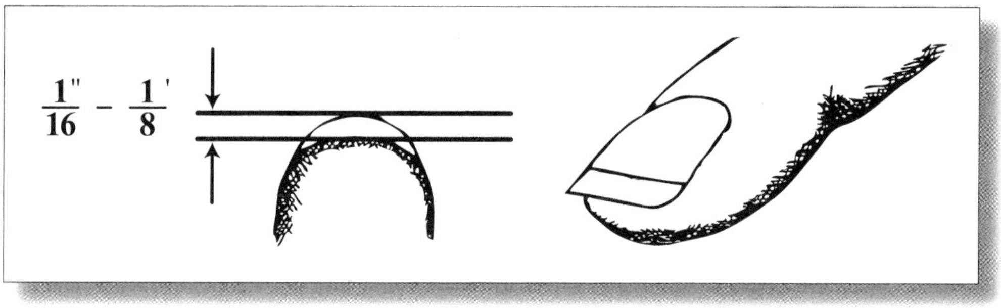

However, in order to get the look of the second illustration, you'll need to adapt the shape to the **arch form** of the nail. Arch form differs from player to player and sometimes between fingers on the same hand. Look closely at your nails head-on, as shown below, to see which arch form they match:

The key to correct shaping is to match the shape (seen from underneath) with the arch form (seen from head-on). In all cases, the peak of the arch is where the nail should appear the longest. If the nail peaks in the middle (arch form A), then the correct shape will be round and symmetrical, just as in the first illustration on this page. If the nail peaks to the left or the right (arch forms B and C), the correct shape will be shown as below:

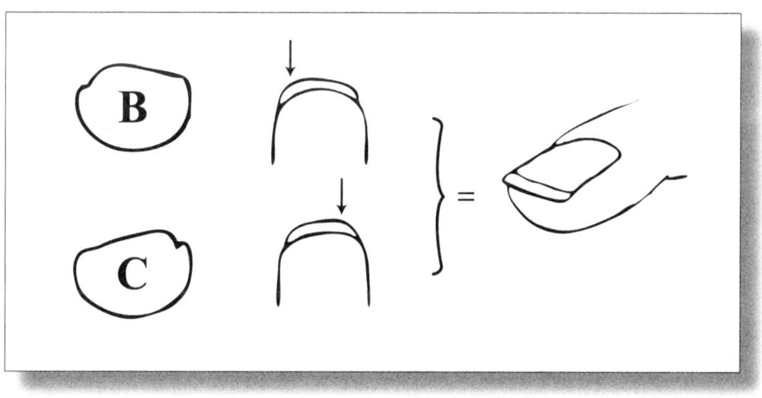

If your nails dip down in the middle as shown below (arch form D), you'll need to file them so that they look flat on the top as seen from underneath:

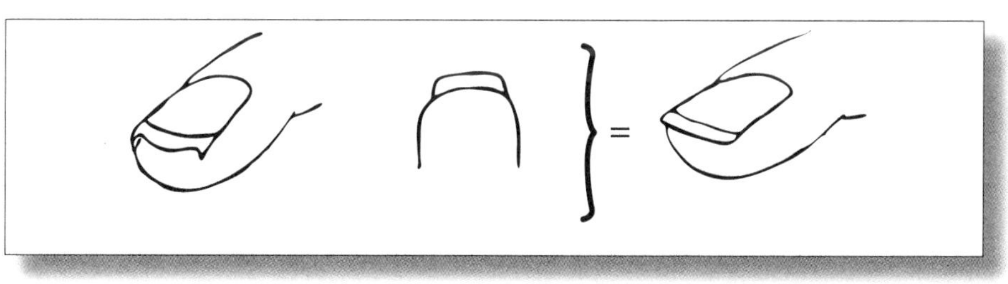

PLAYING WITH THE THUMBNAIL

Good players vary in how they use the thumb. Even the same player will often use different kinds of thumbstrokes consciously or unconsciously to vary the tone. Depending on how you make the nail-to-string contact, there are three kinds of strokes:

① You can make contact (C) the same way you do for the fingers, close to the edge of the nail, and release (R) at the midpoint (illustration 1)

② You can make a double-contact at the midpoint and the edge, and release in between them (illustration 2); or

③ You can make contact at the midpoint and release toward the edge (illustration 3).

The *third* option is the one preferred by most players for their basic stroke. However, you should experiment to see which feels best and produces the best tone.

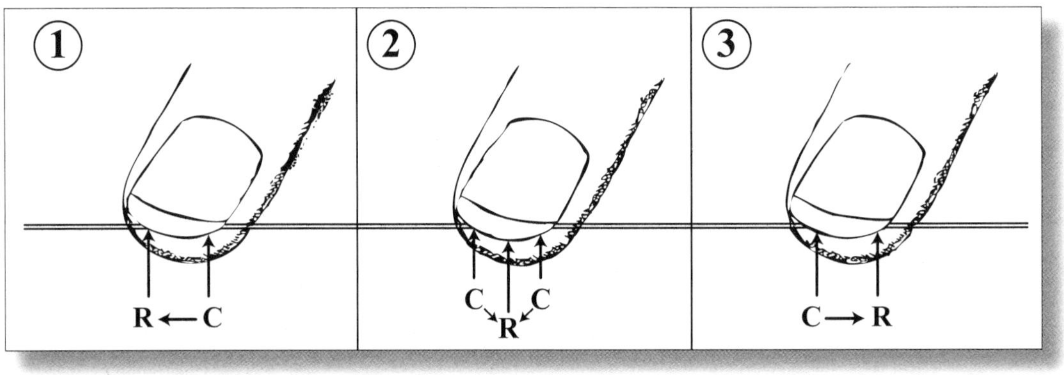

Generally speaking, the thumbnail should be filed according to its arch form just like the fingernails, and should project 1/8–1/4 inch beyond the tip. The relatively greater breadth of the thumb also partly determines the correct nail shape. For a broad thumb with a flattish nail contour, the correct shape will resemble illustration Ⓐ; for a somewhat narrower thumb with a more highly arched nail, the correct shape will look more like illustration Ⓑ:

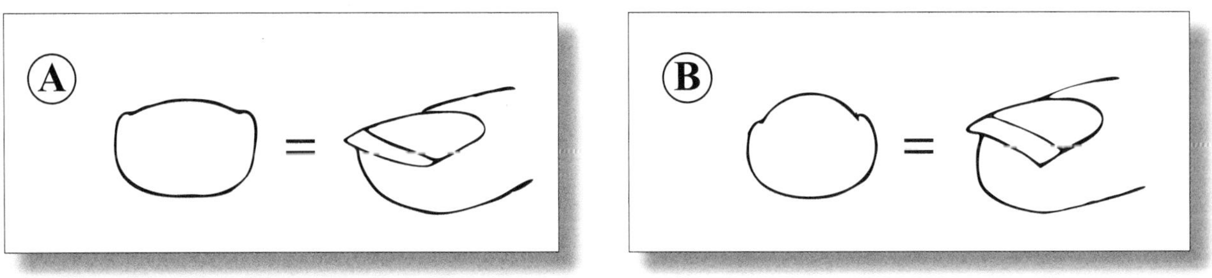

This section will provide you with enough information to start playing with your nails to good advantage. For a more detailed discussion, see Chapter 4 of the author's *The Art of Classical Guitar Playing* (Summy-Birchard Music, 1980), a reference text which continues to be widely used in college and conservative guitar programs.

BOOK 3
PREFACE—From Intermediate to Advanced Playing

If you've completed *Book 2* of this method or were already at that stage of development, you're ready to move up to a level defined by the best players. This means that you'll be learning some valuable new techniques that require good practice habits and patience to develop.

This new edition of *Book 3* will introduce you to those techniques in detail and provide plenty of exercises and music to develop them. If at all possible, you'll also need to be playing with fingernails as explained in *Book 2* (pp. 126–128). The use of nails is now universal and, with few exceptions, good players use nails filed and shaped as illustrated there.

Some techniques and concepts introduced in this new edition include the following:

- Mental anticipation as the key to accurate and efficient technique
- Goal-directed left-hand movements
- Dynamic stroke preparation, known generally as "planting," and its value for good tone
- The use of dynamic stroke preparation in playing arpeggios ("simultaneous planting" and "sequential planting")
- Precise coordination (i.e., synchronization) of the right hand with the left
- The development of confident, reliable speed in scale playing
- The "secrets" of optimal barred chord and slur technique
- The *real* secret of effortless, efficient fingerboard position shifting
- The techniques and uses of damping

As in the first edition, *Book 3* provides introductions to the remaining commonly used keys, the upper fingerboard positions, the techniques of artificial harmonics and flamenco, and more. The music includes solos from several periods, some of the author's compositions, and duets to enhance the study of the upper fingerboard.

Like the section on fingernails in *Book 2*, the genesis of many concepts and techniques in this book can be found in the author's *The Art of Classical Guitar Playing* (Summy Birchard Music, 1980)—a book which has had widespread influence on guitar teaching and playing for decades. In *this* book, they've been further developed, clarified, and methodized for easy and effective use by 21st-century students and their teachers.

I'm grateful for having been provided this golden opportunity to update my ideas in a fresh new format, and also for the synergistic input from the fine students who helped me "road-test" it. Many thanks also to the master teacher-performers who generously read the manuscript and made valuable suggestions for its improvement—Douglas Niedt (who also provided the photos for *Book 3*), Frank Koonce, Louis Lawlor, Michael Jones, and Judy Handler. A special debt of gratitude is due to Judy for her superb recordings of all the pieces for the book/audio version of *Book 3*. A well-degreed protégé of legendary guitarist Oscar Ghiglia, she teaches in Connecticut and performs extensively with her husband Mark Levesque, who also did a masterful job with the recording.

And now let's get started!

The Concept of Dynamic Preparation

1. "Before anything else, *preparation* is the key to success."
   —Alexander Graham Bell

2. *Dynamic, adj.* Marked by usually continuous and productive activity.
   —Merriam-Webster

Dynamic Preparation—a term you'll see repeatedly in this book—is a powerful concept with various applications to the study of the classical guitar. So, what does it mean? Well, look again at the quotes above—the twin reference points which frame its meaning. It's a state of mental and bodily readiness that makes all physical actions easier and more efficient than if initiated "cold" from a more passive state of mind and body. For example, consider a batter waiting for a pitch, a tennis player anticipating the serve, or even a pet cat crouched and ready to pounce on a mouse toy. In all such cases, the muscles needed to move quickly and effectively at the right moment are being *primed* by mentally anticipating the upcoming movement.

The phenomenon of **priming** was discovered by physiologists in the 1930s, and research since then has proved its value in performing reflex-based tasks or learning new psychomotor skills. Although sports performance is the most obvious area of application, music performance is no exception. That's why you'll find lots of references to priming in the teaching literature under headings such as visualization, movement imagery, mental anticipation, aim-directed movement, seeing with the mind's eye, and so forth. The concept of dynamic preparation embraces all these meanings, and *dynamic preparation is the key to a superior classical guitar technique.*

Let's start with how you change chords, and consider each change as a journey from point A to point B. Like all trips, exactly *how* you'll get there is important, so having a good route in mind before you leave makes more sense than just relying on your sense of direction and luck to get where you want to go efficiently. In other words, having a clear mental image of *how* to get from one chord to the next beats merely relying on unthinking reflex movements drilled in by rote practice. Based on Gerhard Mantel's groundbreaking insights into mastering the cello—whose size, shape, and demands on the left hand are similar to those of the guitar—the most appropriate term for fingerboard movements based on laser-focused mental imagery is ***Goal-Directed Movement (GDM)**. The secret of GDM is to "see" the constantly changing fingerboard formations in the mind's eye as clearly as chord diagrams, and the most graceful, efficient way to get from one to another as clearly as a road map.

Grace and efficiency go together like a pair of shoes—i.e., the one implies the other. For example, consider how the slow-motion replays in TV sports broadcasts demonstrate this correlation for all to see. Movements which in real time appeared frantic—a diving pass-catch, a surprise layup, a winning overhead smash, a perfect Triple Lutz—look as fluid and graceful as underwater ballet when played back at half speed. What this means is great news for classical guitarists! By reverse-engineering the process and practicing for graceful efficiency of movement in "super slo-mo," as described on the next page, you'll instill conditioned reflexes that add up to a confident, relaxed style of performance at much higher speeds.

*See Gerhard Mantel, *Cello Technique: Principles and Forms of Movement* [1965], tr. by Barbara Thiem (Bloomington: Indiana University Press, 1975), "Part One: Goal-Directed Movement," pp. 3–40.

For an illustrative example, take the common G-C-D7-G chord sequence shown below in notes and chord diagrams. Read through it a few times to commit it to short-term memory. Then practice it cyclically—G-C-D7-G, G-C-D7-G, etc.—following the steps listed below.

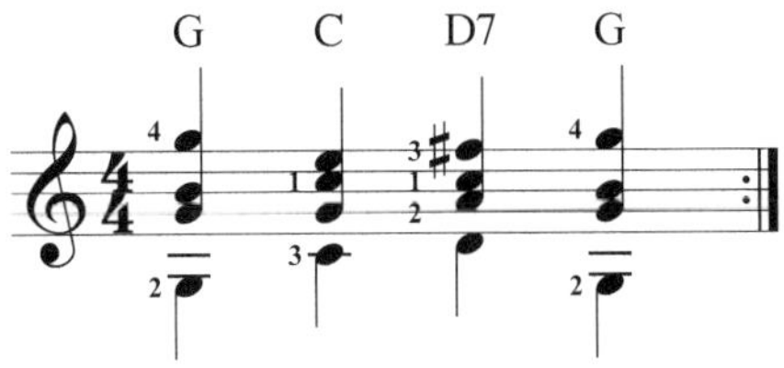

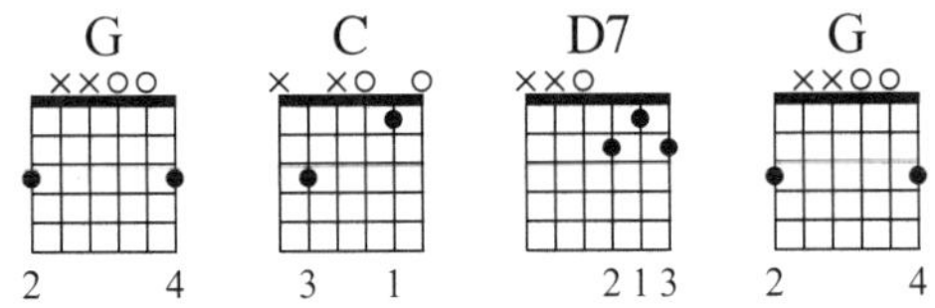

[1] Play very slowly—less than half tempo—and don't try to follow a beat. Allow enough time between movements to concentrate on their *movement style*, not just their target chord.

[2] Play *softly*. Because of the sympathetic neural linkage between the hands, the left hand naturally tends to work harder when the right hand plays more forcefully.

[3] Have a clear *mental* image of the next chord formation *before* releasing the one just played. Look at the frets the new chord will occupy; visualize the exact shape the chord will take and the exact form of movement needed to get into the new formation.

[4] Release the fingers but *don't* relax them *fully*. Keep their curvature, with the tips pointed at the fingerboard, while repositioning the hand and *molding* the fingers into the new chord shape.

[5] Then, as if the fingers were pegs dropping gently into holes drilled to receive them—like some classic Playskool toys—press down the strings and play the chord. Press *no* harder than needed to hold the notes cleanly and securely—don't "kill" the strings the way many players do in the mistaken belief that it's the right way to play.

[6] Practice until each hand position and chord shape appears to flow *seamlessly* into the next, just like the bodily movements in those "slo-mo" replays of exciting moments in ball games and competitive individual sports like tennis and figure skating.

This invaluable practice technique should be used for all the pieces and exercises throughout the book. Although there are others we'll study, GDM is the single most important form of dynamic preparation for the left hand. When you've mastered it and can use it confidently to learn new pieces as well as practice, it will provide a quantum leap in your *overall* technique.

Exactly the same may be said of the dynamic preparation techniques for the *right* hand you'll also learn in this book, which begins next. If all this is new to you, don't worry. Just follow the step-by-step directions carefully, be patient, and you'll be very pleased with the results—in fact, maybe even amazed.

DYNAMICALLY PREPARED FINGER-STROKES AND HAND POSITIONS

Right-hand finger-strokes are dynamically prepared by seating the nail(s) firmly against the string(s) and taking up some string-slack *before* executing the strokes. You can compare this process with archery: (1) the **preparation** is like notching and partly drawing an arrow; (2) the **execution** is like completing the draw and releasing it. Most commonly known as "planting," preparation yields benefits such as accuracy, efficiency, good tone, and speed. It's also the key to a **legato** style of playing in which the notes seem connected like tiny links on a fine gold jewelry chain.

Preparing and executing are defined also by how nails engage the strings during a stroke. As shown below, there's a **contact** point (C) and a **release** point (R). The flesh contact—from *above* the string only—serves to cushion the nail contact. The contact point for *i, m,* and *a* is near the thumb-side edge and the release is near the center, as seen in illustrations 1 and 2 below. For *p*, it's just the opposite: contact in the *middle* and release near the *outside* edge, as in illustration 3.

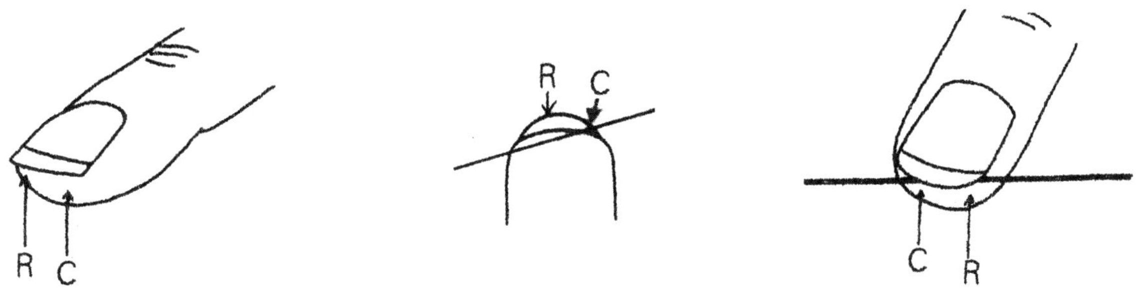

(1) *(2)* *(3)*

Fingernail seen from left side (1) and beneath (2), and thumbnail from above (3).

The three illustrations below show what dynamically prepared hand positions will look like to you:

(1) In the *right*-hand position, note how *p-i-m-a* have been molded into a compact playing unit. The thumb operates most efficiently when tucked in as shown, with the tip turned back, while the **lateral compression** of the fingers counters their common (and harmful) tendency to splay. This position also enhances right-hand stability, accuracy of touch, and consistency of tone color.

(2) The dynamically prepared *left*-hand position is just the opposite. With your fingers *already* hovering over the fret spaces like this, finding and holding notes is much easier than when the fingers aren't curved and spaced in this ready-to-play position. If you practice them conscientiously, the scale and slur exercises in this book will make it feel quite natural.

(3) The last illustration shows the natural alignment of hand, wrist, and forearm that you get when you make a fist. Since leverage and energy are transmitted most efficiently from the arm to the fingers when they're well-aligned, the fist provides a good conceptual model for *both* hands.

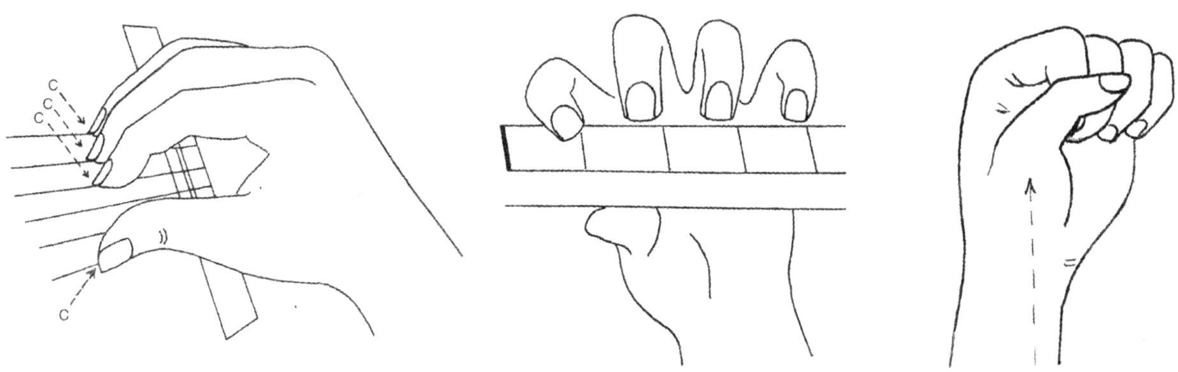

(1) *(2)* *(3)*

(1) The right hand on the strings in a planted, ready-to-play position with nails locked on. (2) The left hand in first position with the first finger on C and the others hovering over the fret spaces. (3) The natural alignment of hand, wrist, and forearm when the hand is comfortably in a fist.

In the next four-page unit, we'll explore the specific dynamic preparation techniques for the *right* hand which lay a foundation for instrumental mastery.

Dynamically Preparing Rest and Free Strokes with *p*:

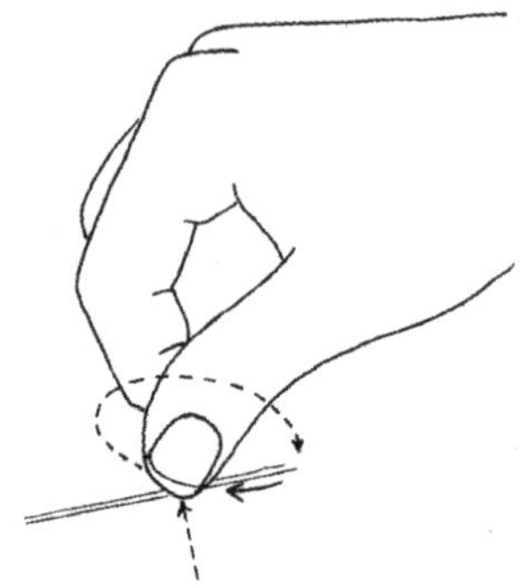

(1) With *i-m-a* planted to anchor the hand, plant *p* on the fifth string. Your hand should now look like the illustration on the previous page.
(2) For rest strokes, push down and to the right with *p* until it glides off the fifth string and comes to rest naturally against the fourth.
(3) For free strokes, use less downward pressure so that *p* barely clears the fourth string and recovers naturally by making a shallow return loop, as if it were bouncing back onto the fifth string.
(4) For both types of stroke, the force should come mainly from the basal joint at the wrist, not from flexion at the mid-joint or tip-joint.

Dynamically Preparing Rest and Free Strokes with *m-i*:

(1) With *p* planted on the fifth string for support, plant *m* on the B string.
(2) For rest strokes, push down and in until *m* glides off the string and comes to rest naturally against the G string. Then do the same with *i*.
(3) For free strokes, aim more toward the palm of your hand so that *m* and *i* barely clear the G string. As shown by the illustration, a good free stroke is more of a downward thrust from the knuckle than an upward pluck.

Dynamically Preparing Your Chord-Strokes:

(1) With illustration 1 on the previous page as a model, plant *p-i-m-a* on open strings 4–1.
(2) Take up the string-slack, balancing the pressure from *i-m-a* with equal force from *p*.
(3) Complete your stroke with a down-and-in "squeeze" that discharges the energy in the partly flexed muscles and feels like a release of tension. The *recovery* should return *p* to its starting point and leave *i-m-a* hovering over the strings, *not* aimed into the palm of your hand.
(4) Practice also with strings 5 and 6 as the basses and listen closely for consistent tone quality and volume.

Correcting a Faulty Position with Lateral Compression

Pictured below are four common variants of right-hand position (a, b, c, and d) that will spoil your efforts to put the instructions above to good use. Each is the product of *dysfunctional* muscular tension, as opposed to the *functional* tension needed to compress the hand into the compact playing unit illustrated on the previous page, with the thumb at about a 45-degree angle to the strings rather than nearly parallel, when the wrist is collapsed as in illustration (d).

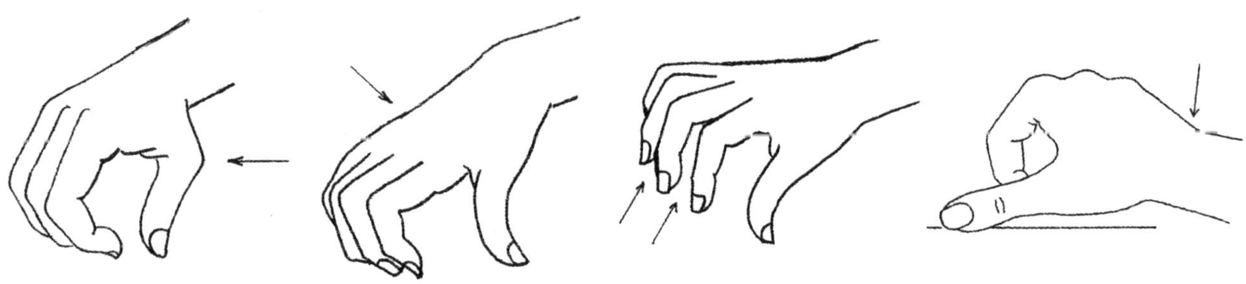

(a) *(b)* *(c)* *(d)*

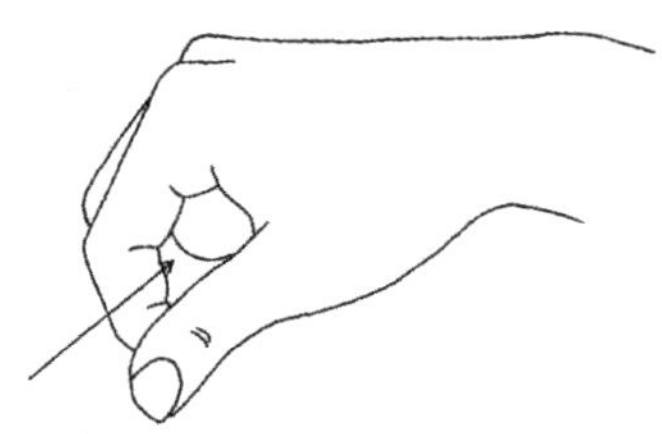

The easiest way to form the correct position is by *laterally compressing* the hand muscles to grip a Ping-Pong ball within your palm as shown to the right. In fact, even a piece of printer paper crumpled into a little ball will serve the purpose just as well. You can actually play quite a bit while gripping the ball, but the real value of this training aid is to mold the hand, thumb, and fingers effortlessly into an optimal position as shown here from your point of view when playing.

(e)

STACCATO PRACTICE

Dynamically prepared strokes are mastered by cutting notes short with **staccato** articulations. This will transform the practice techniques described earlier into conditioned reflexes and lay the foundation for truly **legato** playing. To learn this practice technique, just follow the "plant-play" prompts in the open-string exercises below, *preparing* on the rests and *executing* on the notes. This will create a moderately staccato effect by cutting the note durations in half.

Also, keep in mind the archery analogy from earlier—most of your effort should be expended on the preparations as you seat your nail(s) firmly and put tension on the string(s). Each time you do that, you minimize the effort needed to complete the stroke(s), and therefore the actual execution will feel more like a release of tension than a plucking action.

With *m-i* Rest Strokes, as in Scale Playing:

[1] Plant *p* on the fifth string and leave it down to anchor your hand.

[2] Plant *m* on the second string and play the B.

[3] Exactly as *m* comes to rest against the G string, plant *i* on the B string.

[4] Play the B with *i* and continue by preparing strokes on the *rests* ("plant") and completing them on the *notes* ("play").

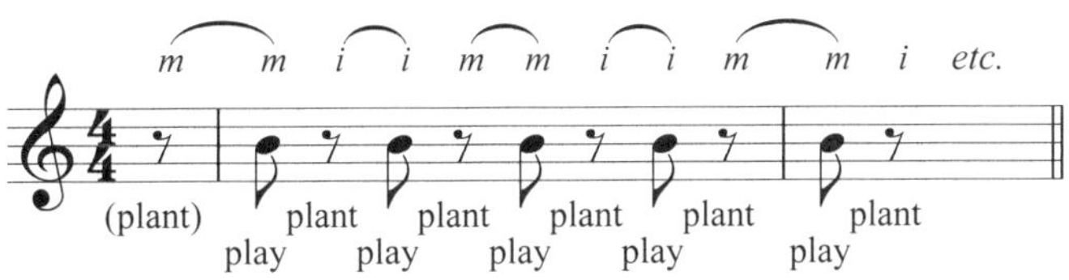

TIP: Don't think of the fast-planting movement as a separate, additional effort. It's triggered and assisted by the finger's natural reflex recovery from its preceding stroke, just like the footsteps when you walk. Consequently, with just a bit of good practice, the simultaneous "plant-play" exchange movement will feel as natural as walking.

With Chords:

[1] Do likewise with staccato *chord* practice by using your natural recovery from one chord-stroke to plant quickly for the next. This will cut the note values by half, except for the bass strings when you change from one to another.

[2] If the change is from string 5 to 4, or 6 to 5, you can **damp** the lower string with the left side of your thumb-tip as you plant on the higher string. As symbolized by the small arrow on each side of the "plant" prompt, just modify your preparation slightly so that the thumb-tip is *sandwiched* between the strings for an instant as the nail is being seated. (Damping a *higher* bass string is a more advanced technique you'll learn later [pp. 174–175].)

COORDINATING (SYNCHRONIZING) THE LEFT AND RIGHT HANDS

Staccato practice also works like magic to coordinate your hands by synchronizing their movements precisely. The secret is to overlap your *left*-hand finger action with simultaneous *right*-hand preparations that mute the string(s) temporarily. Then, you complete the stroke(s) at the moment the new note or chord is pressed down and recover by planting for the next note or chord. That will also trigger the *left* hand's next movement, so that the result is a succession of dynamically paired reflex movements which are synchronized together like windshield wipers.

The prompts in the exercises below, combined with the four-step approach to mastery for each of them, will accustom you to this invaluable style of practice. If it seems awkward or confusing at first, don't worry. Just follow the prompts and let your autonomic nervous system do the rest.

With Chords:

To learn synchronized chord-changing, use the easy A minor chord progression below.

[1] With *p-i-m-a* already planted on the correct strings, play the initial Am chord.

[2] On the rest ("plant/change"), plant for the Dm and make the chord change while the strings are damped. Be sure your thumb plants on the bass string for the *new* chord, not the one just played.

[3] On the next beat ("play"), play the Dm and recover by planting for the Am with E bass.

[4] Do likewise for each subsequent chord change, and repeat. Use the left side of your thumb-tip to damp string 5 on the change from Am to Dm and string 6 on the change from E7 back to Am.

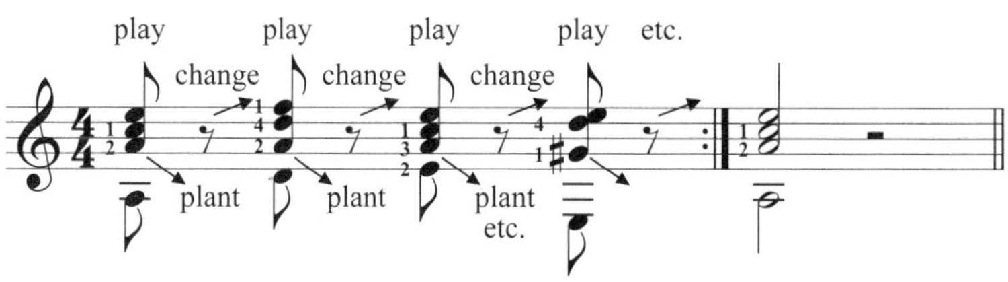

With *m-i* Scales:

[1] In scale practice, coordinate each left-hand finger's "attack" (or "fretting" of the next note) with the right-hand finger's plant for the note—in the chromatic scale pattern below, *i* + 1, *m* + 2, etc., on the rests ("prepare"). The two movements will thus be bound together by *one* shared playing impulse.

[2] Complete the stroke ("play") and release the *i* or *m* resting on the G string for its next plant. The release will also trigger the synchronized movement impulses in step [1] for the *next* note.

[3] In ascending, leave down each left-hand finger so they'll be in place for the descending part of the scale.

[4] In descending, simply *release* each left-hand finger exactly as *m* or *i* plants on the rests ("prepare") and then play the new note, which is already in place. Continue to the end and repeat.

TIP: The rhythmic feel of this process and the sense of constant physical contact with the strings can be compared with swinging hand to hand on a playground overhead ladder or even pedaling a bicycle.

DYNAMIC STROKE PREPARATION IN ARPEGGIOS

To consolidate your command of dynamic right-hand preparations, we'll use some more of Mauro Giuliani's *120 Daily Exercises for the Right Hand*, introduced in *Book 2*, pages 70–71.

Simultaneous Preparation (The "Full Plant")

As symbolized by the vertical bracket in the music example here, plant for the basic *p-i-m-a* arpeggio just as you would for a **block chord**. Then play each finger in turn and repeat the cycle. **Simultaneous planting**, also known as "block planting," is used for ascending arpeggios and the ascending notes in complex arpeggios.

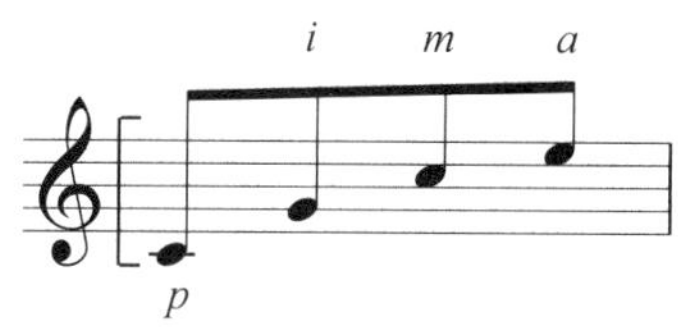

TIP: Oftentimes, students will unconsciously release the planted position of *a* when *m* plays, or even both *m* and *a* when *i* plays. Since you'll lose the benefit of dynamic preparation whenever that happens, be sure to keep *m* and *a* well-planted until they have to play.

Practice the basic *p-i-m-a* exercise below very slowly, synchronizing your hands properly on the chord changes from C to G7 and back. By damping the strings, planting ensures that chord changes will be smooth and relaxed, with no unwanted string noise.

Consecutive Preparations ("Sequential Planting")

The secret of dynamic preparation for descending arpeggios is to plant your fingers consecutively by overlapping each *execution* with the next *preparation* impulse. When done carefully, the seamless connection between neuromuscular impulses will make your fingers feel like they're *chained* together. Usually called "sequential planting," the technique is symbolized here by the horizontal brackets which link consecutive notes in this basic *p-a-m-i* arpeggio:

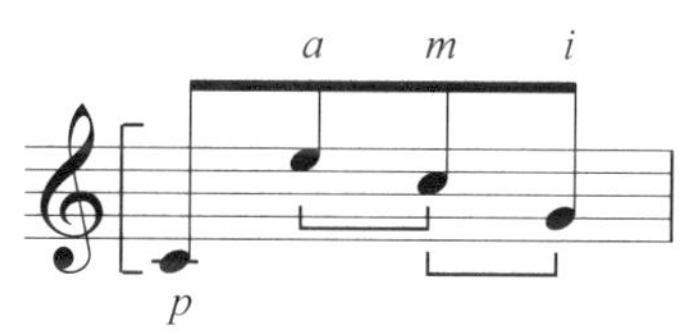

Use the following four-step approach to practice the *p-a-m-i* exercise below:

[1] Plant *p* and *a* simultaneously on C and E, and play the C.

[2] As you play the E with *a*, bring *m* smartly into a planted position on the B string with enough force to seat the nail firmly and take up some slack on the string.

[3] As you play the C with *m*, do the same with *i* for the third string.

[4] As *i* plays the G, complete the cycle by simultaneously planting *p* and *a*.

TIP: When these movements are well-executed, your fingertips will feel like they're actually *sticking* to the strings the way your boots will stick to the ground when walking in mud or snow.

Fine-Tuning Your Preparation Technique with Arpeggios

The following Giuliani exercises will further develop your planting technique with various combinations of ascending and descending preparations. Also, from here on, you *won't* need to simultaneously plant your thumb and the next finger(s) to play, except at the start of an exercise. Once you've begun, it's more efficient to let *p* make its own preparation, triggered by the preceding finger-stroke. *Then*, as *p* plays, its recovery movement (shown on p. 134) will sympathetically pull the next *finger(s)* to play into the correct planted position. Synchronizing your thumb and finger preparations this way will generate a dynamic rotary cycle like that of a waterwheel.

We'll revisit the concept of dynamic preparation in the sections devoted to other essential left- and right-hand techniques, but now it's time to move on to some music and new music concepts!

3/8 Time and Thirty-Second Notes

Just like 6/8 time, in **3/8** time, eighth notes get one beat and sixteenth notes get a *half* beat. **Thirty-second notes** divide a beat into *fourths*, as shown:

Count music in 3/8 as indicated below. In bars 5 and 6, notice that you count dotted sixteenth/thirty-second notes just like dotted eighth/sixteenths in 3/4 or 4/4.

In Aguado's etude below, dotted sixteenth/thirty-second note figures are used as a rhythmic *__motive__. Note also the composer's use of third-beat *rests* as phrase endings. To play these musical silences, just plant for the next chord while simultaneously relaxing your left-hand finger pressure. Since this is an almost intuitive damping technique, with just a bit of practice it will feel entirely natural.

Estudio

Dionisio Aguado
(1784–1849)

*__TIP:__ Motives are short musical ideas whose repetition in a piece helps to unify it.

Barred Chords

In this section, we'll start with a brief practical review of partial barring (introduced in *Book 2*) with a couple of enjoyable etudes, and then tackle the more difficult full barre. As explained in *Book 2*, barres are identified by the letter C (for Spanish *ceja*, "bar"), plus the fret number. In this book, the *type* of barre is indicated by the fret number (in Roman numerals) preceded by fractions for the number of strings covered. Thus, for a *2nd*-fret barre, the possibilities are: 1/3CII (*two* strings), 1/2CII (*three* strings), 2/3CII (*four*), 5/6CII (*five*), and CII (*all six*).

Barred Chord Etude 1

Charles Duncan

Andande M.M. ♩ = 88

Barred Chord Etude 2

Charles Duncan

Andante M.M. ♩ = 88

THE FULL BARRE

The easiest way to learn the full barre is to start with the fingerings for the Am and E chords shown to the right. With the barred first finger in place of the nut, these movable chord grips can be played up to the 10th fret. Practice changing them back and forth, and be sure to keep your fingers joined together on the changes!

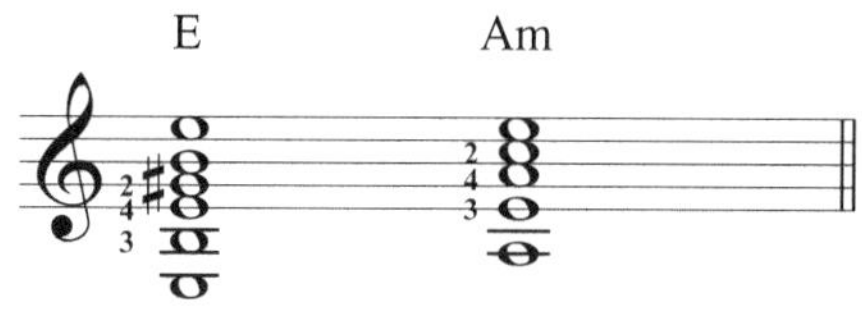

Barred at the 1st fret, they become the F and B♭m chords shown below. Practice as follows:

[1] Make the re-fingered E chord; *then* slide it up a fret and clamp down the barre at the 1st fret.

[2] Strum the F chord in the first photograph and change to the B♭m shown in the second.

[3] Keep your fingers joined on the change, place them simultaneously, and strum the B♭m.

[4] Finally, practice changing the chords back and forth *without* lifting the barre.

TIP: In five- and six-string barres, the leverage comes mainly from the *knuckle* joint. Therefore, you'll need to keep the finger rigid from knuckle to tip with no "give" in the tip-joint or middle joint.

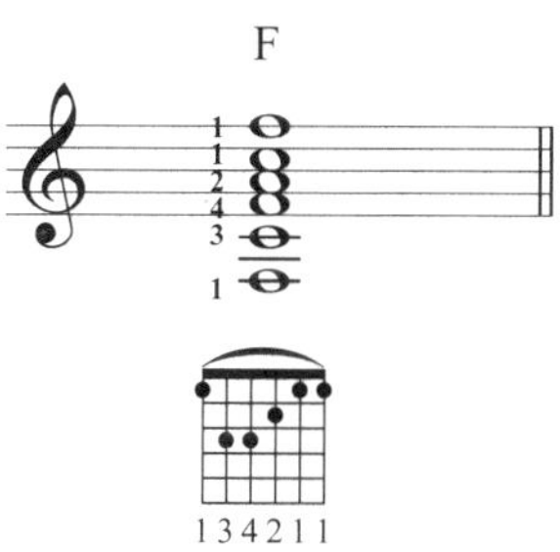

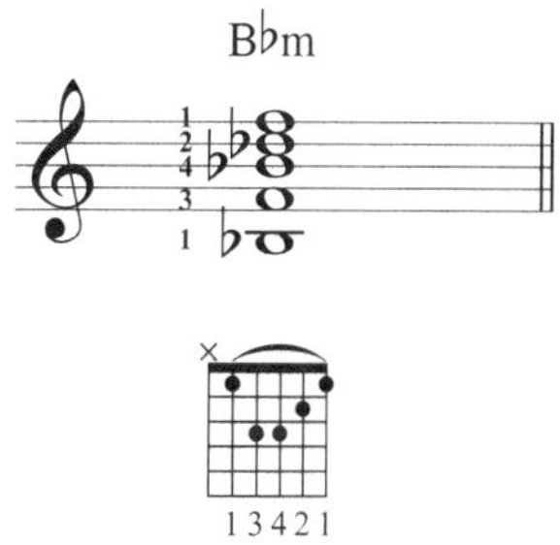

Refining Your Grip for Best Leverage

Students often press too hard with the thumb and try to keep the first finger unnaturally straight. These common errors strain the muscles and waste effort by not providing efficient leverage. You can avoid them by observing the following fine points:

[1] Pressure from the ball of the thumb provides only part of the force needed for a good grip. Most of it comes from **(a)** the adductor and interosseous muscles *between* the thumb and forefinger, and **(b)** the arms, by pulling back slightly against the counterforce from the chest. A tendency to pull back a bit is perfectly normal anyway; just experiment with it until you can feel the leverage relieving the strain on your hand and stop there. With practice, the muscles between your thumb and first finger will get bigger and your barred chord playing will become easier.

[2] Look closely at the photographs, and notice how the first finger presses slightly on its outside edge, rather than completely flat. At the lower frets, this small outward rotation of the finger is natural, and increases its leverage. As you move up the fingerboard, the finger will naturally flatten out, and the extra leverage will come from the better alignment of the hand and upper arm at the higher frets.

The Key of F Major

Since keys with *more* than one flat don't use many open-string fingerings and rely mainly on barred chords, there's not much classical guitar music in those keys. However, with only one flat (B♭), the key of F has some, and its relative minor (Dm) is a commonly used key.*

[1] Memorize the two-octave first-position F scale and practice with staccato articulations. Use the *a-m* as well as the *m-i* fingering to strengthen *a* and improve its independence from *m*. For most players, the *a* finger requires considerable extra work to develop its playing potential.

[2] Memorize and practice the following F major *cadence* slowly, combining GDM (p. 132) with conscious planting to synchronize the hands (p. 136). Formal cadences consist of a short sequence of the primary chords that define any given key—the tonic (I), subdominant (IV), and dominant or dominant seventh (V or V7). The chords are usually in root position, except for the tonic 6/4 chord (tonic over the fifth scale tone) that sometimes precedes the V7 chord as it does here.

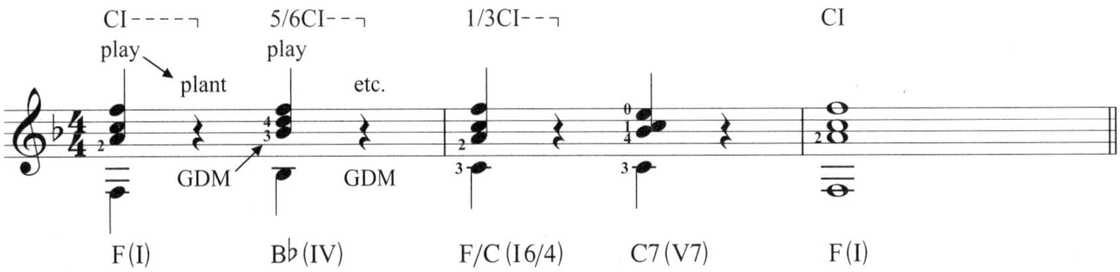

[3] Practice the following scale *pattern* exercise built on the ascending F scale. Pattern exercises provide an enjoyable form of scale practice with benefits such as enhanced fingerboard IQ, left-hand agility, and right-hand scale speed. Don't neglect to practice also with *a-m*!

*__TIP:__ For good examples in both F and Dm, see the author's *A Modern Approach to Classical Guitar Repertoire, Part One*. For examples of pieces in the much less-used key of B♭ (two flats), see Fernando Sor's famous "Etude 19" in *Twenty Studies for Classical Guitar*, ed. Andrés Segovia (Hal Leonard), and the author's etude "Reverie" in *A Modern Approach to Classical Guitar Repertoire, Part Two*.

Carulli's light-hearted etude below provides an opportunity to use articulations for musical effect by dramatizing the repeated rhythmic motive introduced in measure 1:

(1) Play the eighth-note chords on beats 3 and 6 *forte* and cut them off quickly by planting.

(2) Then, play the already-planted quarter-note chords on beats 1 and 4 somewhat softer and hold them for full time value. When well-learned and played with less effort to create contrast, the effect will be a colorful, interesting, *legato* melodic line.

TIP: The visual symbols for staccato and legato notes are dots and dashes, just like Morse code ("dit-*dah*," etc.). Look for them in the first line as a guide to phrasing for the whole piece.

Etude in F

Ferdinando Carulli
(1770–1841)

The Key of D Minor

[1] Memorize and practice the extended one-octave Dm scales in **(a)** open position, and **(b)** second and third positions. As explained in *Book 2*, the melodic minor is the form preferred for scales.

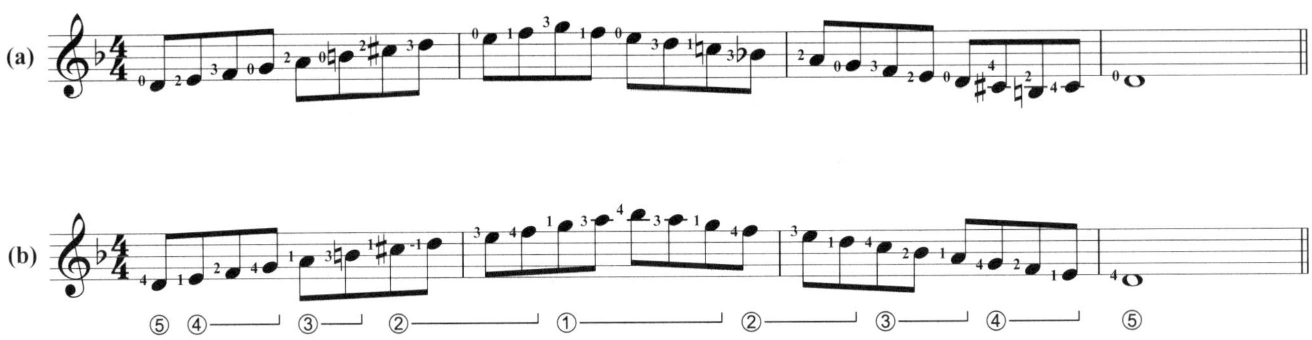

[2] Memorize and practice these Dm cadences using both GDM and conscious synchronization.

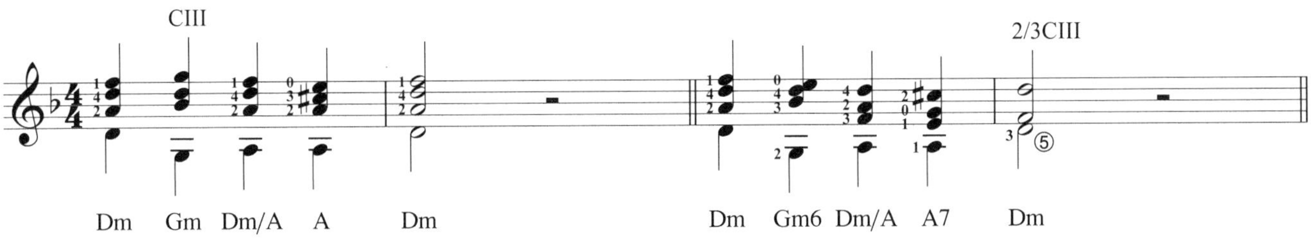

The charming "Minuet" below is a harpsichord piece by England's finest composer of the early Baroque period (the late 17th century). A popular dance form that emerged during Purcell's times, the *minuet* was used both for instrumental solos and as a movement in extended works.

Minuet

Henry Purcell
(1659–1695)

TIP: The fingering in measure 1 is called a *campanelas* fingering (Spanish, "little bells") because of the shimmering resonance created by the overlapped tones. Here, and like the similar fingerings in the last line, it captures the transparent sonority of the harpsichord better than a standard fingering.

USING REST STROKES WITH THE THUMB

Free strokes with *p* are the norm for most playing, but rest strokes are often used for various purposes. To cultivate the technique, practice the lower octave of the F major scale as follows:

[1] Plant *p-i-m-a* with the thumb tucked in and the nail firmly seated, as shown on page 133.

[2] Push down and in from the thumb's basal segment, with supplementary pressure from the mid-joint and tip-joint to control the stroke. Bring the tip to rest on the fifth string.

[3] Recover and plant for the next note with the natural, efficient movement illustrated on page 134.

Gaspar Sanz, the premier guitarist of 17th-century Spain, was the author of the first published guitar method (1674), and the *pavana* was a favorite dance of the aristocracy. In the first measure, try using rest strokes with *p* to bring out the dramatic quality of the descending bass line.

Pavana

Gaspar Sanz
(1640–1710)

The Fifth Position

Book 2 covered position playing in the second and third positions. In this book, we'll explore the upper fingerboard—an intimidating "twilight zone" if you visualize it as just a *longitudinal* array of notes up to the 12th fret or higher. In contrast, the dynamically prepared approach to reading and playing above the 4th fret is based on secure knowledge of three overlapping, *lateral*, home-base positions—the fifth, seventh, and ninth. The twelfth position can be saved for after you've mastered these interlocked four-fret grids on the free fingerboard.

The fifth-position notes on the first string, as shown to the right, are A (5th fret), A♯/B♭ (6th fret), B (7th fret), and C (8th fret). Notes on the other five strings are the same as in first position, but now they are found on the next lower string as shown below for the 2nd- and 3rd-fret notes.

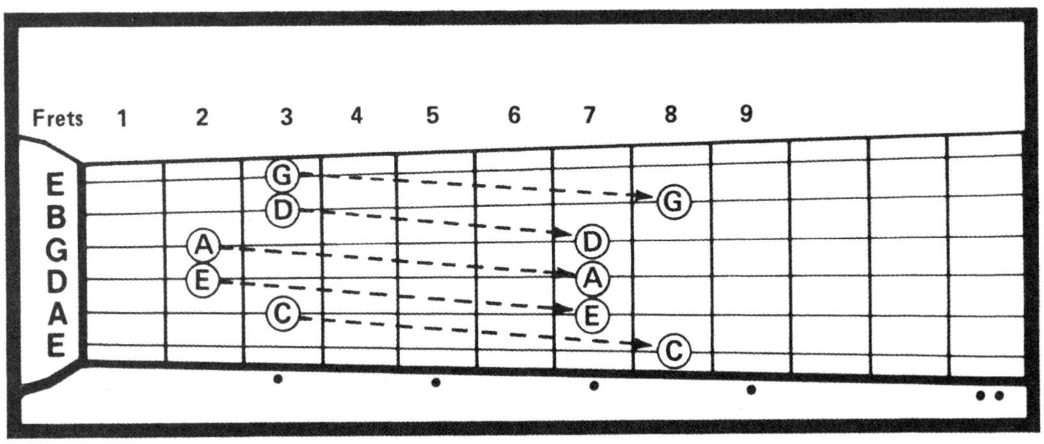

TIP: Remember the "rule of five"—first-position notes are located *five* frets higher on the next lower string, with one exception. Because of how the guitar is tuned, first-position *B-string* notes are *four* frets higher on the G string. For ready reference, the chart below shows *all* the notes in fifth position.

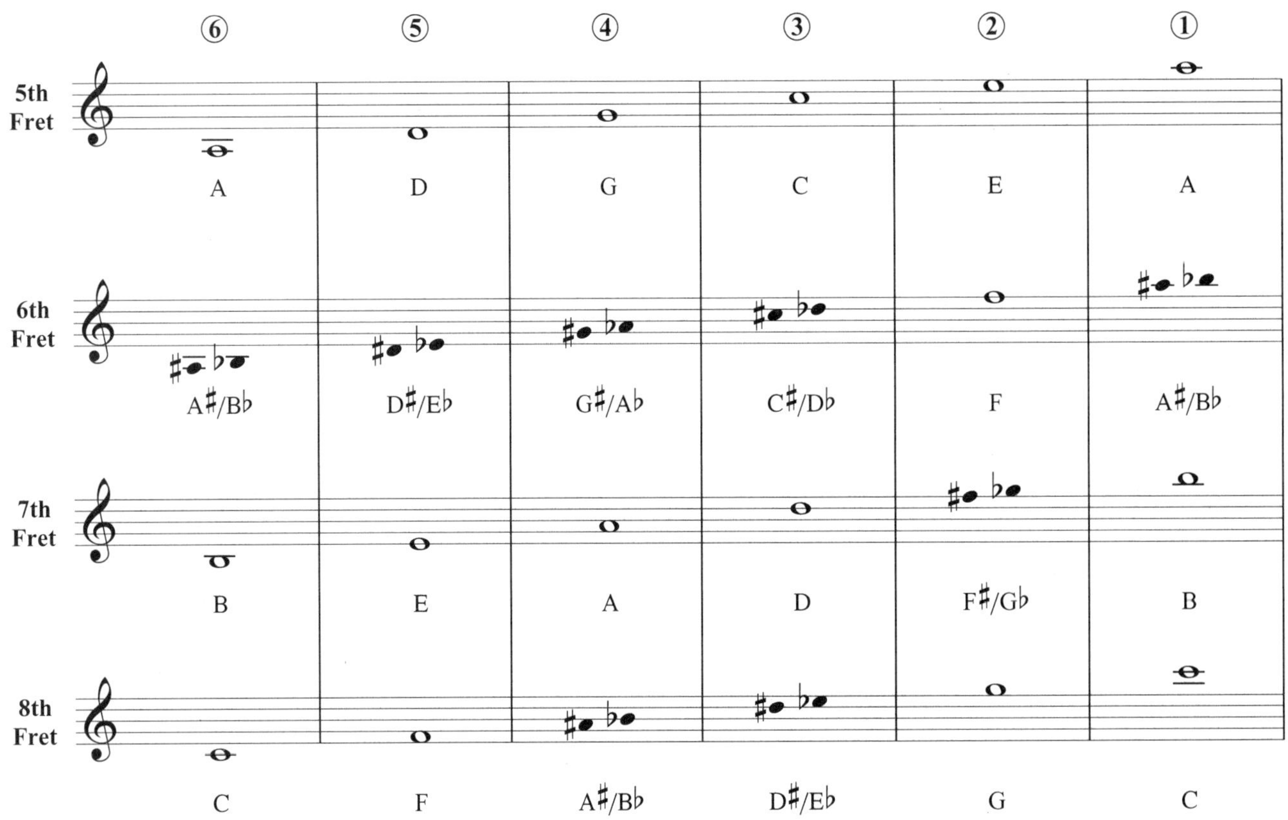

FIFTH-POSITION SCALE PATTERN STUDIES

Since they're based on logical sequences of scale motives, pattern studies are great for learning the lateral note-grids of the upper fingerboard. Practice the patterns below with the fingers curved and spaced as shown on page 133, and *without* letting them uncurl when they lift. Instead, your fingers should pivot from the knuckle only so that they won't have to flex inward on the return. Correct finger movements are simply up and down, like the pistons in automobile engines.

TIP: In the right-hand fingering, note the reversal of *m* and *i* which occurs at the midpoint of each study. By making this simple change of sequence, you'll avoid awkward **cross-fingerings** on the descending string changes (i.e., where *m* rather than *i* would have to play the lower string).

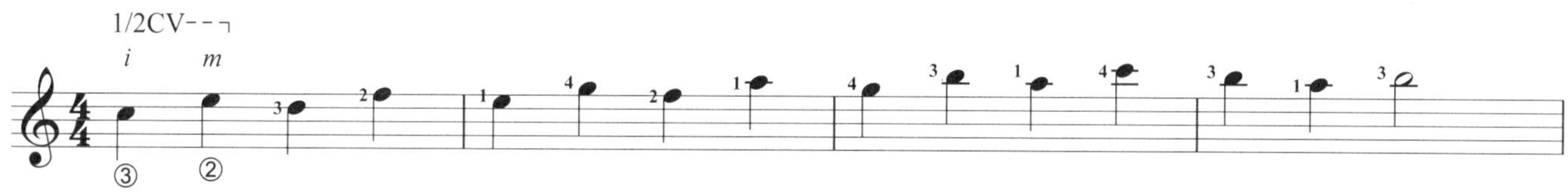

The Pivot Shift

Position playing sometimes requires a one-fret excursion to the next lower or higher fingerboard position. Since the distance to be covered is so small, usually you can just leave the thumb fixed as the pivot for a hand movement that doesn't involve the whole arm. In such cases, you make the shift either by **(a)** a finger-slide, or **(b)** a contraction from the wrist, as indicated in the Am and G scale patterns below. Practice both until these economical shift movements feel natural.

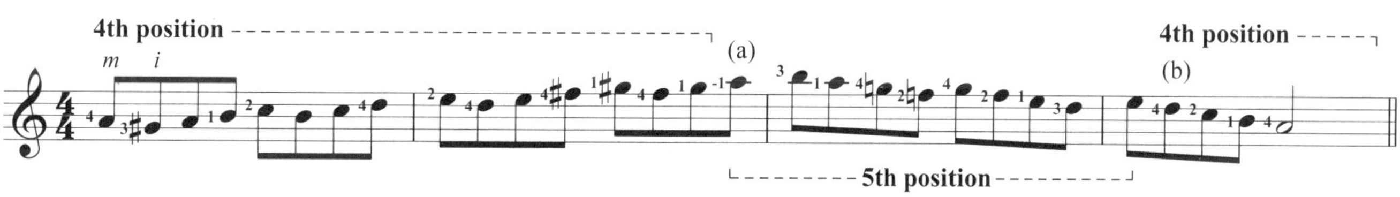

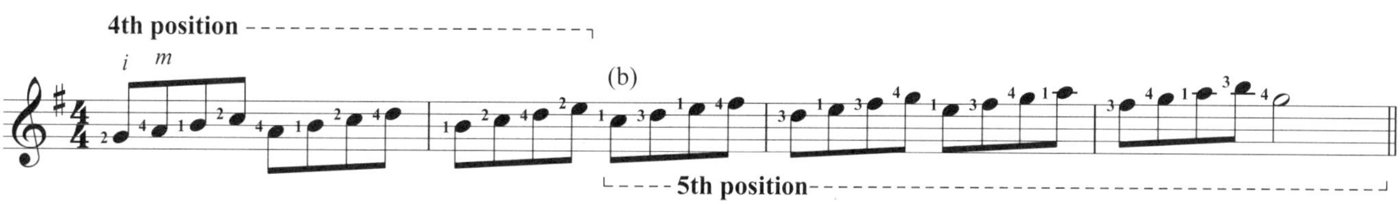

The two-octave C scale below provides a logical model of the fifth-position note layout that will help orient you to the position as a secure home base. Memorize and practice it with extra attention to the *fourth-finger extension* used for B on string 4. Like pivot shifts, such extensions are also used in position playing from time to time. Be sure to keep your first finger anchored on the fourth-string G to maintain the stability of the position as you reach for the B.

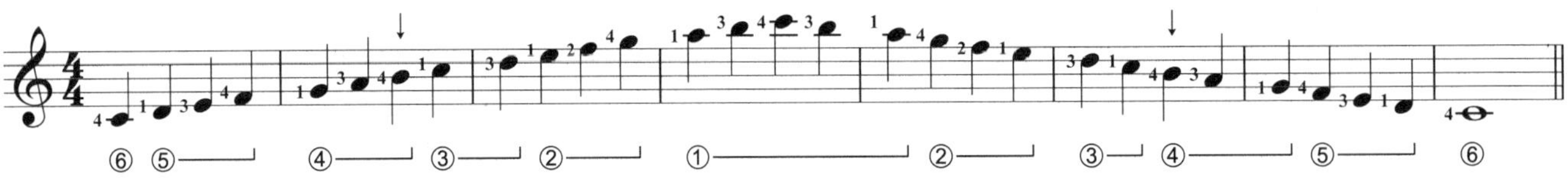

TIP: The melody of "Joy to the World" is based entirely on the higher octave of the above scale.

Joy to the World

G.F. Handel
(1685–1759)

Allegro M.M. ♩ = 76

With different lyrics, this romantic gondolier's song from 19th-century Naples is well-known as a traditional Yuletide carol, especially in Scandinavia. Although it's based in the fifth position, note the fourth-finger extension in measure 6, which in *this* case pulls the hand into sixth position for just a moment. In the next measure, you'll return to fifth position with a small pivot shift from the wrist (type b). In measures 11–15, pivot shifts that also include the finger-slide (type a) provide a smooth, comfortable fingering while retaining the security of the home base.

Santa Lucia

Traditional Italian Song

Moderato M.M. ♩ = 84

Dynamically Prepared, Goal-Directed Shifts

Unlike pivot shifts, changes of fingerboard position require movement of the *whole arm*. Since the weight of the arm and the inertial forces involved are significant factors, that's a problem in itself. When coupled with a lack of mental anticipation, chances are that the shift will be hurried, jerky, and stressful. In contrast, good shift technique is fluid, graceful, and stress-free. But how?

Guide fingers will always help, but the secret of effortless shifting is another form of dynamic preparation and goal-directed movement (GDM). First, *visualize* the new fingerboard formation as clearly as a chord diagram. Then, rather than move the whole arm as a fixed unit, *divide* its movement like a baseball pitch into a beginning, middle, and end. The movements for ascending and descending shifts will be different, but in both the elbow is the point of control. Its movement precedes the hand's, and the resulting inertial forces propel the hand effortlessly toward the new position.

The illustrations below will give you an idea of the arm, elbow, and hand movements needed for ascending and descending shifts. Practice both types in "super slo-mo," as follows:

[1] For shifts to a *higher* position, **[a]** start with a little backswing of your elbow that sets it in clockwise motion. At that point, moving inertia will take over, and **[b]** as the elbow adducts toward the body, **[c]** transport the hand easily to its destination. The result is a shift that feels as if your hand is floating into its new position.

[2] For shifts to a *lower* position, **[a]** start by abducting your elbow away from the body to a point beneath the new fingerboard position. Then, with the elbow as a pivot for the forearm's pendular movement, **[b]** use a *counter*-clockwise upper-arm rotation that will **[c]** "float" your hand into the new position while **[d]** the elbow falls naturally back toward the body.

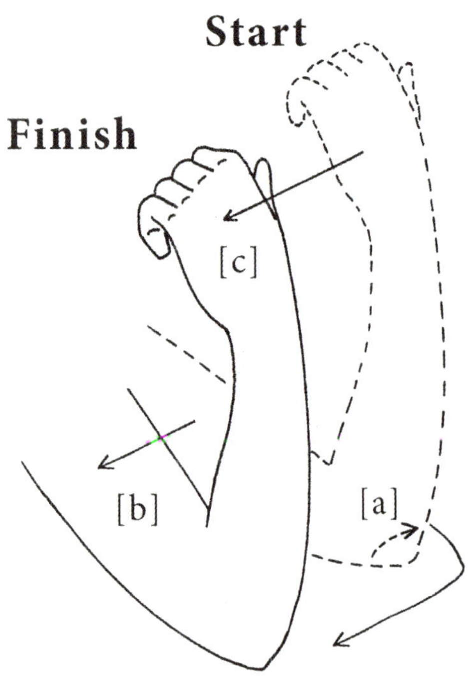

(1) Ascending

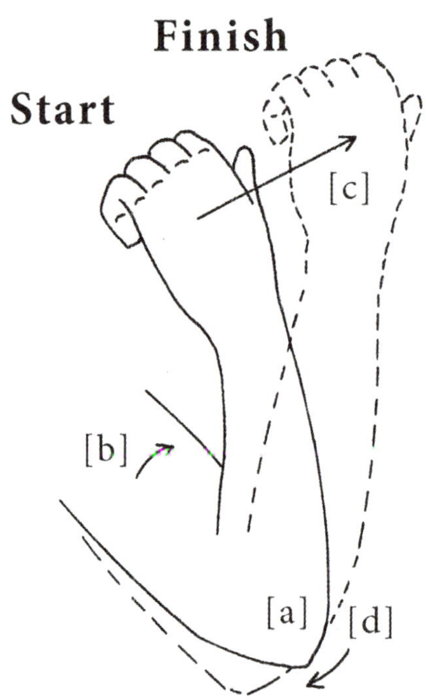

(2) Descending

✔ **TIP:** Remember that the elbow *always initiates the movement.* In ascending, it describes a small clockwise semicircle that generates enough momentum to get your hand to the target fret with no further effort. In descending, it achieves the same objective by torquing the hand in the *opposite* direction with a gentle see-saw movement of the forearm. For both types, your eyes should *lead* the hand. Don't fall into the trap of just *tracking* the hand's movement with your eyes!

CHORD AND SCALE SHIFTS

Use the following approach to memorize and practice the two cadences in F. Take your time on the shifts, making sure to *lead* the hand with your eyes. Once you've mastered the proper movement forms, the brain's motor areas will take over and transform them into graceful, reliable reflexes.

[1] Plant after each chord, look toward the target fret, and visualize the new chord.

[2] For *ascending* shifts, start the backswing with your elbow; for *descending* shifts, move the elbow away from the body and toward a point beneath the new fingerboard position.

[3] In ascending, "float" the hand to its new position by completing the elbow's outward rotation. In descending, use leverage from the elbow's adduction back toward the body for the same purpose.

[4] Carefully shape your fingers into the new chord form as you approach the target position.

[5] Press down the fingers and play the chord.

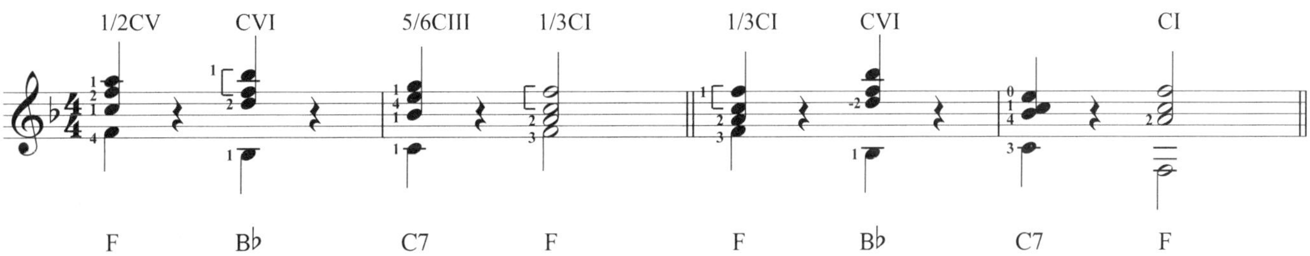

Practice the following C and F scales likewise, while noting the differences from chord shifts:

[1] Since only one string is involved, the shift is simpler and requires somewhat less energy.

[2] The *first* finger serves as a guide to the fifth position in each case. As indicated by the dotted-line brackets, *leave it down* as an anchor to stabilize the position until it's needed to play again.

PRACTICING ARPEGGIATED PIECES WITH BLOCK CHORDS

As for most arpeggiated pieces, practicing the charming study by Francisco Tárrega on the next page in the form of *block chords*, as shown below, will shortcut your mastery of it. This particular use of dynamic preparation will enable you to hear and see the underlying chord structure, sharpen your visualization of how it lies on the fingerboard, and concentrate on your left hand's goal-directed movement forms. When coupled with aggressive planting to perfect the synchronization of your hands, your technical command of the piece will be secure. Then, when practicing it as written, you can focus on bringing out the melody with the *a* finger's heavy down-and-in push into the string, called a *half*-rest stroke (see *Book 2*, p. 82). Where added melodic emphasis is called for, use *full* rest strokes as indicated by the accent marks (>).

Using the Tip-Joint Hinge Barre

This piece will also introduce you to the tip-joint **hinge barre**, an easy technique used intuitively by good players when needed. In measures 10 and 14, simply flatten your index finger's tip-segment to grab the F on beat 3—*while still holding the C*—by collapsing the arch of your tip-joint. Then, on the fourth beat, "hinge" back up onto your tip to play the open string E, while *still* holding the C.

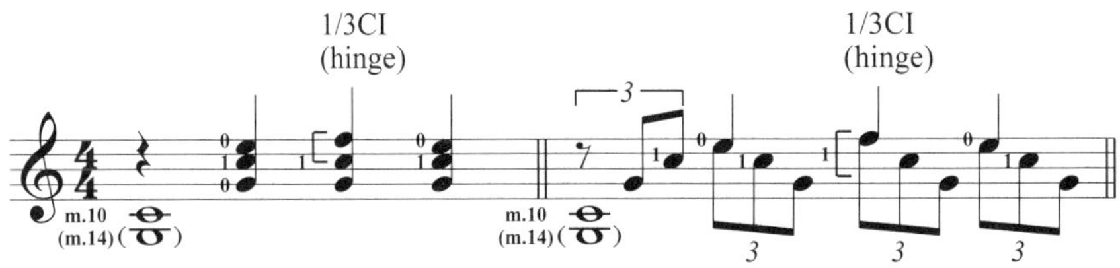

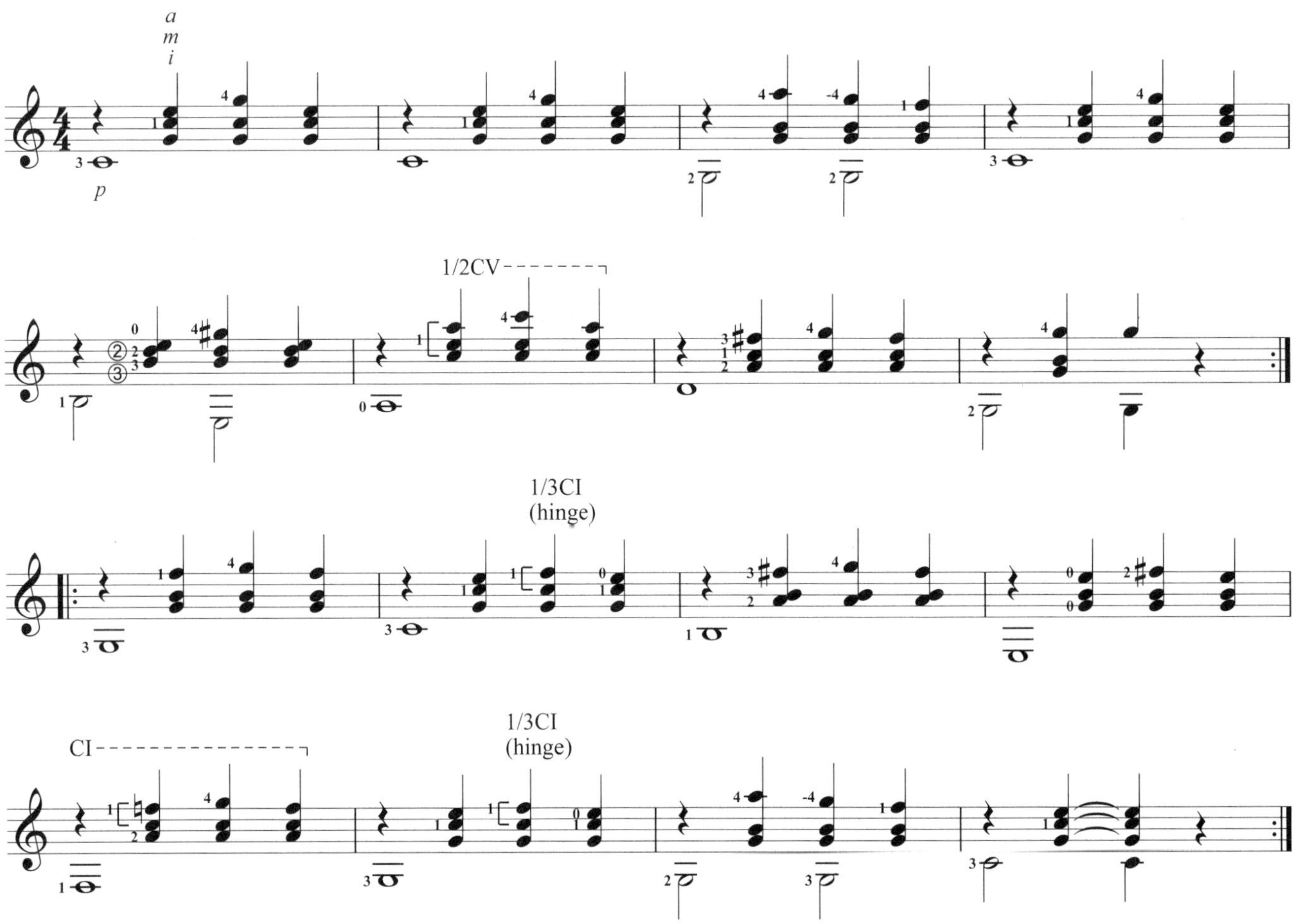

Study No. 1

Francisco Tárrega
(1852–1909)

Andante M.M. ♩ = 80

The following "Leccion" (Spanish, "lesson") by Sor provides an excellent practice model for stress-free shifting, with the tips shown below the piece as a working guide—they're keyed to the numbers you'll see over several measures. The *alla breve* time signature (𝄵), known as "cut time," means that the count is based on the *half* note—*two* relaxed beats to the measure instead of a frantic four.

Leccion in Am

Fernando Sor
(1778–1839)

[1] Use a regular descending shift (not a pivot shift) to reach the G♯.

[2] Note how naturally the out-and-in elbow movement transports the hand to the first position, while the open E masks the shift.

[3] Plant *p* on the A string as you dynamically prepare the shift back to fifth position with a little backswing of the elbow.

[4] Note how easily the clockwise elbow rotation propels the hand back to the 5th fret.

[5] Here, the out-and-in elbow movement torques the first finger into position on the 3rd fret without stress, while the *campanelas* fingering at the end of the measure masks the shift.

[6] Observe the dynamics indicated and hold the climax chords for slightly more than full value.

[7] The musical climax here is challenging, but the shifts are all facilitated by a guide finger, including the first. (Note how it glided silently up to fifth position.)

Carulli's dramatic D minor prelude also provides a great opportunity to prove the benefits of practicing arpeggio pieces minus the arpeggiation. When you can sight-read it fluently, practice in the form of *p-i-m* block chords while concentrating on the left hand's goal-directed movements and the right hand's extra-firm preparations before position shifts.

Prelude in Dm

Ferdinando Carulli
(1770–1841)

The following composition by the author is in the Romantic style made famous by early 19th-century piano composers such as Beethoven, Schubert, Schumann, and Mendelssohn. The melody should be emphasized with the deliberately solid half-rest stroke. At the points of extra melodic significance indicated by the accent marks, a full rest stroke would be best.

Remembrance

Charles Duncan

The author's "Song Without Words," also in the 19th-century Romantic style, recalls some of Felix Mendelssohn's beautiful "Songs Without Words"—a series of short, lyrical piano solos which have long been favorites in the piano repertoire. The piece also provides various opportunities to practice your goal-directed, dynamically prepared shift technique in an interesting form.

Song Without Words

Charles Duncan

Andante con moto M.M. ♩. = 56

Dynamic Slurring

Like position shifting, dynamic slur technique includes the sympathetic participation of muscles from the wrist to the shoulder. Rigid hand and arm positions therefore should be avoided, and the palm of your hand should stay close to the edge of fingerboard so the wrist can remain straight (see again on p. 133). When slurring on the lowest strings, let your palm touch the edge of the fingerboard.

ASCENDING ("HAMMERING ON")

[1] Curve and space your fingers as illustrated on page 133, so their tips point straight down.

[2] Use "Micro-GDM" to aim their attack at a spot right behind the metal fret, where the purchase on the string is best and a clean slur is therefore the easiest. Try for a sharp, percussive impact that you can actually *hear* as a crisp note articulation.

[3] Use the muscles in the heel of your hand, pivoting from the wrist, to support the finger-attack. Especially when hammering on with the fourth finger, you should feel those muscles contract into a power-source for the movement. Some rotary play of the forearm, pivoting from the elbow, will also help maximize the force transmitted to your fingertips.

[4] Avoid the common pitfall of pivoting the fingers from the knuckle only. Dynamic ascending slurs are powered also by energy from the wrist, elbow, and shoulder.

DESCENDING ("PULLING OFF")

[1] Curve and space your fingers the same way, with the tips right behind the metal frets.

[2] The correct finger action is a lateral flex of the tip which actually *plucks* the string. A common error is weak tip-joint flexion—a goal-directed pull-off is aimed straight into the palm.

[3] Since this motion can *also* sound the next higher string inadvertently when slurring on any string but the first, play these slurs as *left-hand rest strokes.* Aim your fingertip straight back so that it bumps into the next higher string and recoils back up into the dynamically prepared attack position.

[4] As with ascending slurs, sympathetic participation of the arm and wrist should be encouraged, not inhibited. Some energetic contraction of the heel of the hand from the wrist, supported by a bit of forearm rotation, will multiply the force available at the fingertip and spare the fingers from having to do all the work.

The exercises on the next page combine ascending and descending slurs in various ways. As shown for Ex. 1, play as far as seventh position by shifting up one fret at a time, and descend the same way. Practice them on all six strings with your metronome, listening for an even division of the beat. To offset the common tendency to rush slurs, practice *also* by dotting the rhythm as shown in the warm-up exercise at the top of the page. This counterintuitive but extremely effective practice technique will retard the slurs and gradually instill the ability to control their timing more accurately.

For Ex. 6, 7, and 8, use this comparable eighth + two sixteenths rhythmic formula to develop control and keep the triplets from galloping:

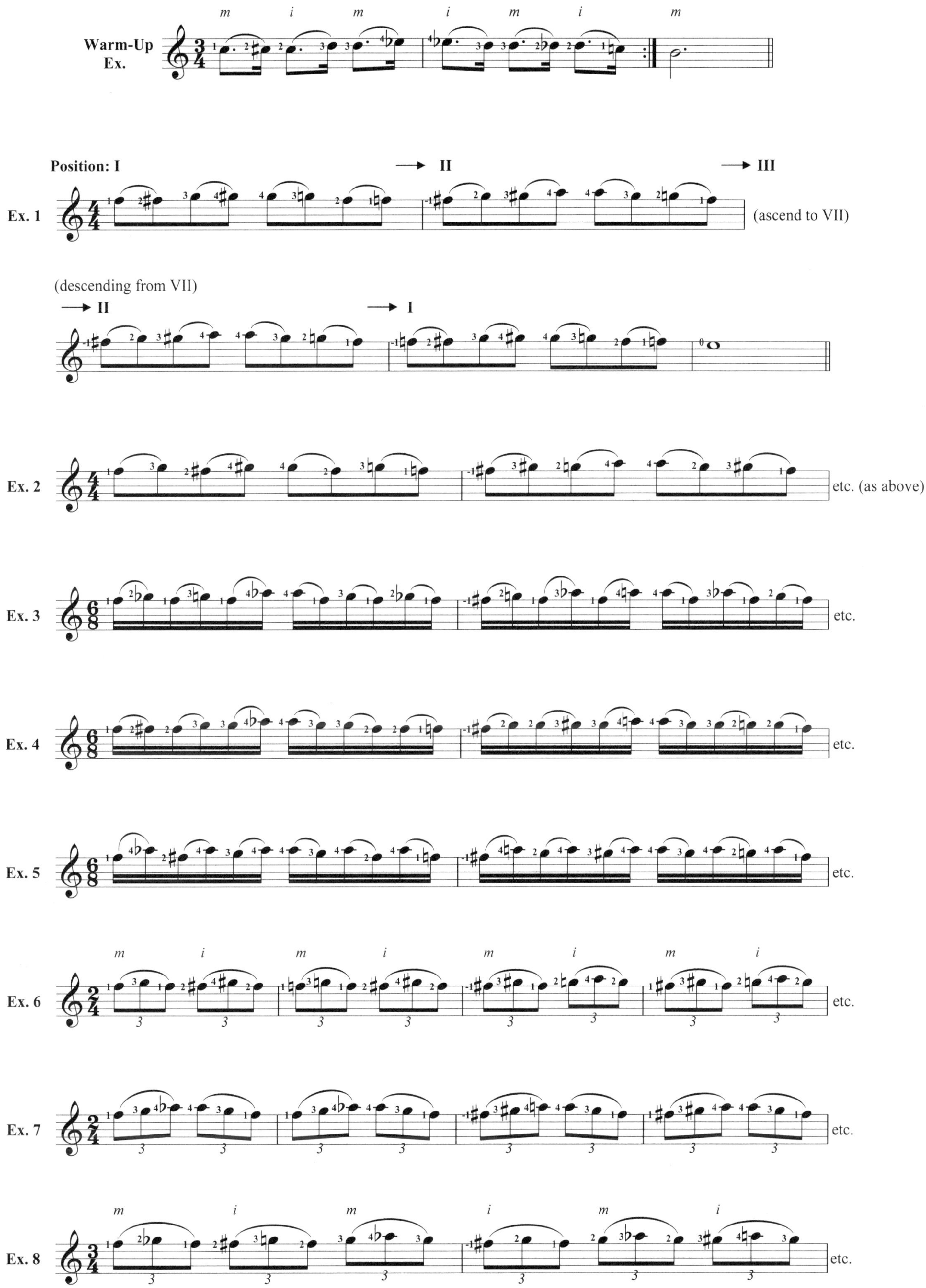

m i m i m i m
Warm-Up Ex.
Position: I
II
III
Ex. 1
(ascend to VII)
(descending from VII)
II
I
Ex. 2
etc. (as above)
Ex. 3
etc.
Ex. 4
etc.
Ex. 5
etc.
m i m i m i m i
Ex. 6
etc.
Ex. 7
etc.
m i m i m i
Ex. 8
etc.

The Key of D Major

The key of D and its relative, B minor, use F# and C# in their key signatures. Both keys are commonly used in classical guitar music, particularly D major. To begin, memorize and practice the extended one-octave D major scales in second and fourth position:

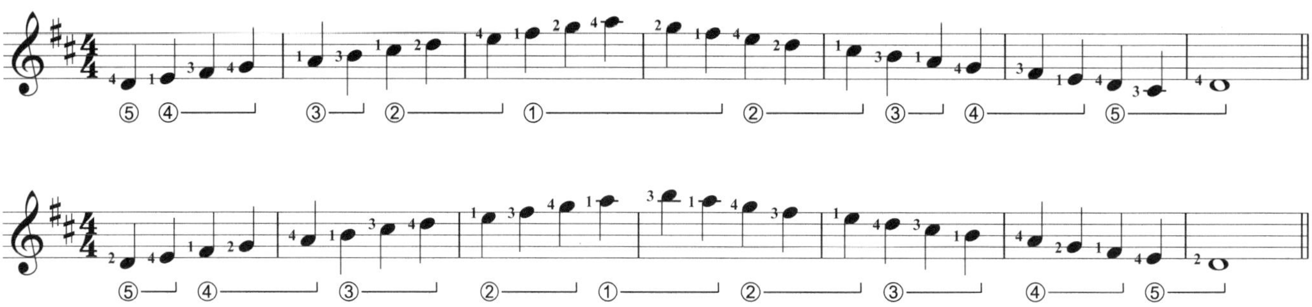

Memorize and practice these D major cadences for clean articulation and synchronization of the hands. Then practice in the broken chord forms which follow them, using precise consecutive preparation technique: play *p*-plant *i,* play *i*-plant *a/m,* play *a/m*-plant *i,* play *i*-plant *p,* etc. Remember the importance of feeling that your fingers are chained together! (See again p. 137.)

In the following scale pattern study, the alternation between fourth and fifth position is made easy by keeping the thumb fixed and using pivot shifts. Note also the right-hand fingering—until the final measure, there are only three cross-fingerings (see the arrows). If the one that would occur in the last measure seems too awkward, you can *drag* your *i* finger through a double rest-stroke as shown. Although not often taught, the "drag-stroke" with *i* is used by many top players.

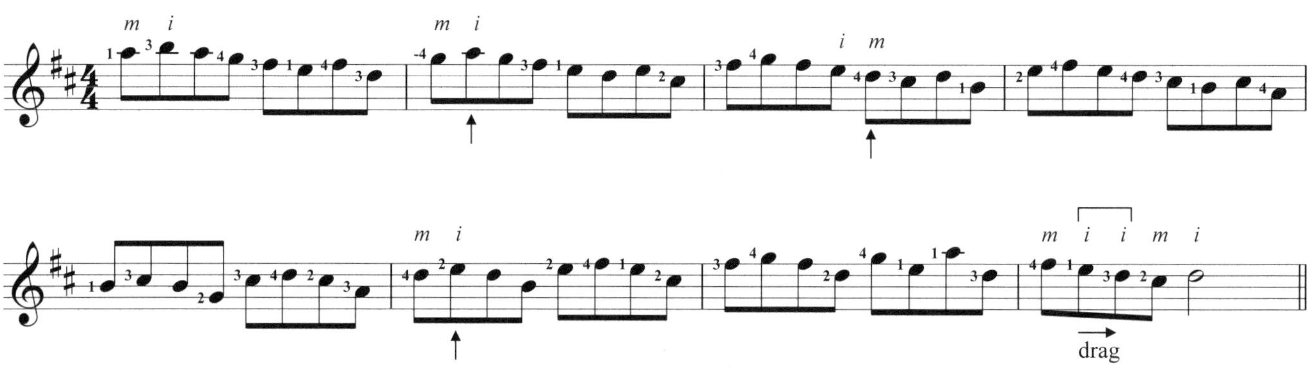

Couperin's "Le Petit Rien" ("The Little Trifle") is a good example of the harpsichord compositions by France's premier early Baroque composer. Frequently, they have whimsical titles that reveal the composer's intentions—here, that the piece is an amusing diversion to be played with a light, sparkling touch. To help create that effect, use the articulations shown in the first measure wherever this important rhythmic-melodic motive occurs.

Le Petit Rien

François Couperin
(1668–1733)

Allegretto M.M. ♩ = 120

Anton Diabelli, a prominent Viennese music publisher as well as a prolific composer, authored numerous attractive guitar pieces. This one is in the style of a popular dance form in which lines of couples faced off *opposite* each other—a "*contra*-dance," known in French as *contredanse*, *kontratanz* in German, and "country dance" in English. It's from one of his many editions of music for the big 19th-century market of European guitar enthusiasts.

Contradance

Anton Diabelli
(1781–1858)

The next piece typifies a fast Renaissance and Baroque dance form in triple meter that was named for its speed, the word for "running" in Italian (*corrente*) and French (*courante*). Not much is known about Carlo Calvi except that he was a prestigious court musician in 17th-century Italy and composed many good pieces for guitar such as this one. (For another, see the author's *A Modern Approach to Classical Guitar Repertoire, Part One.*)

Corrente

Carlo Calvi
(c.1610–1670)

Moderato M.M. 𝅗𝅥. **= 56**

Embellishment: Common Ornaments

Book 2 introduced the use of single and double grace notes as melodic ornamentation. We'll revisit them here and then go on to the other most common embellishments.

The grace note is usually the upper neighbor to the one it embellishes and is played with a pull-off. Although written before the beat, it's played *on* the beat simultaneously with any lower tones:

Double grace notes use either the upper *or* lower neighbor to decorate the main tone. If using the lower, this ornament is known as a **mordent** and is played by pulling off and hammering on. If it's the upper neighbor, it's called an **inverted mordent** and is played by hammering on and pulling off.

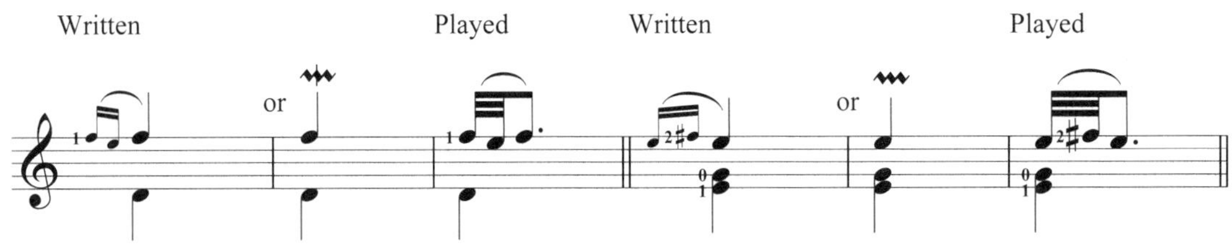

Both types are played simultaneously together with any lower notes, and can be written either in small, cue-sized notes or indicated by signs. For the mordent, the sign resembles a tilde bisected with a stroke symbol (𝆝); for the inverted mordent, the stroke is omitted (𝆝). The mordent was used very frequently in music written before 1800, while the inverted mordent has been a common embellishment since then.

✔ **TIP:** Just like grace notes, mordents succeed by tricking the ear, which naturally gravitates toward the main tone. Consequently, when well-played, they sound as if the main tone falls *on* the beat, *not* a fraction after it!

In contrast, the **appoggiatura**—an upper or lower neighbor to the main tone—borrows *half* of the main tone's time value, thereby creating a brief dissonance. It can be written out or indicated by a small note *without* the diagonal stroke used for a grace note. The examples below exemplify its usage to decorate cadences: **(1)** is from Bach's "Minuet in G" (from *A Modern Approach to Classical Guitar Repertoire, Part One*); **(2)** is the second ending to de Visée's "Minuet" on page 167.

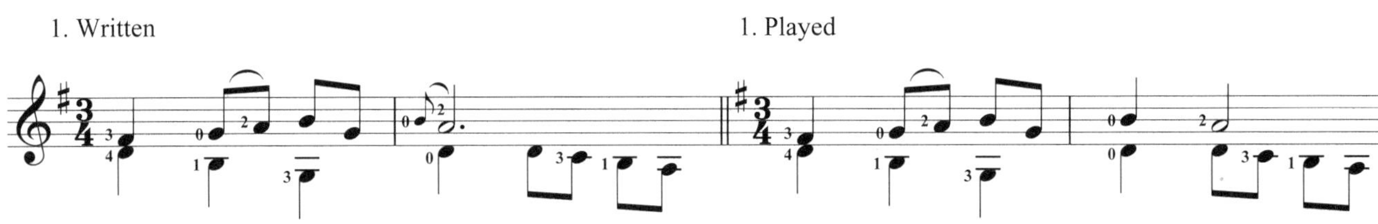

To these embellishments may be added the **turn**—a group of four notes played as a continuous slur: **(1)** upper neighbor, **(2)** main tone, **(3)** lower neighbor, and **(4)** main tone. Its symbol is a letter "S" on its side, written over the main tone and played as shown in the first measure below. If written *between* that note and the next one, it's played as shown in the second measure. Turns originated in the late 17th century and remained a standard ornament well into the 19th century.

Finally, there's the **trill** (***tr***)—a series of rapid alternations between a main tone and its upper neighbor. The modern trill begins on the main tone, but in music written before 1800, trills usually began on the upper note to create more dissonance with the underlying harmony. The "***tr***" sign is often followed by a wavy line to indicate the trill's duration, and the traditional way to execute trills is with a continuous slur. A more recent innovation is the use of **cross-string trills**, which are especially appropriate in Baroque music—see the Weiss "Sarabande," page 173.

Trills can be used to decorate any note long enough to accommodate them, but their most common use is to dramatize phrase endings. In the first example below, the trill finishes with an eighth note that dynamically anticipates the tonic resolution. In the second, the trill finishes even more dynamically with a turn that anticipates the resolution. As shown in the first example, the number of notes in a trill depends largely on the tempo, and thus, the amount of time available.

Ex. 1

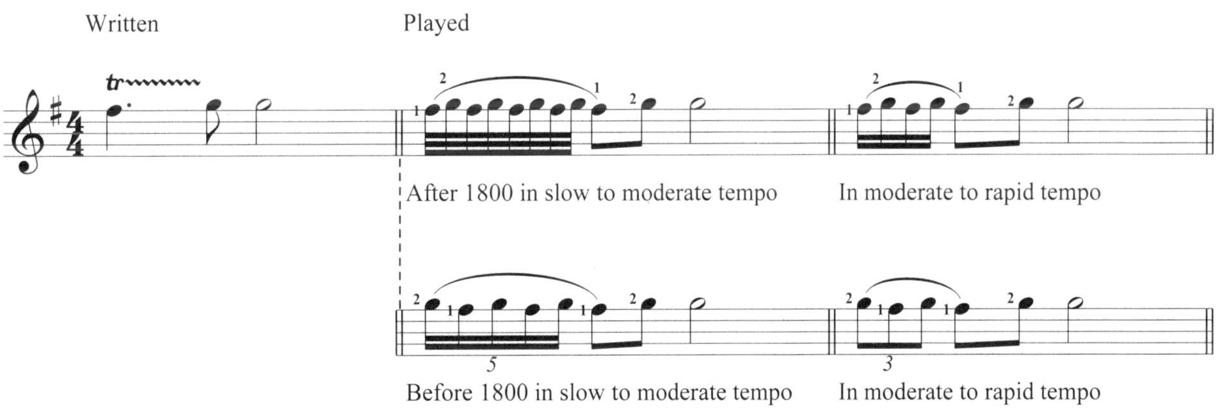

Ex. 2

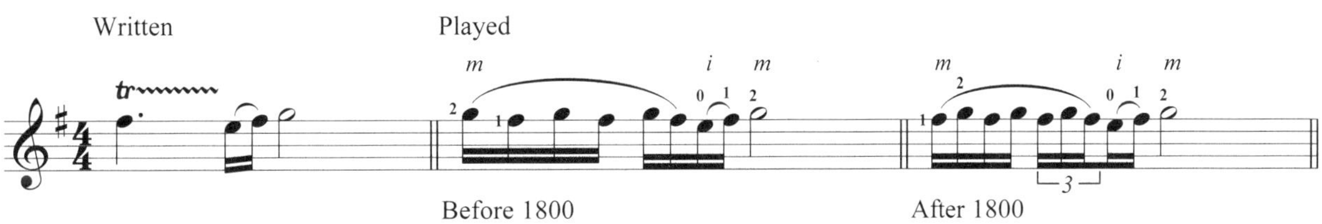

What we've covered provides a foundation for playing music that calls for embellishment, but to pursue the subject further, there are many print and online resources. For example, Frank Koonce's *Johann Sebastian Bach: The Solo Lute Works* (Neil Kjos, 2002) contains a practical overview of Baroque ornamentation, and for cross-string trills, various reliable tutorials are available on YouTube. The best scholarly guide to the subject is Frederick Neumann's *Ornamentation in Baroque and Post-Baroque Music* (Princeton University Press, 1983).

Besides being a fine composition, the piece below is from the first book of printed music for the guitar's immediate ancestor, the Spanish *vihuela—El Maestro* by Luis de Milán (1536). The slow, stately *pavana* (English, *pavan*; French, *pavane*) was a favorite dance form among the Renaissance aristocracies of Europe, which is probably why de Milán included six of them in his book.

TIP: Although this is a challenging piece, the new time signature shouldn't be a problem. It's counted just like 3/4, except that in 3/2 the *half* note gets one beat and *quarter* notes get a *half* beat.

Pavana No. 6

Luis de Milán
(c.1500–1561)

Andante M.M. 𝅗𝅥 = 82

On the next page, the author's piece is a tribute to the great Baroque lutenist Sylvius Leopold Weiss (see p. 173). Written in the style of his dreamy-sounding Preludes, it utilizes *campanelas* fingerings (p. 144) to create the overlapping sonorities of the Baroque lute. In contrast, the "Minuet" by Robert de Visée exemplifies the style of the French five-string Baroque guitar, including the highly ornamented repeat of the last four measures. A popular court musician during the reign of Louis XV, de Visée's compositions are now favorites among contemporary Baroque guitarists.

Prelude in the Style of S.L. Weiss

Charles Duncan

Poco Lento M.M. ♩ = 84

Minuet

Robert de Visée
(1655–1732)

Moderato M.M. ♩ = 120

The Key of B Minor

Although not used so much as its relative major, there's a goodly number of fine classical guitar pieces in the key of Bm. To learn this key, begin with the following two-octave melodic minor scale. On the ascending and descending position shifts, remember to look ahead and lead with the elbow.

Memorize and practice the following cadence and arpeggio exercise. When playing the arpeggios, concentrate on sequential planting and well-prepared chord changes (see pp. 135–136).

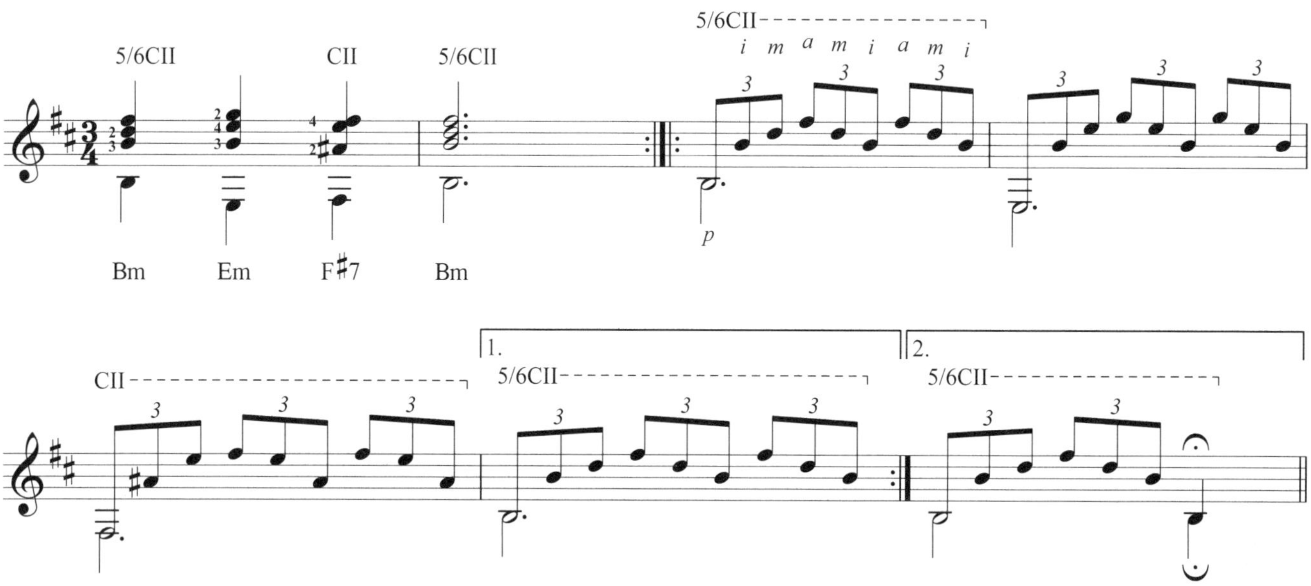

THUMB DEVELOPMENT AND SCALE PLAYING WITH *p-i* ALTERNATION

Because of its natural strength and versatility, the thumb can be a powerful weapon in your arsenal of right-hand technique if you cultivate its capabilities. Besides bass-note emphasis with the rest stroke (p. 145), there are two more techniques it's time for you to learn: **(1)** rest-stroke bass notes in arpeggios for emphasis and right-hand stability, and **(2)** *p-i* alternation to play bass-string scales or scale fragments.

[1] Practice the previous arpeggio exercise with the rest-stroke thumb technique described on p. 145. Leave *p* resting on the next higher string, and synchronize its recovery for the next stroke with the last stroke of the *i* finger in each measure (see again p. 138).

[2] Practice the lower-octave Bm scale below with free stroke *p-i* alternation. Use small, well-controlled *p* strokes alternating smoothly with the *i* strokes, like left and right windshield wipers. Because *p-i* alternation requires no change of hand position, it's usually the best way to play short melodic passages on the bass strings.

Fernando Sor has been called the "Beethoven of the guitar," and even his smaller pieces suggest why. This beautiful composition captures the serenity that Beethoven's slower, quieter pieces are famous for and reflects how the key of Bm itself helps to create that mood.

Lento

Fernando Sor
(1778–1839)

"Dropped D" Tuning

For music in the keys of D and Dm, the sixth string is often tuned down to low D. With the string tuned a whole step lower, its notes will be two frets *higher* than in standard tuning:

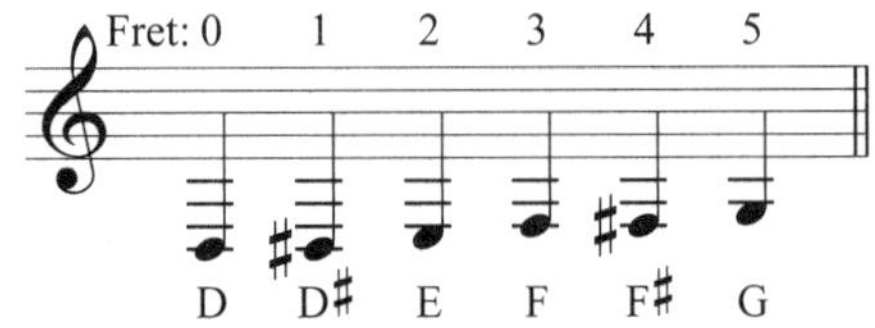

To tune down by ear, lower the string to well *below* D. Then, bring it back up *slowly* while playing it alternately with the open D string. As the sixth string tightens, listen for the clash of overtones to flatten out until you hear a single "thick" D tone with no dissonant oscillations.

Memorize and practice these lower-octave D major and minor scales using *p-i* alternation. For further thumb development and enhanced musicianship, accent the first beat of each measure by using rest strokes. Cultivating rest strokes with *p* provides various benefits in musical control.

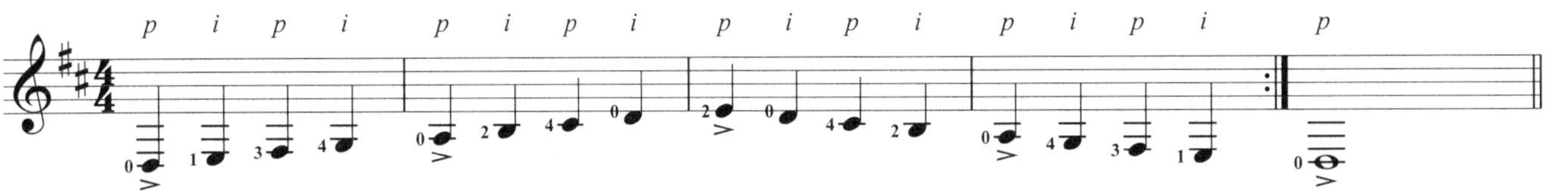

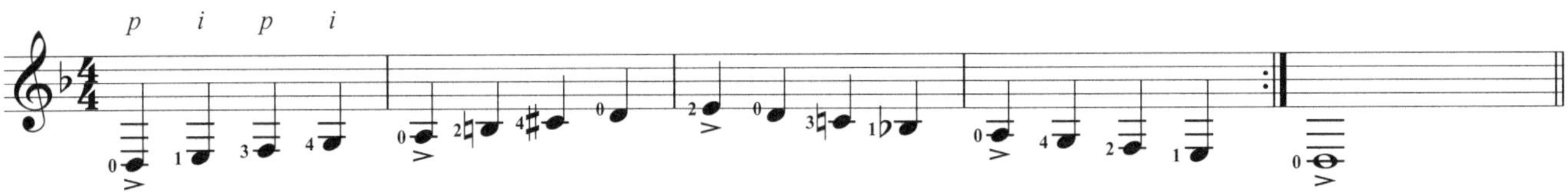

The dropped-D, two-octave major scale provides a good opportunity for learning how to play *m-i* bass-string notes without the ugly sound of nail-scraping. First, memorize it; then, practice with the technique explained below for changing the angle of your strokes.

CHANGING YOUR ANGLE OF ATTACK IN SCALE PLAYING

The illustrations here show the range of angles to the strings your *m-i* strokes can make, from perpendicular to around 30 degrees from perpendicular. Changes of angle are produced by *tiny* changes of wrist-curvature, and by varying your attack as shown, you can equalize the tone on the treble strings: angled to the full extent for string 1, slightly less for string 2, and still less for string 3. By continuing this process on the bass strings, you can *also* eliminate the scratchy tone produced by the friction between your nails and the metal string-winding. When you get to the fifth and sixth strings, the perpendicular stroke will be *parallel* with the metal winding, so that even these strings won't scrape against your nails. (You'll save wear and tear on your nails, too.)

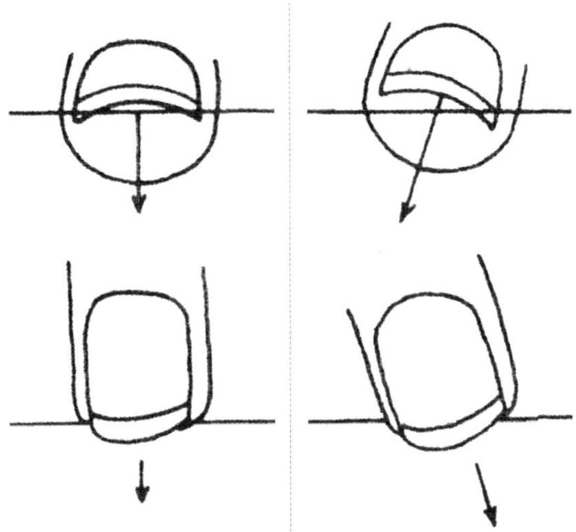

6th string attack *1st string attack*

Many fine Renaissance lute pieces are by unknown composers, and this is one of the best. The *gigue* (known in England as the "jig") was a very fast dance, normally in triple meter, that in the Baroque era became the standard concluding piece for instrumental suites (see p. 178). In order to play it confidently, master it first at half speed, with graceful, economical left-hand movements, solid right-hand stroke-preparations, and perfect synchronization of the hands on chord changes.

Kemp's Jig

Anonymous
(16th-century England)

⑥ = D

Allegro M.M. ♩ = 138

USING HINGE BARRES

The tip-joint hinge barre you used on page 152 illustrated the value of hinge barres to sustain a bass note while playing an open first- or second-string melody note. When these needs are reversed, you can use the underside of your *knuckle* joint, as shown, to play the treble note while playing the open bass string. Then, clamp down the *lower* part of your finger for the subsequent bass note. In the next piece, both types are used in measure 9; instructions for playing them are at the bottom of the page.

The composer of "Bianco Fiore" (Italian, "white flower") was a 16th-century Italian dance-master whose compositions were transmitted to the modern world by the musicologist Oscar Chilesotti and made famous among guitarists by Andrés Segovia's recordings. The short trills called for in measures 4 and 12 are written out in footnotes 1 and 2 beneath the music.

TIP: This version is somewhat closer to the original lute music than the Segovia and Parkening recordings.

Bianco Fiore

Cesare Negri
(c.1535–1605)

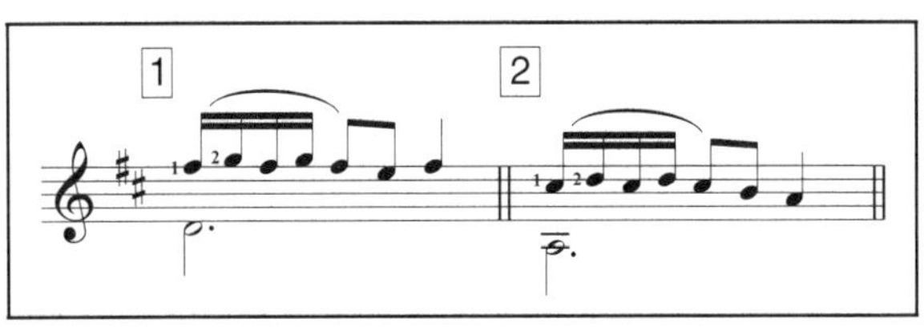

*On the first beat, use the underside of your knuckle-joint as shown in the photograph to play the 1st-string F♯ while simultaneously playing the open D. On the second beat, clamp down the rest of your finger to make the Bm chord. Then, on beat 3, hinge up on your fingertip to play the open E while sustaining the bass B through the bar line.

The "Sarabande" from Weiss's beautiful *Sonata 34* calls for a relaxed, flexible tempo to express its intense emotion. The slowest dance form of the times, the *sarabande* typically served as the slow movement in Baroque instrumental suites. The trills called for in the music are written out below the piece and numerically keyed to the places where they're used. (Note that the *first* is used only on the *repeat* of the A section.)

Sarabande

S.L. Weiss
(1686–1750)

⑥ = D

Adagio M.M. ♩ = 66

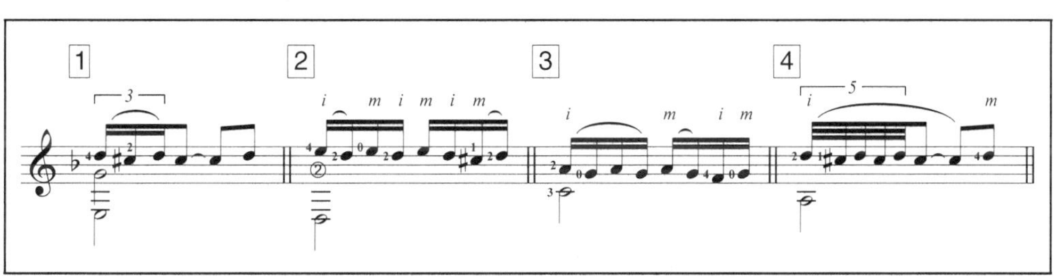

Damping (Muting) Techniques

As in the "Estudio" by Dionisio Aguado (p. 139), damping is used to honor the musical silences which sometimes are part of a composition. Its other most typical use is to eliminate overlapped bass-string sonorities when they create harmonic confusion or spoil a melodic line in the bass.

[1] The most intuitive, efficient way to silence unwanted resonance from the *next lower* bass string is the one introduced on page 136. That is, you use the *left side* of the thumb-tip by sandwiching it between the strings for just an instant as it makes nail contact with the higher string.

[2] The other way is to reach back and touch the vibrating string lightly with the tip of the thumb right *after* playing the new note. It's also the best way when the string to be damped isn't the *next* lower one—for example, the E string after playing the D string.

TIP: Look at the illustration on page 134 of how *p* recovers from a free stroke. The *damping movement* is essentially the same as this natural *recovery movement.*

The examples below illustrate both methods. The second method permits the previous note to overlap the new note slightly, but by such a small fraction that it's not even noticeable.

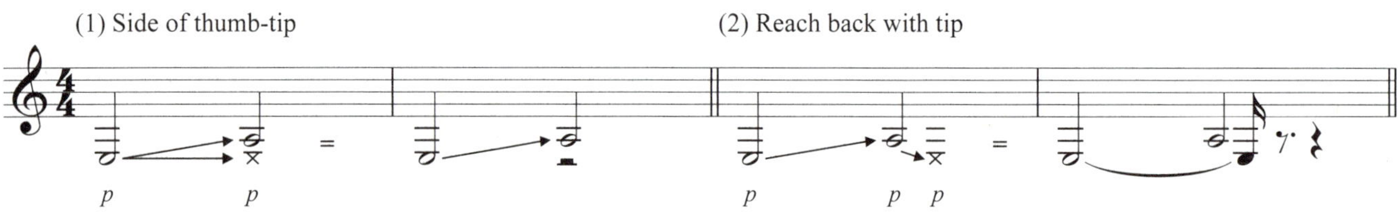

[3] To damp the next *higher* bass string, **(a)** you can use a rest stroke with *p* when the thumb is playing by itself, as in arpeggios. If it's playing together with other fingers, as in a chord, **(b)** you can "bounce" the thumb-tip up onto the higher string as a modification of its recovery. **(c)** The back of a *left*-hand fingertip also can be used when the next note to be fingered is on the *next lower* string. For a chord, **(d)** you can even add the finger that *would* play that string in the standard whole-chord formation but isn't needed in the music. The examples below illustrate each of these techniques except for **(c)**, which is explained further on the next page.

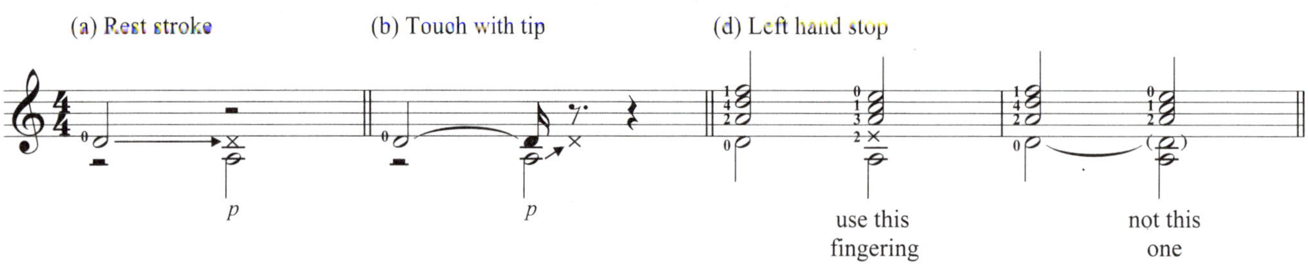

[4] Occasionally, an open *treble* string will need damping. In such cases, either **(a)** pre-planting with *a* or *a-m*, or **(b)** using the back of a *left*-hand fingertip works well, depending on the situation. These techniques are so intuitive that many players use them unconsciously to keep their melodic lines clean; both are discussed further on the next page, where we'll revisit Purcell's "Minuet" (p. 144) as a practice model. There are *ten* numbered places where a note will over-ring the next unless damped; solutions are listed numerically below the music.

Henry Purcell
(1659–1695)

Andantino M.M. ♩ = 96

[1] To keep the open E from over-ringing the D, plant *a* together with *m* on strings 1 and 2, which also prepares *a* for the *next* E (method [4a] from previous page).

[2] To keep the open D from blurring the C, "kiss" the fourth string with the back of your third finger as it "plants" to hold down the C (method [3c]).

[3] To prevent a harmonic clash with the implied B♭ chord here, kiss the open E with the back of your fourth fingertip as it makes the second-string D (method [4b]).

[4] As you plant *p-i-a* for the F chord, use the left side of your thumb-tip to silence the fifth-string A from the preceding measure (method [1]).

[5] Once again, the strong resonance of the open E needs to be stopped to prevent dissonance—here, with the implied Dm chord. The best way is to plant *a* along with *p* and *i*, leaving it planted for the E in the *next* measure while you play the notes in between (variation on method [4a]).

[6] Here, damping is *not needed* since note decay will minimize the lower string overlap. Also, the faint sonority of the A will reinforce nicely the implied Dm chord which ends the section.

[7] To play this important rest, plant *p* for the D on the *next* beat as *a* plants for the first-string A.

[8] Here, kiss the D string with the back of your first fingertip as it makes the C♯ bass—an easy left-hand bass-stop using method [3c].

[9] Likewise, silence the D with the back of your *third* fingertip as it frets the fifth-string C (method [3c]).

[10] Here, damping the A *is* necessary in order to provide a clean entry for the D.C. al Fine. Just lean your thumb back when planting *p* and *m* so that it momentarily touches the A string (method [1]).

If all of this sounds like a tall order, just take each occasion for damping by itself without worrying about the rest! The effort is primarily mental, and where the mind leads, the fingers will follow. By gradually applying these techniques to other pieces, you'll polish your performance style and take your command of dynamic preparations and goal-directed movements to a yet higher level.

The Keys of A Major and F♯ Minor

The key signatures of A major and F♯ minor use three sharps—F♯, C♯, and G♯. Because of its pleasing middle register and the readily available open strings, A major is often used in classical guitar music. Memorize and practice the following second- and fifth-position scales and cadences.

TIP: The second-position scale form is the same as the fifth-position C scale (p. 148), but the fingering differs slightly to make up for the wider fret spaces. Instead of using a fourth finger extension to play the lower octave G♯, it's easier and more effective to use pivot shifts to first position and back.

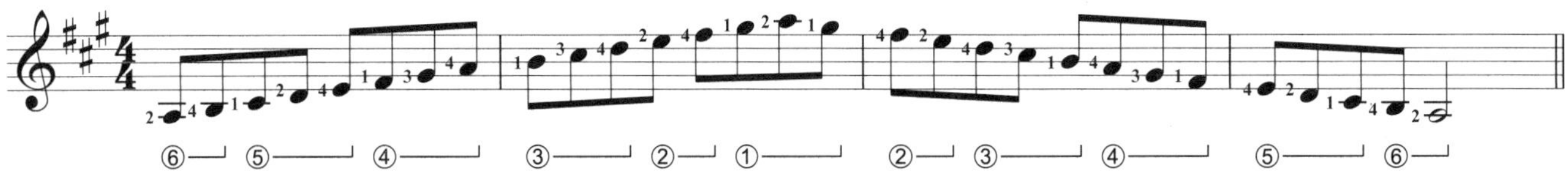

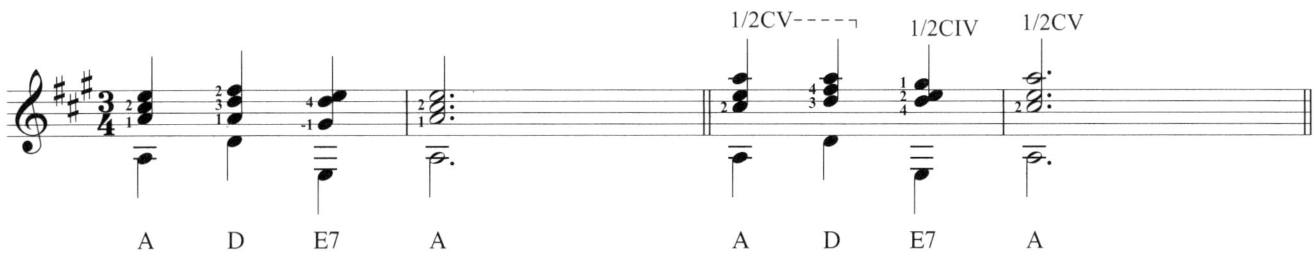

F♯ minor is not a home key for classical guitar music, but incidental use of it occurs from time to time, as in the "Gigue" on page 178. To gain familiarity with this key, memorize and practice the following F♯m scales: **(1)** the first-position scale, which uses a conventional fingering with open strings; and **(2)** the second-position movable scale, used for other minor keys as well (for example, the seventh-position Bm scale on p. 180).

(1) First-position scale

(2) Second-position movable scale

Memorize and practice the previous cadences in the following arpeggiated forms:

*2nd time, let ring into final bar.

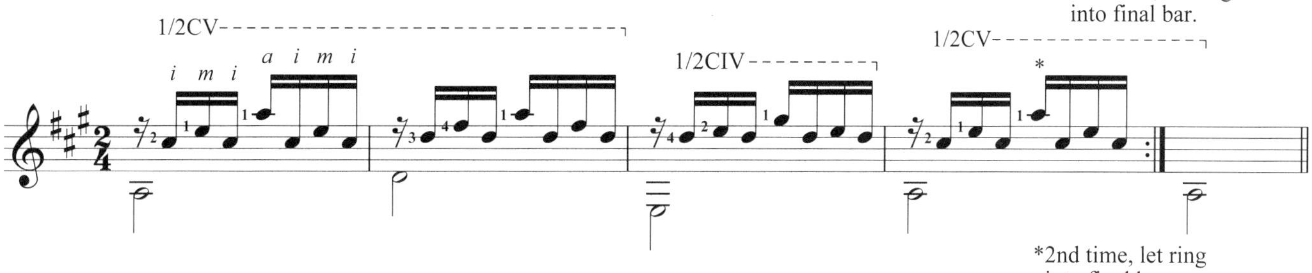

*2nd time, let ring into final bar.

John Dowland was the greatest of the lutenist-composers who flourished during the English Renaissance—the "golden age" of English music, as it's called. Much of his best music is melancholy-sounding; this piece is a fine example of his more playful moods. The rhythm contains a variety of figurations, so be sure to count accurately when you're learning it.

Mistress Winter's Jump

John Dowland
(1563–1626)

A contemporary of Bach and Weiss, Giuseppe Antonio Brescianello was an Italian Baroque composer whose works included a collection of 18 partitas for *colascione*, an Italian lute tuned like the guitar. The "Gigue" below is a good example of the many fine pieces in the collection and provides a great workout for both hands. Observe the fingering carefully, including how the A string in measures 4 and 16 is damped—the method described in **[3d]**, page 174.

Gigue

G.A. Brescianello
(1690–1758)

Allegro M.M. ♩. = 56

The following composition is based on the romantic French bistro music of the earlier 20th century—the musical culture that produced such legendary artists as Edith Piaf and Django Reinhardt. The most popular all-purpose bistro instrument was the charming small accordion known as a *concertina*, and the piece is designed to capture its characteristic performance style.

Bistro Waltz

Charles Duncan

The Seventh Position

As the fifth position is the anchor position of the upper fingerboard, the seventh is the pivotal position. Besides serving as a secure way-station between the fifth and ninth positions, it's used commonly for guitar music in several keys. The new notes are at the 9th and 10th frets as shown:

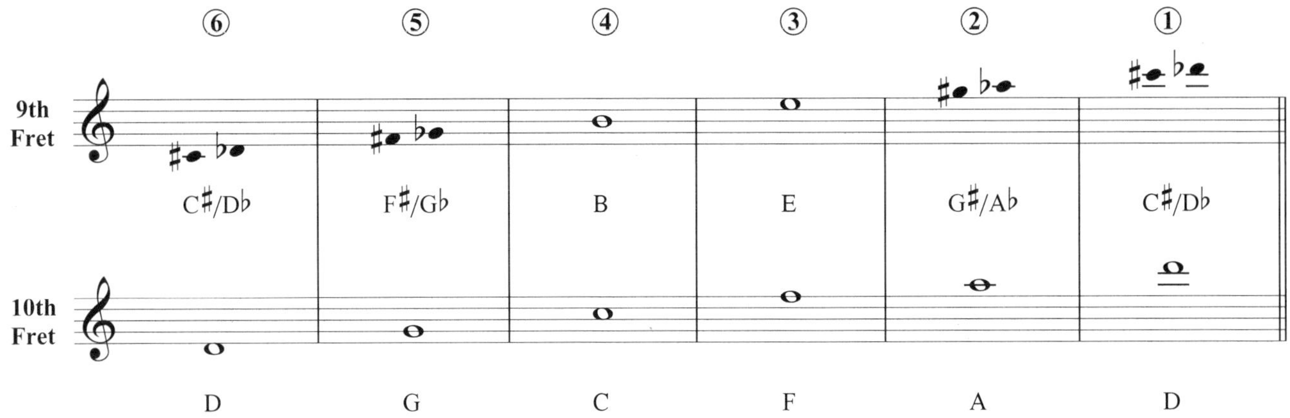

To get well-acquainted with the seventh position, practice the following two-octave D, Bm, and C scales using conscious GDM. (Their scale *forms* are the same ones you learned on page 176.)

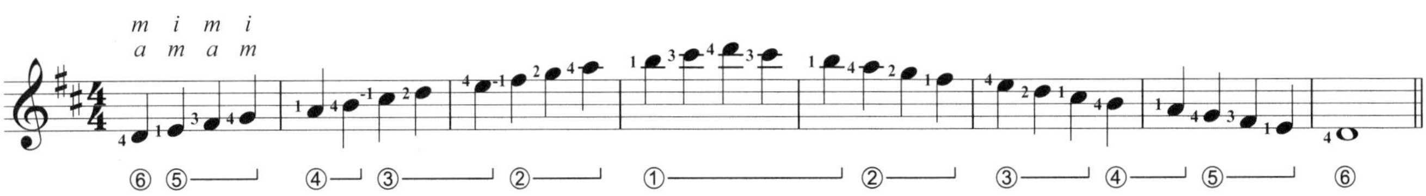

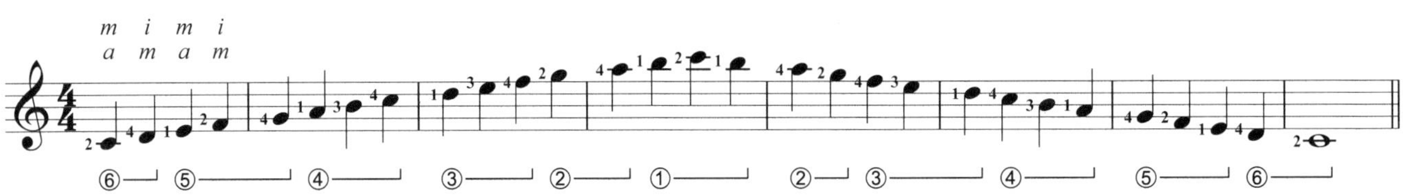

Practicing Beethoven's famous "Ode to Joy" (*Book 1*, p. 35) in the interesting split-octave melodic format below will also help accustom you to seventh position as a secure home base.

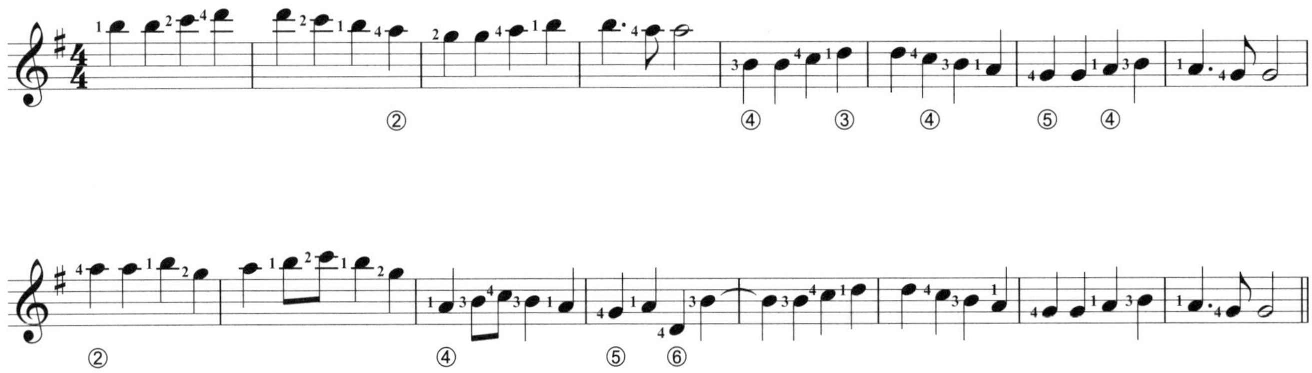

In this small masterpiece by Sor, you'll be using seventh position and also a **slide-slur** with your fourth finger on beat 4 of measure 9 (see the asterisk). This easy technique is used all the time by steel-string players and has uses in classical guitar playing as well.

✔ **TIP:** To make the two-fret slide from G to A sound as clean as the hammer-on that precedes it, use yet another form of GDM. Aim your slide for the *6th* metal fret as a *backstop*, and increase the *pressure* on your fingertip as it crosses the *5th* fret.

Andantino

Fernando Sor
(1778–1839)

M.M. ♩ = 120

This great Mexican folk classic provides a good fifth- and seventh-position workout because of how the melody is harmonized—*thirds* in the "A" section and *sixths* in the "B" section. It also introduces you to the kinds of Spanish harmony and rhythm you'll be playing later (pp. 200–203).

La Llorona

Traditional Mexican
arr. Charles Duncan

OTHER USES OF THE HIGHER POSITIONS: NATURAL HARMONICS

Harmonics are chime-like tones produced by lightly touching a string right above the metal fret. **Natural harmonics** are available at the 4th, 5th, 7th, 9th, 12th, and 18th frets. By using the more advanced technique of **artificial harmonics**, they can be played also at the other frets (see p. 204).

Harmonics are written in the form of diamond-shaped notes an octave *lower* than their actual pitch and identified by the abbreviation "Arm." (Spanish, *armonico*) plus their fret number in Roman numerals. The notes you can produce effectively with this technique are shown below:

Arm. XII

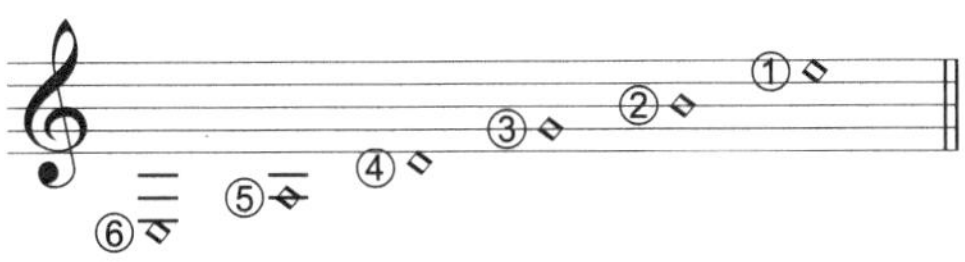

Arm. VII & XVIII

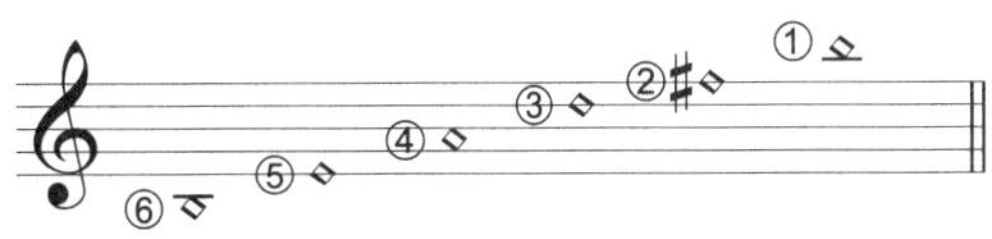

Arm. V

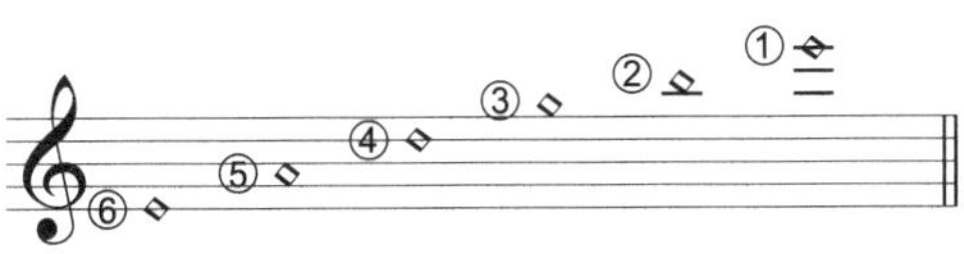

Arm. IV & IX

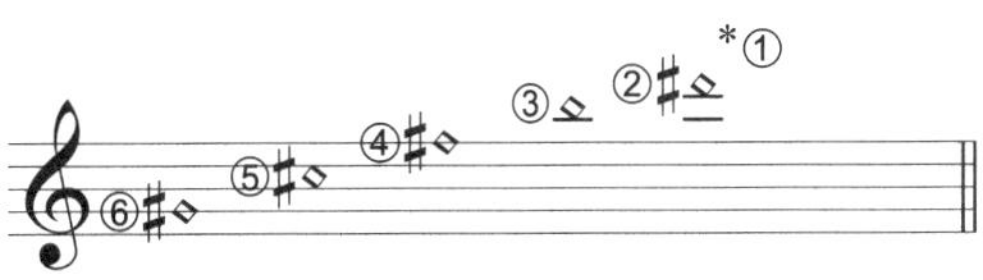

*No usable harmonics on string 1.

Harmonics at the 12th fret are the easiest to execute cleanly. Follow the steps below to learn how, starting with the D string—it's the most responsive for this purpose.

[1] *Touch* the string with the fleshy underside of your second finger's tip-joint, *not* the tip itself.

[2] Make sure the fingertip is directly *over* the metal fret, not behind it as in normal playing.

[3] Pluck the string close to the bridge and *immediately* afterwards lift the fingertip off the string.

[4] Practice on the other strings until you can produce clear, consistent "chimes"; then do the same for harmonics at the other frets. For the clearest sound, always pluck close to the bridge.

Tuning with Natural Harmonics

As shown below, bass-string harmonic notes at the *5th* fret reappear at the *7th* fret on the next higher string. Notice also that the *7th*-fret B and E on strings 6 and 5 are exactly the same pitches as the open second and first strings. These natural matching-tones provide an excellent way to tune your guitar accurately, assuming your *6th* string is tuned to the correct pitch.

Arm. V = Arm. VII

[1] 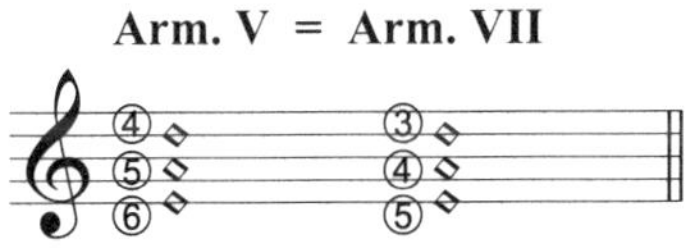

Arm. VII = open strings

[2] 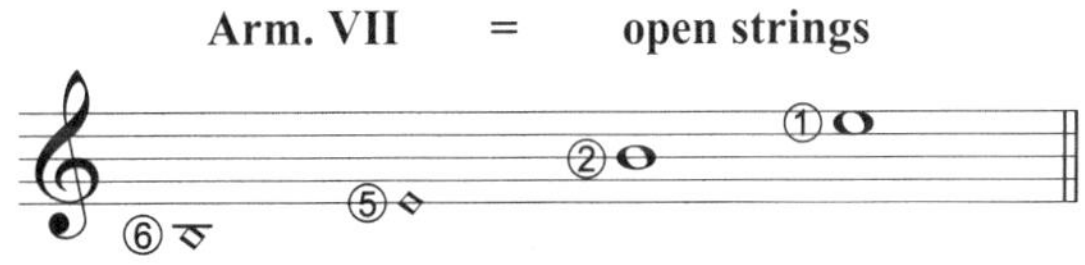

[1] To tune strings 5, 4, and 3, pluck the 5th-fret harmonic on the next *lower* string, and while it's still ringing, pluck the *7th*-fret harmonic on the string to be tuned. With both harmonics still ringing, adjust the higher string's tuning key while listening for a perfect match with no dissonant oscillations. Repeat until you hear only a single "thick" tone.

[2] To tune the second and first strings, use the same procedure to match their natural pitches with the corresponding 7th-fret harmonics—string 6 for the B string and string 5 for the E string.

The Keys of E Major and C♯ Minor

The keys of E major and C♯ minor have four sharps as their key signatures—F♯, C♯, G♯, and D♯. Despite the number of sharps, E major is one of the best classical guitar keys because of the many open-string fingerings you can use and the extra resonance they afford. Memorize and practice the following two-octave first-position scale and fourth-position extended one-octave scale.

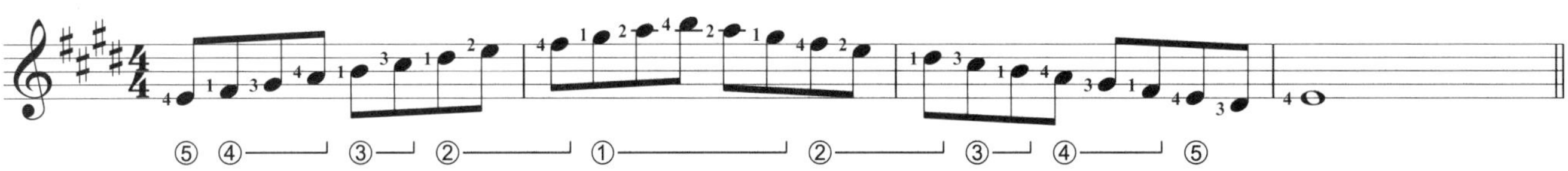

Memorize and practice their corresponding cadences with GDM. Practice the first one *also* as the *p-i-m-a-m-i* exercise shown, concentrating on your "sticky-fingered" planting technique which makes the fingers feel like they're chained together (see again pp. 137, 160).

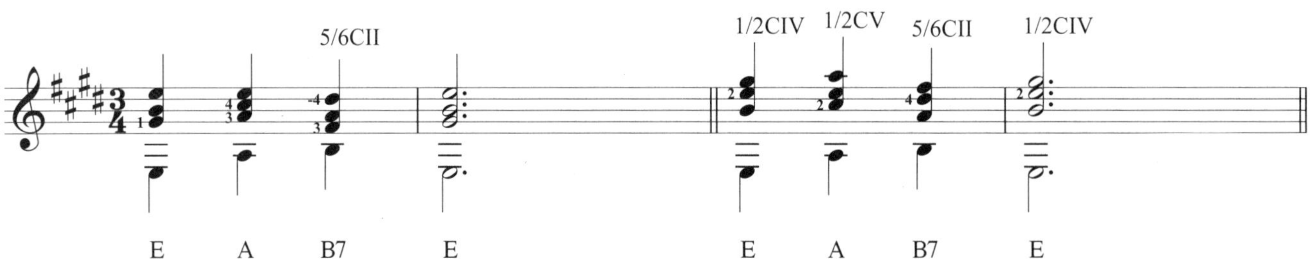

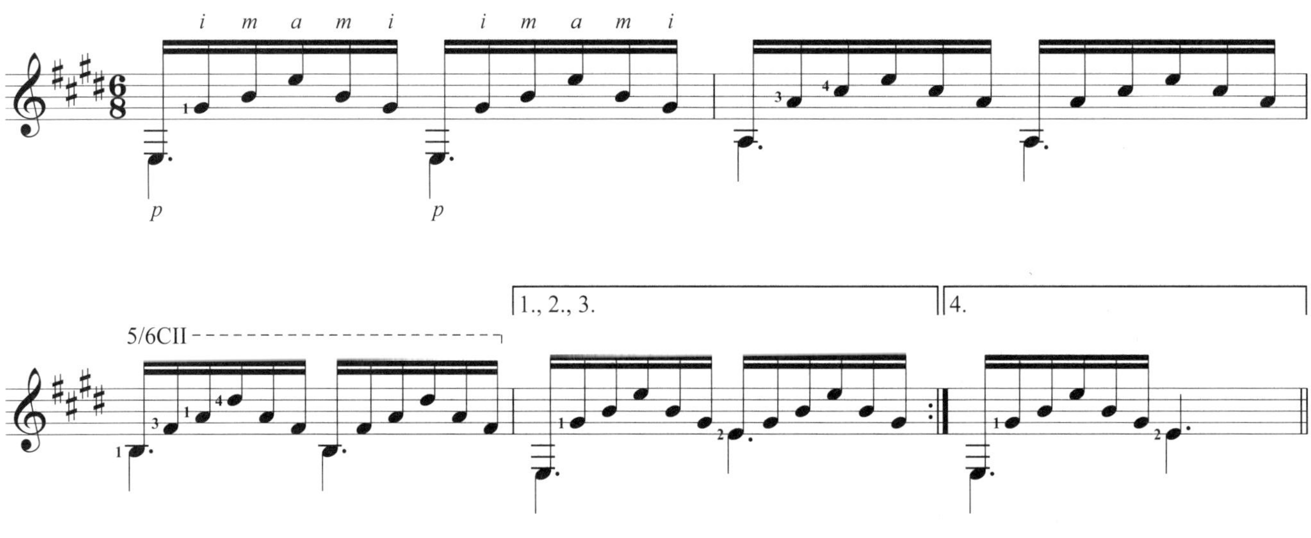

Like F♯m, C♯m is not a home key in classical guitar music, but incidental use of it is common—for example, in measures 10–12 of the duet on page 186. Memorize and practice the following two-octave C♯m scale—it's also a movable scale form used in other keys as well.

Carcassi's lively "Waltz" makes an enjoyable introduction to music in the key of E, and although not difficult, measures 9–12 are tricky—they'll need extra practice. In the long "B" section, use the half-rest stroke to make the melody *sing* (see again pp. 152, 156). On the dramatic leaps from F♯ to B (at the asterisks), **[1]** dynamically prepare the shift with your elbow's backswing on the F♯, **[2]** lead off with it on the open B, **[3]** fix your gaze on the fourth *position* (not just the 7th *fret!*) as the target, with your first finger as an anchor on G♯, and **[4]** finish with a *full* rest stroke on the climax tone (the high B).

Waltz

Matteo Carcassi
(1792–1853)

Like the stylistically similar "Ode to Joy" in Beethoven's Ninth Symphony, the triumphant theme of the finale to Brahms's First Symphony is one of the greatest song-tunes in orchestral music. On the repeat, play it somewhat louder and a tiny bit faster to dramatize the feeling of sublime, heroic courage which Brahms conveys so well in musical language.

Theme from the First Symphony

Johannes Brahms
(1833–1897)

Allegro non troppo M.M. ♩ = 132

“Cavaquinho” (“kahva-*keen*-yo”—a small Brazilian folk guitar) is based on the universally popular Brazilian jazz style known as *bossa nova*. Since it’s quite syncopated, count the rhythm aloud while playing until you’re comfortable with it. (For further practice in playing syncopated modern music, see the author’s *Pop Classics for Fingerstyle Guitar* [Hal Leonard].)

Cavaquinho

Allegretto M.M. ♩ = 88

Charles Duncan

Attitudes of the Left Hand: Longitudinal and Lateral Configurations

Let's recall the two principles of a dynamically prepared left-hand position as introduced on page 133: **(1)** The natural alignment of the hand and forearm which provides maximum strength and comfort. **(2)** The longitudinal spread of well-curved fingers which balances the hand, channels leverage to the weaker third and fourth fingers, and provides easy coverage of a whole fingerboard position.

Now it's time to add a third—the way you move easily and naturally from *longitudinal* attitudes of the fingers, such as the Gmaj7 pictured below, to more *lateral* configurations like the D9 chord to its right. How can that be done *without* a stressful bending and curving of the wrist?

(1) Rotate out, ab*duct elbow*

(2) Rotate in, ad*duct elbow*

The secret is to keep a *loose arm*. Rather than abandon the natural alignment of the hand and forearm, combine forearm rotation with some elbow play. **(1)** For the change from Gmaj7 to D9, use a quarter-turn of *outward* rotation, accompanied by a slight abduction of the elbow away from the body. **(2)** For the return to Gmaj7, use the equivalent *inward* rotation, supported by a slight *ad*duction of the elbow back toward the body. In the photographs and musical illustrations above, the arrows indicate how efficiently the hand and fingers are torqued into the correct position by this leverage from a loose arm. Use the following exercise to practice the movements correctly.

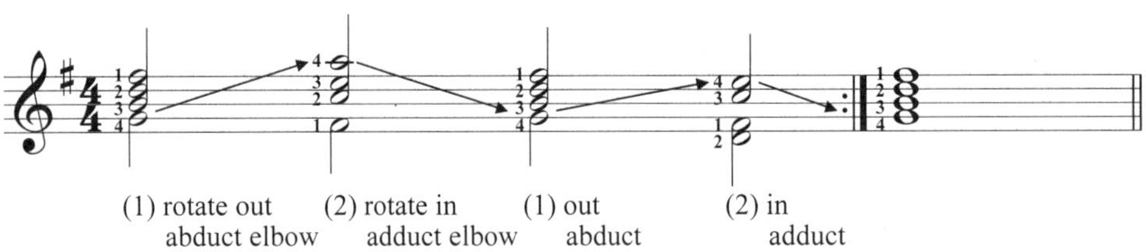

These techniques apply to any situation in which you need to change back and forth between comparable configurations. The next exercise, which uses the fingers in pairs (1 and 3, 2 and 4), is a good example. Practice until you can play it smoothly with the supportive movements indicated.

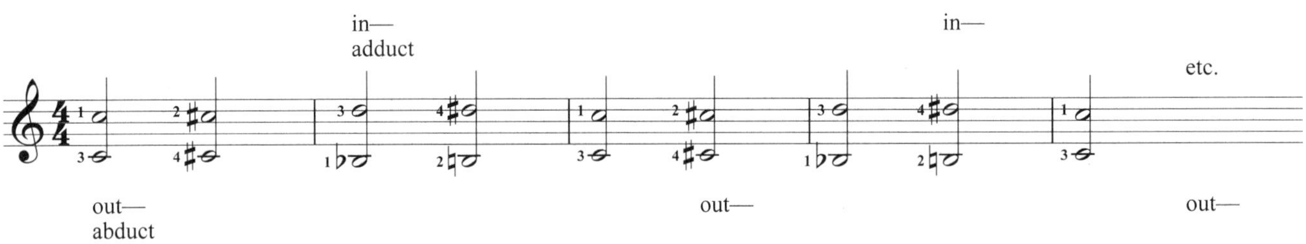

TIP: Hold down each pair of fingers until the next pair completes its exchange movement and is touching the strings. At no time should *both* pairs of fingers lose contact with the fingerboard!

INCREASING LEFT-HAND STRENGTH AND AGILITY

Besides slur and scale pattern exercises, there are exercises designed specifically to develop left-hand strength and agility. On this page and the next, you'll learn some of the most valuable.

The "Spider"

This exercise is named for the way the fretting hand looks like a tarantula crawling up the fingerboard. In each cycle, the paired fingers exchange configurations just as in the previous exercise, assisted by the same "loose arm" technique. Practice in first position as shown in the first line of music. For variety and endurance, ascend chromatically to seventh position as shown in the *second* line.

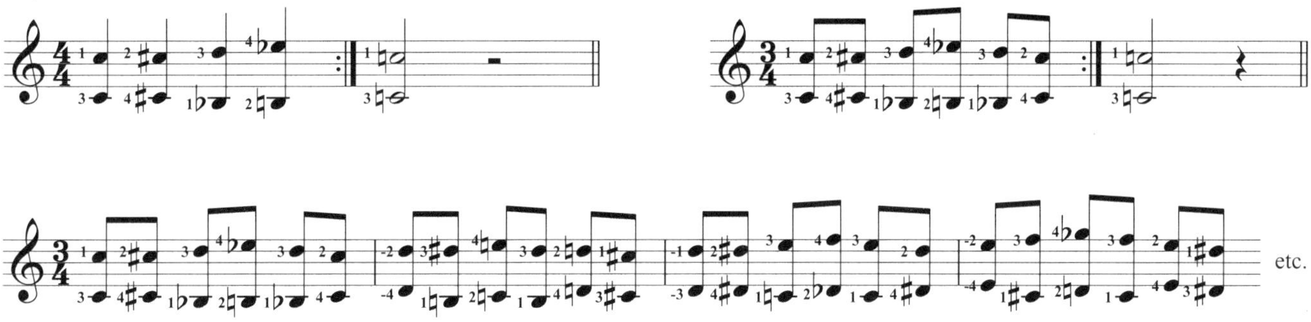

Chromatic Octave Scales

You'll gain additional strength and agility by practicing exercises based on the first-position chromatic octave scale. First, memorize and practice the scale with careful GDM, being sure to hold down the notes just played until the next pair of fingers touches the strings. As in the "Spider," use the correct forearm and elbow movements to support your hand and finger action.

When the scale is memorized, practice the following pattern exercise. When it's memorized as well, try constructing a few more for yourself. Inventing pattern exercises will strengthen your mental command of left-hand movements and your ability to think ahead.

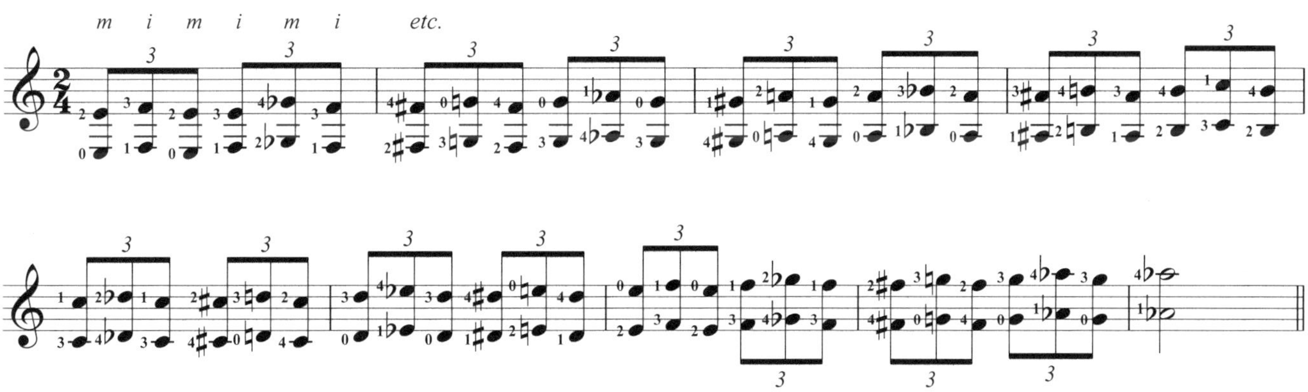

BARRED CHORD PRACTICE

As noted earlier (p. 141), building up the muscles between your thumb and forefinger will improve your barred chord expertise dramatically. The following exercise is great for that purpose, and also provides excellent arpeggio practice. When you can play it cleanly, add the four patterns following it to your practice and then try inventing some of your own for more variety. Within a few weeks, you'll see real gains in strength, plus a more dynamic arpeggio technique.

Alternative Arpeggio Patterns

1.
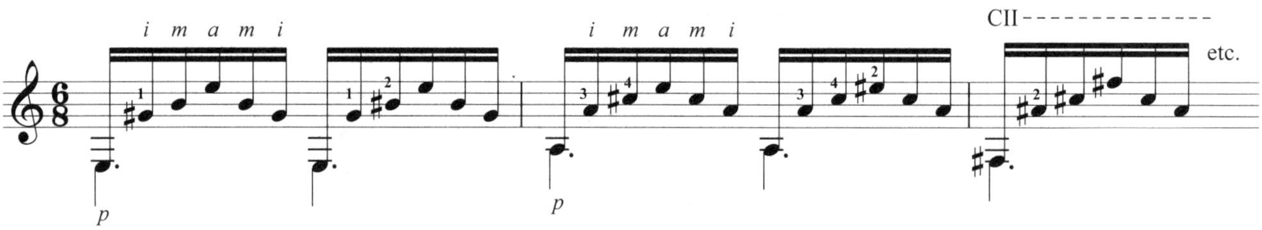

2.
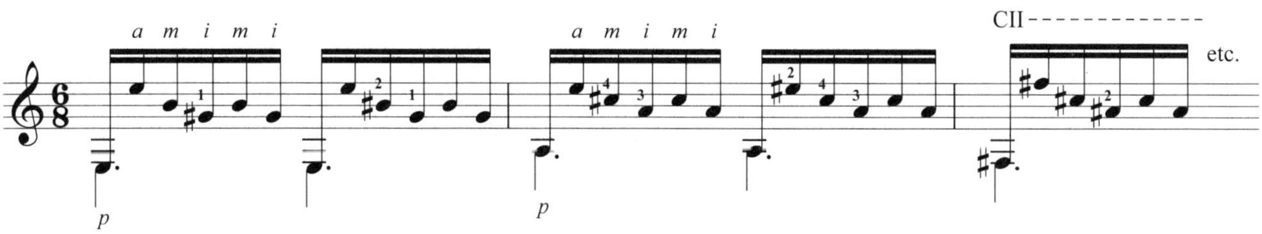

3.
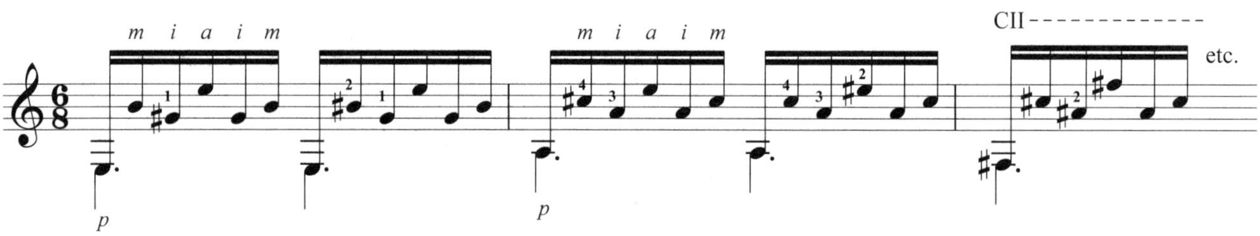

4.
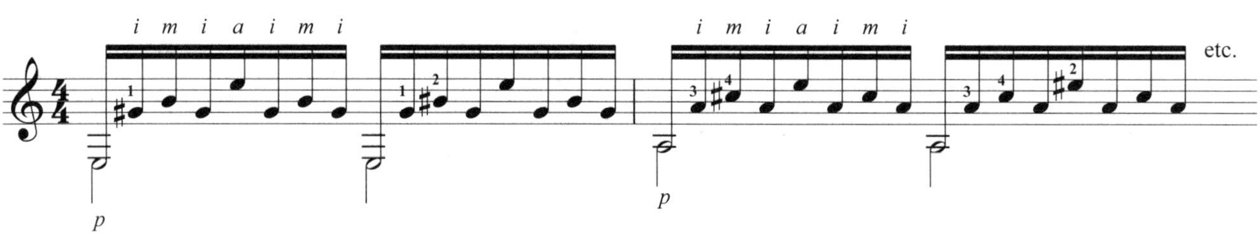

Ninth Position and Beyond

The terminal position of the free fingerboard is the ninth, and besides the 9th- and 10th-fret notes you learned in seventh position, it includes the following layout of 11th- and 12th-fret notes. Notice that the 12th-fret notes are the same as the open strings but an octave higher:

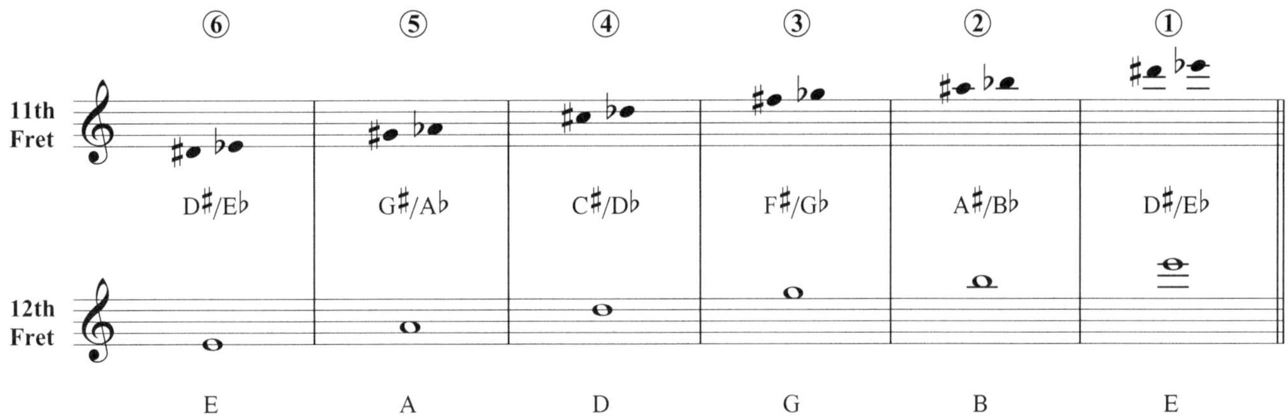

The following notes beyond the 12th fret are available on the first string and require a relocation of the hand to where the neck of the guitar joins the body. Although most of the guitar repertoire doesn't go beyond ninth or tenth position, you'll occasionally see these highest notes in advanced level compositions.

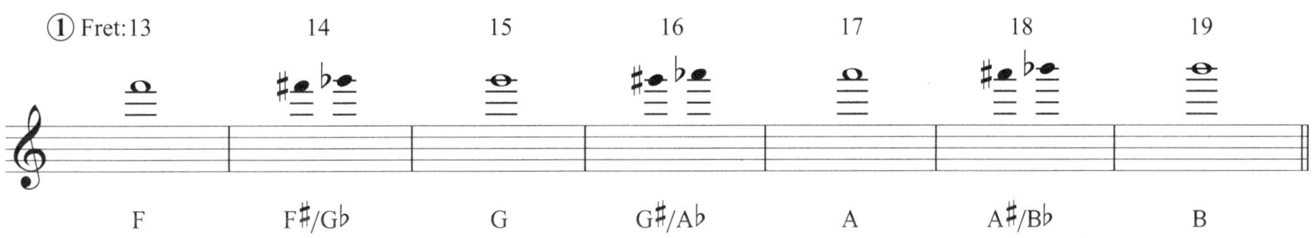

Memorize and practice the following ninth-position scales: **(1)** the two-octave D major scale and **(2)** the extended one-octave A major scale. **(3)** Then do the same for the two-octave E major scale, which begins in *sixth* position and shifts to ninth position for the higher octave.

What better way to get used to playing in ninth position than with the most famous classical guitar solo of all time? First recorded in 1897, during the 20th century it gained international popularity as a concert classic and motion picture theme. It's also known in several different versions, but the one below is the most traditional, including the title (Spanish for "Anonymous Romance").

[**1**] Practice it *first* in the form of block chords as shown below. In the process, you'll see that the E *major* "B" section will need extra work—especially the shifts. Also, in its fourth measure, notice the C double sharp—it's the same tone as a D natural. However, for correct musical spelling, **double sharps** (𝄪) and **double flats** (𝄫) are used in the sharp and flat keys, respectively.

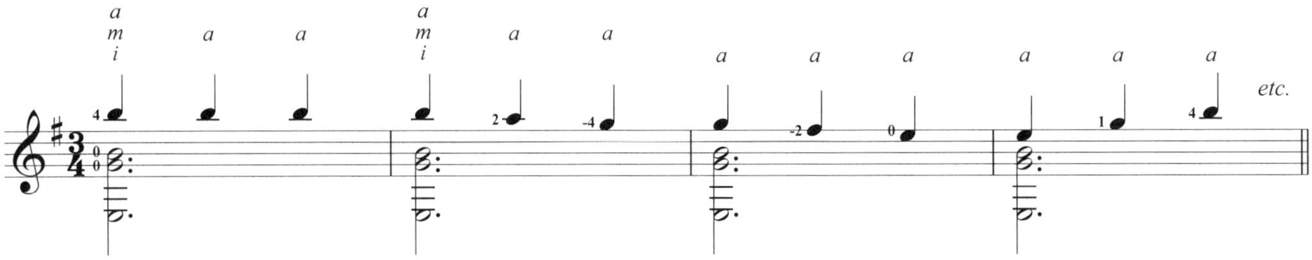

[**2**] Next, work on it with *precise* sequential planting so that each finger in the cycle feels like it's being pulled quickly into its prepared position by a strong magnetic attraction. Be sure also that *p* and *a* plant simultaneously just before the first beat of each measure, and in the case of position shifts, before the left hand leaves the chord it's holding.

[**3**] Finally, accent the melody as indicated in the first measure. Although this is customarily done with rest strokes on each melody note throughout the piece, an equally valid approach is to use mainly *half*-rest strokes and save the full rest strokes for points of greater musical emphasis.

Romance Anonimo

Anonymous
Spanish

A

Moderato M.M. ♩ = 108

*This notoriously tricky shift can be cleaned up by separating the bass and treble as shown here, so that the open A neatly covers the shift. Be sure to play the A slightly *before* the beat and the C♯ *on* the beat to keep the rhythm intact.

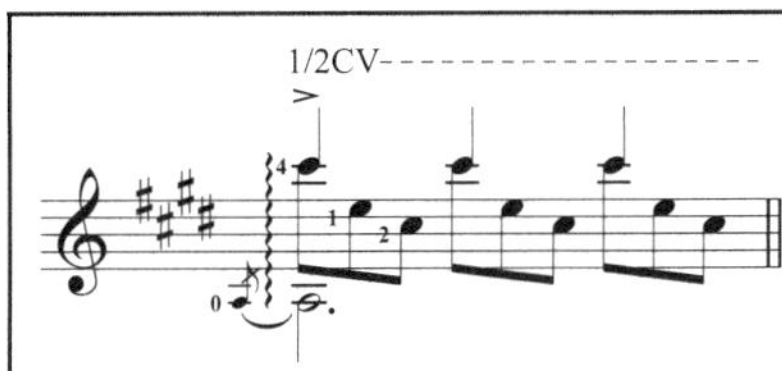

**This unobtrusive but effective reversal of the G♯ and B enables a much cleaner shift to the cadential B7 chord by covering the movement with the open B string.

Until they reach an advanced level, classical guitar students would probably think of Mauro Giuliani as the composer of numerous etudes and beginner-to-intermediate pieces. However, in his tragically short life, Giuliani also composed a huge body of concert music which has been rediscovered and recorded by many of the top players. The following short masterwork provides a gateway to that repertoire, as well as practice in using the highest positions of the fingerboard.

Andantino Grazioso

Mauro Giuliani
(1781–1829)

1/3CV
a píacere (freely)
a tempo
1/3CV
1/2CII
CII
1/2CII
1/3CX
dolce
poco rit.
1/2CII
5/6CII
a tempo
1/2CII

Although it doesn't make very much use of the upper fingerboard, the famous "Bourrée" from Bach's *Lute Suite No. 1* will challenge your technique and musicianship in various ways. Follow the practice scheme below as a guide to mastering this great piece.

BOURRÉE: STEPS TO MASTERY

[1] Practice with an enhanced GDM that includes two consecutive changes. Thus, as you play the first notes (E over G), visualize your left hand executing not just the F♯ bass and melody notes on the "and" of beat 4, but also the G over E across the bar line on beat *1*. Do likewise for the subsequent changes on beats 2 and 3 and keep going by counting and visualizing "four-and-*one*," "two-and-*three*." Break the piece into its well-defined four-measure phrases as practice units and look for some impressive gains in left-hand security and mental command after a few days.

[2] Fast contrapuntal pieces such as this will test your right-hand accuracy to the limit. Therefore, when practicing at 75% speed, plant more aggressively than usual in order to ensure right-hand security and precise right-hand/left-hand synchronization. Because of its residual imprint on motor memory, practicing with forceful, super-staccato articulations at 75% speed leads to more accurate, relaxed playing when this demand is lifted at performance speed.

[3] The articulation marks in the first two measures serve as a guide to phrasing the piece—"dit-dit-*dah*, dit-dit-*dah*," etc. However, when playing the downbeat quarter notes, play *no louder* than on the upbeat eighth notes—in fact, when practicing slowly, play them *softer* just to be sure. This will help you avoid the stiff, boring metric accents that are as instinctive as clapping, and contribute to the "long line" (i.e., the vocal quality) of the four-measure phrases.

[4] To offset the complex left-hand demands of this piece, you'll need to double down on your dynamically prepared chord-changing and shifting technique (pp. 136, 152, 188), especially in its more difficult passages. The *most* difficult is the dramatic four-measure conclusion, where the counterpoint is intensified by the close-packed overlapping motives in the bass and treble parts. This beautiful but risky grand finale will benefit the most from such practice in "super slo-mo."

[5] Embellishment is used for the three cadences where you'll see a short trill in small sixteenth notes tied to the principal tone. Play the trills and the concluding mordent (on the final E) as shown:

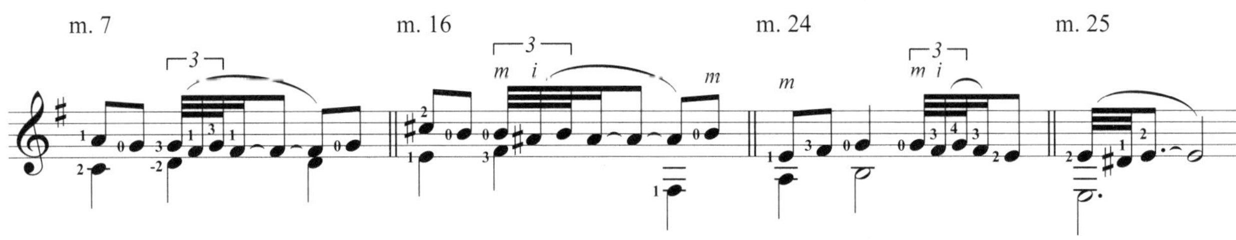

✔ **TIP:** Note that the first trill is played entirely with a slur, while the second and third use the adjacent open string for the *first* note. This hybrid technique, used also in measure 8 of the Weiss "Sarabande" (p. 173), creates effective trills where neither pure slurring or cross-string trilling would be as easy or sound as good.

Bourrée

J.S. Bach
(1685–1750)

Allegro M.M. ♩ = 132

Right-Hand Development: Faster Scales and Arpeggios

In both hands, the secret of speed is the **economy of movement principle**—the less motion needed to accomplish a given task, the less time needed for it. Although you can increase left-hand economy by deliberately restraining excess movement, for the right hand, the easiest and most effective way is with staccato practice. When playing staccato, you automatically restrict the distance covered by the fingers by absorbing the recovery movement into your next preparation.

STACCATO PRACTICE WITH INCREASING METRONOME SETTINGS

[1] For both scales and arpeggio exercises, prepare each stroke decisively, with firm fingernail engagement. Increase the metronome settings until you can no longer distinguish between planting and playing, record your speed, and use it as a benchmark of your progress. Although maximum speed can't be increased voluntarily, *controlled* speed (i.e., with planting) definitely *can*, and for each gain in controlled speed, there's a small derivative gain in maximum speed.

[2] For practice models, use the following arpeggio pattern and one-octave G scale. Then, apply the technique to **(a)** various arpeggio exercises and pieces (pp. 137, 138, 153, 157, 160, 168, 176, 184, 190), and **(b)** scales and scale-pattern exercises (pp. 144, 147, 151, 160, 168, 176, 180, 184, 191).

Reflex-Based Modes of Dynamic Preparation

To complement your staccato practice, *reflex-based* forms of dynamic preparation are a great way to gain additional fluency. These include **(1)** dotted or staggered rhythms, and **(2)** speed bursts. Since they're reflex-based, you don't need to make any effort to plant—just take it for granted.

[1] The dotted and staggered rhythm exercises which follow can also be applied to the repertoire of scale and arpeggio exercises listed above. Practice them using these rhythmic formulas at progressively higher metronome settings.

TIP: The ligatures you'll see in the music are *not* slurs or ties. They've been inserted to make the note-connections easier to see as tightly linked upbeat-downbeat groupings, irrespective of how they're beamed. Thus, in the first measure of exercises **(a)** and **(b)**, the way to count is "*One,—* ta-*Two,*—ta-*Three*," etc.

(a)

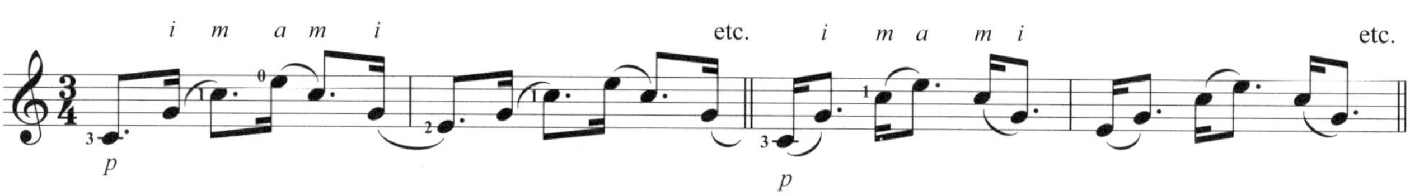

(b)

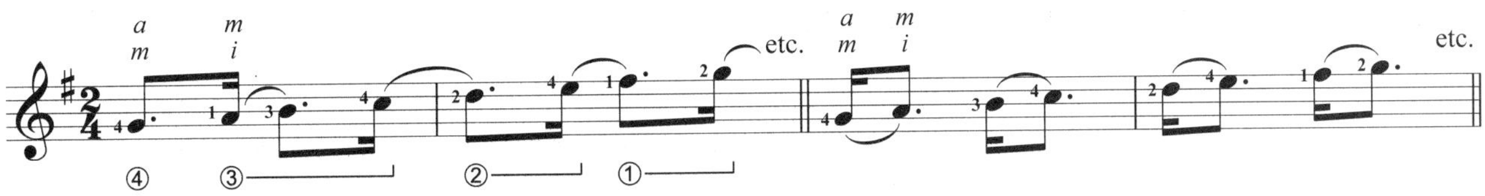

(c)

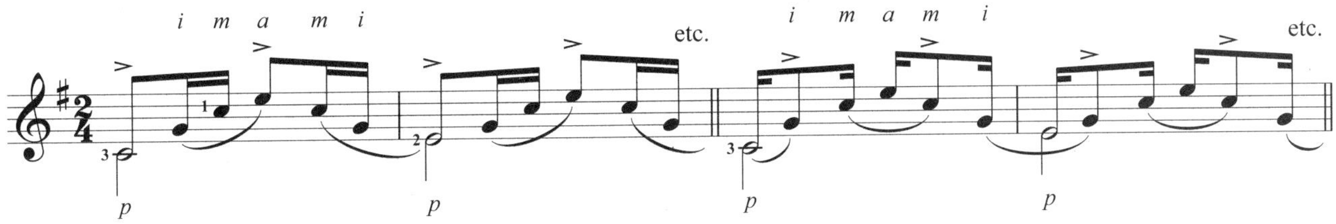

(d)

[2] Speed bursts employ dynamic preparation in the form of micro-relaxations between groups of fast notes, comparable to the breaths taken between groups of arm-strokes in freestyle swimming. Practicing bursts like those below at increasing metronome settings will improve your overall fluency in playing scales and arpeggios, because you'll be learning to cluster several notes under a single playing impulse. With only one act of will needed to play all of them, there will be a net speed gain proportional to the savings in mental effort expended on their execution.

Flamenco Rasgueado

Book 2 introduces students to flamenco playing—the Phrygian modes on which it's largely based, the basic *rasgueado* with *i*, and the *malaguena* as one of its most traditional dance forms. In this section, you'll be introduced to the next level of rasgueado playing, the use of hemiola as a rhythmic device, and another traditional dance form called the *peteneras.*

Like the up-and-down strokes with *i*, the basic four-finger flamenco "roll" is highly percussive and rhythmically exact. To play it, **(1)** anchor your thumb on the face of the guitar and clench your fingertips into the palm of your hand. **(2)** Starting with the little finger (*c*, for *chico*), *snap* the fingers out of your palm as shown below, making sure each finger comes to a full extension.

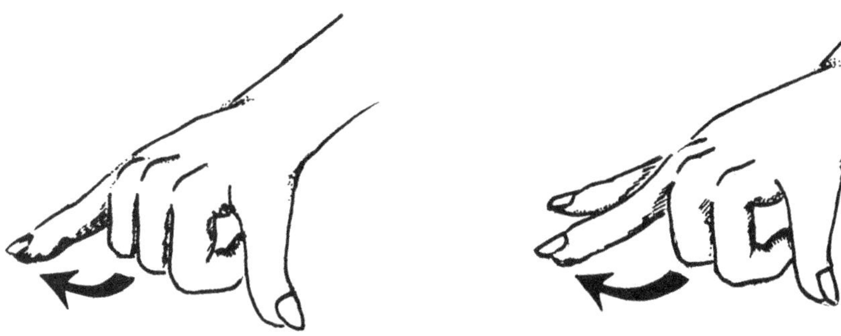

continue with *m*, then *i*

Note below that each finger strikes approximately three strings, and that the *c-a-m* strokes form a triplet which serves as an upbeat to the downbeat with *i.* Although often written this way, to save space, the broken chord symbol is also used. Thus, the second measure sounds just like the first.

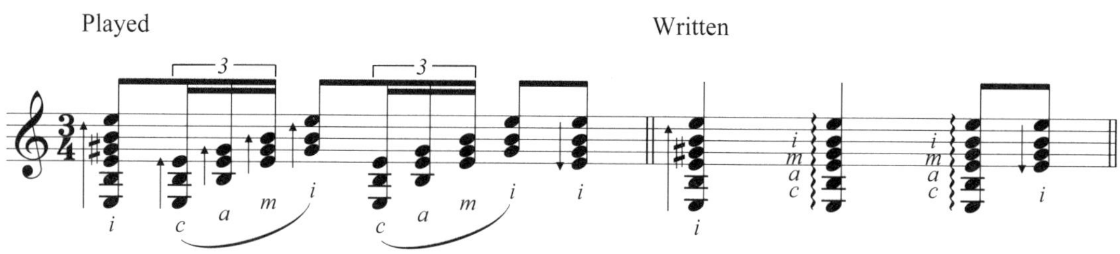

In addition to its use of the Phrygian mode and rasgueado technique, the rhythm of *peteneras* is based on hemiola, another typical feature of flamenco music. **Hemiola** consists of an alternation in triple meter between 3/4 and 6/8 rhythms, which only *looks* confusing. To play it correctly, simply count a steady beat in eighth notes (i.e., "1-2-3-4-5-6") with the note-groupings and accentuations shown below that make it alternately 6/8 (**1**-2-3, **4**-5-6) and 3/4 (**1**-2, **3**-4, **5**-6):

TIP: Practicing this rasgueado also serves as a valuable workout for the weak extensor muscles on the back of the hand. Although their only natural function is to open the hand, in classical guitar playing, they power the recovery from all finger-strokes. Rasgueado practice will strengthen them with a form of resistance-training that benefits your overall right-hand technique.

Peteneras

Traditional Flamenco

Adagio M.M. ♪ = 176

Like flamenco, the spirited folk classic "El Vito" comes from the Andalusian region of southern Spain, uses the Phrygian mode, and includes hemiola in its rhythm. Unlike "Peteneras," however, its notation is 3/4 throughout except in the middle and end of this arrangement, where it alternates with 2/4. This unusual meter *also* only looks confusing. Since quarter notes are exactly the same length in *both* time signatures, just use your metronome and play on each click. For how to count the hemiola, see the last line of music below.

TIP: In measure 7, you'll see a **cross-string slur**, another type which sometimes can be very useful. To play it, pluck the C on string 2 and hammer the B♭ on string 3 energetically and decisively. If your hammer-stroke is sufficiently percussive, the connection between the two notes will sound like a normal slur.

El Vito

Traditional Spanish
Arr. Charles Duncan

5/6CI
2/3CII
1/2CII
mf
poco rit.
a tempo
p
cresc. poco a poco
ff

Artificial Harmonics and Tremolo

You've learned how to play open-string harmonics by touching an open string over the frets where they naturally occur (p. 183). For *fretted notes*, you can create the node which divides a string into vibrating halves with your right hand alone. The resulting pitch is an octave above the fretted note, and notes played this way are known as **artificial harmonics**, or "octave harmonics." To learn the technique, follow these steps:

[1] With your left hand, finger the C♯ at the 2nd fret of the B string.

[2] As shown in the photograph, extend your *i* finger as if you were pointing and touch the string *twelve* frets higher at a point directly over the metal fret (here, the 14th fret of the B string).

[3] Simultaneously pluck the string with your *a* finger, as also indicated. Unlike normal free stroke, this specialized plucking action requires a curled finger and a flex from the middle joint.

[4] Immediately lift your *i* finger so that the harmonic can resonate freely.

[5] When you can play consistently clear harmonics, alternate between C♯ and the open-string B without watching your left hand. Keep your eyes on the tip of *i* as it switches back and forth between the 12th and 14th frets.

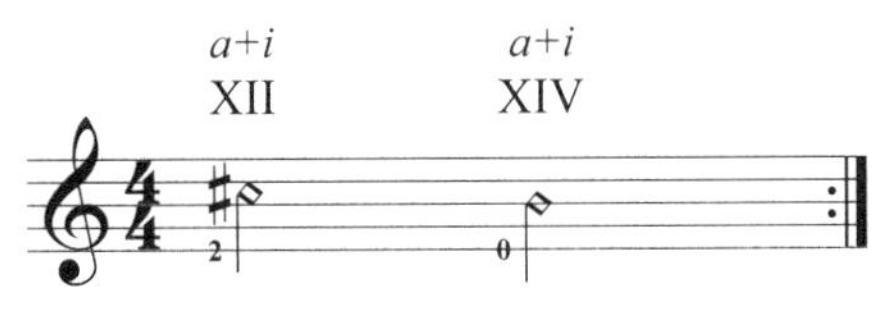

✓ **TIP:** To produce a clear harmonic, make sure your *i* finger stays straight in order to maintain the proper distance between the *a* and *i* fingers, and also ensure solid tip-contact with *i*.

To master the technique, practice this extended one-octave E major scale while watching your right hand and using conscious GDM. Memorize and practice it by itself first so that you can rely on the *feel* of the fingering while concentrating on accurate right-hand movements.

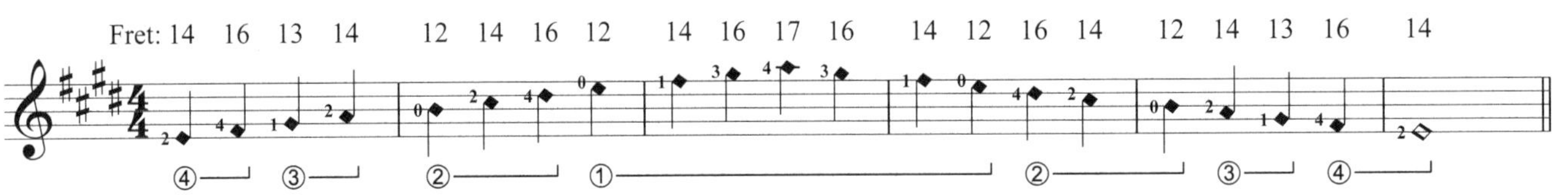

✓ **TIP:** The secret of goal-directed point-and-pluck movements is to *lead* the pointing index finger with your eyes, as if they were *pulling* the fingertip to its destination over the right fret.

Treble-string harmonics can be combined with regular bass-string notes to create a charming music box sound. To support the melody without competing with it, play the bass notes very softly, using the fleshy left underside of your thumb-tip instead of the nail. This most famous of Christmas carols is ideally suited to the technique and will provide a good introduction to it.

✔ **TIP:** Practice the piece without harmonics until it's well memorized, so that you can count on accurate left-hand movements while focusing your attention on the right hand's complex activity.

Silent Night

Franz Gruber
(1787–1863)

TREMOLO PLAYING

The last piece in this book, an original arrangement of "Greensleeves," will introduce you to the **tremolo** technique—the magical illusion of a duet between the guitar and an instrument like the mandolin which can sustain a continuous melody with fast up-and-down picking. However, like most magic tricks, there's a simple secret—basically, it's a *p-a-m-i* arpeggio in which *a, m,* and *i* play the *same* string. Therefore, your practice will need to focus squarely on the rotary cycle of consecutive right-hand preparations needed to create the illusion. Practice it thoroughly with deliberate sequential planting and staccato articulations as explained on pages 137, 160, 184, and 192. Look for those sensations of your fingers feeling chained together and sticking to the strings as evidence that you're practicing effectively.

Practicing Tremolo for Control Without Aggressive Planting

When the piece is memorized and you can play it at 108 BPM or faster, practice it also with two *reflex-based* modes of dynamic preparation:

[1] With the dotted rhythm shown:

[2] As written, but by accenting *m* with a more forceful stroke than the *a* stroke.

These two practice techniques will check the universal tendency of tremolos to "gallop" as they approach the entirely reflex-based performance speed, by closing the neuromuscular gap between well-controlled playing and accurate reflex playing.

Greensleeves

Traditional English
Arr. Charles Duncan

Andante Grazioso M.M. ♪ = 126–138

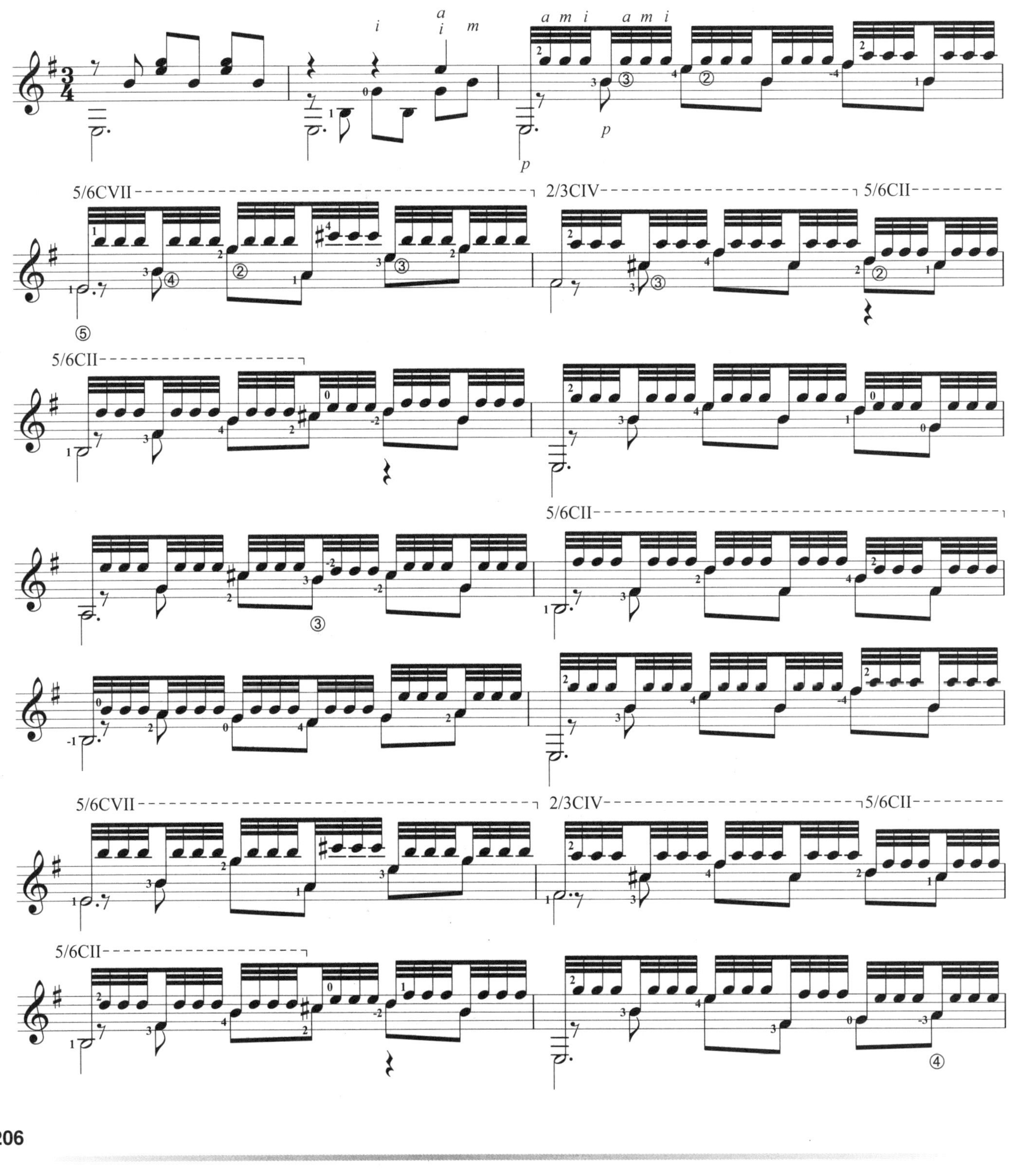

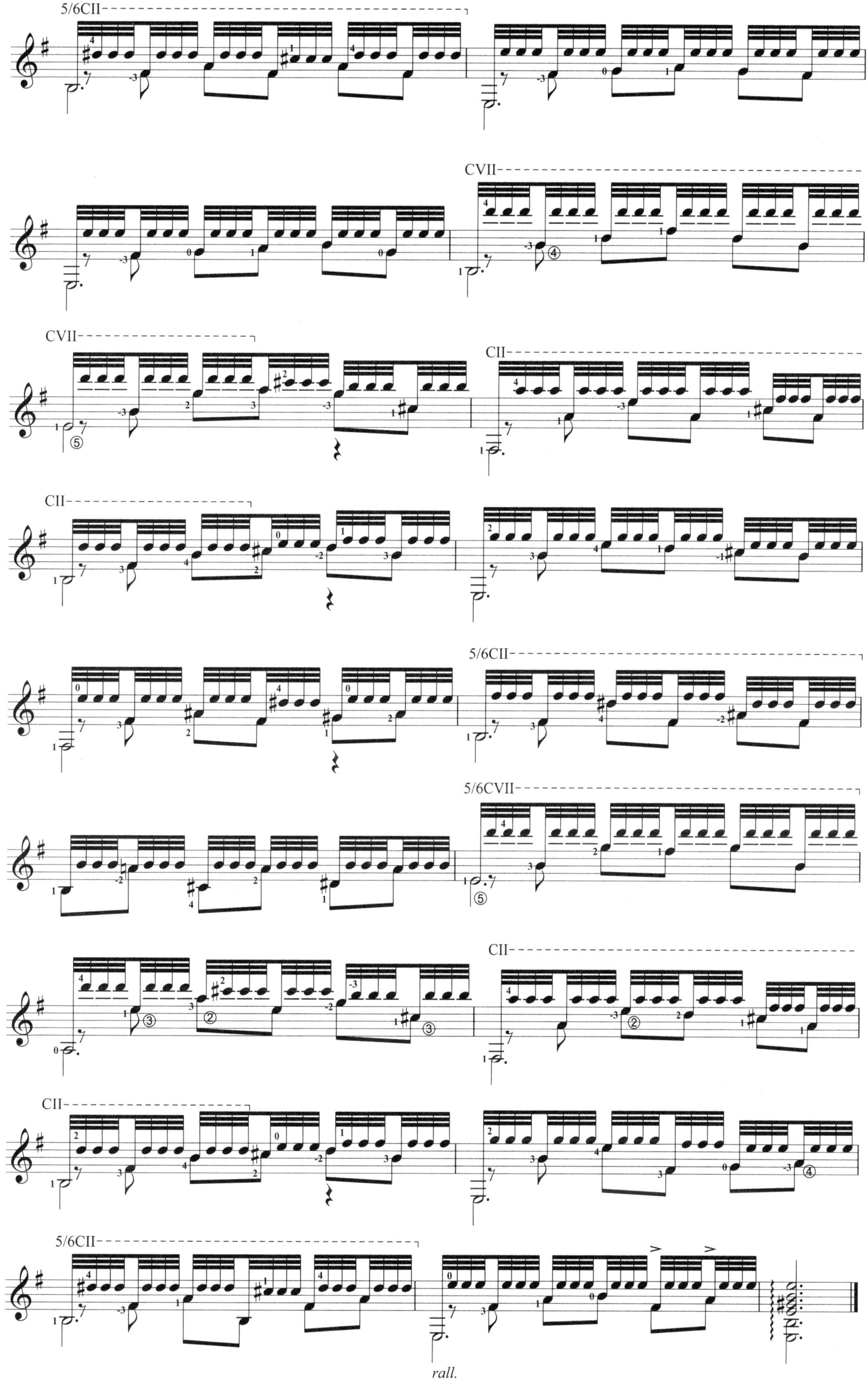
5/6CII
CVII
CVII
CII
CII
5/6CII
5/6CVII
CII
CII
5/6CII
rall.

Continuing Your Study

Students who have completed this book should be ready to start exploring the advanced guitar repertoire. Of the various ways to do this, the best would be to use some standard anthologies of etudes as a bridge to the highest levels. The following widely used classics are recommended:

(1) **Required Studies for Classical Guitar**, ed. Jerry Willard (Hal Leonard, 2008). This comprehensive collection contains Mauro Giuliani's *120 Studies for Right-Hand Development*, as well as many other etudes and recital pieces by Carcassi, Sor, Carulli, and more. The Giuliani studies used on pp. 137–138 cover the essential styles of arpeggiation, but the sheer number and variety of Giuliani's arpeggio patterns is an asset. Working on just 10–15 a week on a rotating basis will keep your practice of arpeggios constantly refreshed.

(2) **Matteo Carcassi: 25 Melodious and Progressive Studies, op. 60**, ed. Paul Henry (Hal Leonard, 1993). Even after 175 years, this book retains its unique value as an instructional work. The etudes are enjoyable, the variety of techniques they cultivate is comprehensive, and their increasing levels of difficulty are well-designed to incentivize a student's progress.

(3) **Twenty Studies for the Guitar by Fernando Sor**, ed. Andrés Segovia (1947; Hal Leonard, 1995). This too is a classic which has withstood the test of time because of its editor's prestige and the musical excellence of the pieces selected. Since its overall level of difficulty is greater, this book provides a fine complement to Carcassi's. Both editions include high-quality recordings of the pieces.

(4) **Etudes Simples (Estudios Sencillos) for Guitar**, by Leo Brouwer (Editions Durand, 2016). For an introduction to modern and contemporary guitar music, this book is unbeatable. The 20 short compositions by one of the finest guitar composers of the late 20th century cover a range of styles (impressionistic, atonal, Afro-Cuban, etc.), and are both instructive and fun to play.

(5) **Villa-Lobos: Collected Works for Guitar**, by Heitor Villa-Lobos (Editions Durand, 2001). The guitar music of this great Brazilian composer is such an important part of the modern repertoire that you should begin learning some of it. Besides their intrinsic value, his pieces serve as a gateway to a vast amount of more recent guitar music. Since most of his *12 Etudes* are quite difficult, a better place to begin would be with the "Choro No. 1," "Etude No. 1," and "Prelude No. 1."

To these valuable works may be added the author's *A Modern Approach to Classical Guitar Repertoire, Part 2* (Hal Leonard, 1985) for a choice selection of intermediate-to-advanced pieces from the traditional repertoire. To learn more about flamenco, the *Hal Leonard Flamenco Guitar Method* by Hugh Burns is the first book to get. And to broaden your understanding of modern music and explore the techniques of jazz playing, the *Hal Leonard Jazz Guitar Method* by Jeff Schroedl is unsurpassed.

Finally, to pursue your technique development to the max, the author's *Classical Guitar 2000: Technique for the Contemporary Serious Player* (Summy Birchard Music, 1993) is highly recommended (see, for example, the Amazon reviews). With a complete, practical scale system, comprehensive slur and arpeggio studies, and exercises for interpretive control—all supported by a thorough explanatory text—it combines the best features of many other technique books into a convenient 91-page package. Also, like its companion volume *The Art of Classical Guitar Playing*, it contains various unique features which even after three decades are not found elsewhere.